REASONS FOR ACTION AND THE LAW

Law and Philosophy Library

VOLUME 43

CRISTINA REDONDO

National Council of Scientific and Technological Research (CONICET), Córdoba, Argentina

REASONS FOR ACTION AND THE LAW

SPRINGER-SCIENCE+BUSINESS MEDIA, B.V.

A C.I.P. Catalogue record for this book is available from the Library of Congress.

ISBN 978-90-481-5301-5 ISBN 978-94-015-9141-6 (eBook)
DOI 10.1007/978-94-015-9141-6

English translation of María Cristina Redondo, *La Noción de Razón para la Acción en el Análisis Jurídico,* Centro de Etudios, Constitucionales, Madrid, Spain, 1996.
Translated by Ruth Zimmerling.

Printed on acid-free paper

To the memory of my parents

TABLE OF CONTENTS

Logic issues in tautologies, mathematics in identities, philosophy in definitions; all trivial but all part of the vital work of clarifying and organizing our thought.

Frank P. Ramsey

PREFACE

The present book is an offspring of my doctoral thesis, presented at Pompeu Fabra University in Barcelona/Spain, in March 1995, and published in Spanish the following year. It is the fruit of several years of work during which I have received stimulating impulses from far too great a number of people to name them all here. A few of them, however, deserve a special mention.

Above all, I wish to thank Ricardo Caracciolo, the director of my thesis – my unfailing teacher, who thought about and discussed with me every single line of the following investigation.

Then, there is Pablo Navarro with whom over the past years I have been sharing the pleasure and attraction some philosophical problems happen to produce. He has provided me with much helpful criticism which permitted me to avoid more than one mistake.

I am also deeply endebted to Albert Calsamiglia and Jorge Malem who made it possible for me to find, at the Department of Legal, Moral and Political Philosophy of Pompeu Fabra University in Barcelona, a wonderful place of learning where I could put my ideas to the test. In this institutional context, I have benefited greatly from the comments of my colleagues at the post-graduate school as well as the other members of the Department. My discussions with José Juan Moreso, Carlos Rosenkrantz and Silvina Ramírez have been of special importance for me.

The publication of this revised English version of my work has been made possible by financial support received from the *Fundación Antorchas* (Argentina) and the *Caja de Madrid* (Spain), for which I am most grateful. I also wish to express my gratitude to Ruth Zimmerling who has put all her intelligence and diligence into the translation. Finally, a heartfelt thanks to Ernesto Garzón Valdés and Francisco Laporta for encouraging and supporting the publication of this book.

Córdoba, May 1999 — Cristina Redondo

PRESENTATION

1. Introduction

One of the main concerns in contemporary legal philosophy involves the idea of law-imposed *duty* and its relevance for action. The interest in this topic is reflected in the discussion of a great variety of problems, all focused on the practical nature of the law. Its analysis presupposes a context of discourse somewhat wider than that of legal theory, and a more general philosophical discussion. The practical relevance of the law has been a subject of reflection in moral philosophy as well as in action theory. Each one of these lines of work has contributed valuable insights into the meaning of 'duty', the possibility of its justification, and its relationship with action.

Some of the most prominent contributions in this field have as their starting point the notion of 'reason for action'. According to them, the concept of *reason* is a necessary element for understanding the relationship between *norm* and *action*. This line of analysis can be approached from several perspectives, some of which have been taken up by those theorists interested in legal questions. This is exemplified by the contributions of H. L. A. Hart, Joseph Raz, or Georg Henrik von Wright, to mention just a few. In the work of these authors, the notion of reason for action plays a decisive role in the explication of the existence of a norm and its practical relevance.

In the following investigation, I will look at different theoretical proposals which use the concept of reason for action in approaching some of the classical questions of legal theory, that is, more specifically, the normativity, the acceptance and the justification of legal norms. For this purpose, the present book is divided into two main parts. The first part contains a general analysis of the concepts of reason and of action. The results of this part are then applied, in the second part, to the analysis of the three questions just mentioned.

2. Meanings of 'Reason'

The word 'reason' is used in different senses, and each one of these senses has been the subject of extensive philosophical reflection. From a methodological point of view, it is useful to distinguish three lines of thinking about this term, referring to

(i) reason as a human faculty,
(ii) reasons for action, and
(iii) reasons as premises of arguments.

Each one of these topics entails substantial problems related to my present purpose. The first part will be dedicated to a discussion of these problems. With respect to *(i)*, the analysis will evolve around the common contraposition of the theoretical and the practical nature of reason as a human capacity. Consequently, the different functions for motivating and guiding action this faculty is said to have or lack will also be treated. With respect to point *(ii)*, I will mainly concentrate on the identification of those elements (reasons) that enable us to explain and justify an action. Finally, with respect to *(iii)*, the discussion will focus on reasons understood as linguistic expressions supporting a conclusion. In that context, I will look at the different kinds of practical arguments reasons can be a part of. This will presuppose, first of all, a discussion of the distinction between theoretical and practical arguments.

These three perspectives of the notion of reason are different, but not unrelated. For instance, what approach to reasons for action one adopts depends on one's conception of reason as a human faculty, as well as on one's conception of reasons understood as premises of an argument.[1] The relationship between the study of premise-reasons and that of reasons for action is the same as that between a logical investigation and other types of theoretical enquiry. Statements of (or about) reasons for action can form part of an argument. What a logical investigation can contribute is a language and the structures of inference for validly formulating such statements. The notion of reason in the sense of premise of an argument is not the same as the notion of reason for action. A premise-reason may express a reason for action, but this does not affect its quality as a premise-reason. Similarly, the existence of a reason for action does not depend on its being formulated as a premise of an argument. This distinction between the two concepts is not always recognized. The similarities and differences will become more explicit in the course of the following detailed analysis of each one of them.

For the purposes of the present investigation, the concepts of reason for action and reason as premise of an argument are especially interesting. Only to the extent that they are affected by the position taken with respect to reason as a human faculty I will also briefly need to treat this latter concept.

3. Reason as a Theoretical Faculty

Philosophers' opinions on this matter, generally expressed in an extremely metaphorical language, reveal their different metaphysical positions and the conceptions they have of what human beings can know and do. According to a more or less uncontroversial thesis, reason is a *formal* faculty. On this conception, the function of that capacity is to connect ideas by way of the application of rules, and its exercise is linked to the acquisition of a specific kind of knowledge, namely *a priori* knowledge. In the words of Paul K. Moser:

---

[1] For the sake of simplicity, hereafter, the expressions 'reasons as premises of an argument' and 'premise-reasons' will be used interchangeably.

„Philosophical questions about a priori knowledge revolve around a trio of long-standing distinctions: the epistemological distinction between a priori and a posteriori knowledge, the metaphysical distinction between necessity and contingency, and the semantical distinction between analytic and synthetic truth."[2]

This triple classification has been the object of a long and heated philosophical controversy. I do not wish to enter into this discussion here. Rather, I will only refer to an epistemological distinction between a kind of knowledge based on evidence provided by experience and another kind acquired through inference from propositions. Normally, the difference between the categorical assertion that some proposition is true and the conditional assertion of the truth of a proposition that follows logically from other propositions is clear.[3] This distinction can be made without taking sides in the controversy about whether there are two independent meanings of truth, and whether reason plays different roles for each one of them.[4]

Traditionally, reason and experience have been considered to be alternative foundations of knowledge.[5] This opposition, in turn, is at the root of a conception which concedes competence to reason exclusively in the realm of the validity of arguments and *a priori* truth. The capacity for having access to experience, i. e., to factual or empirical knowledge, is thus attributed entirely to the senses.

From this point of view, the characterization of reason as an epistemic faculty is the consequence of a conception of reason as a formal capacity for connecting propositions by following rules. The elements connected by reason are abstract entities. Reason links propositions, not the facts propositions refer to. The possibility of assuring the truth of such propositions derives from the formal relations reason is able to establish between them, and not from their correspondence to facts. Valid relations are defined by rules or principles which stipulate under what conditions a proposition can be inferred from others, regardless of their material truth or falsity.

It should be noted that the application of such formal rules enables us to assert the truth of analytic as well as of synthetic propositions. The fact that reason is a purely formal capacity should not be taken to say anything about the kinds of propositions it can relate to each other. The truth of a synthetic proposition can perfectly well be established by stating certain logical relationships between propositions. All we must say is that this truth is conditional, i. e., it depends on the truth of the propositions we start from. Although from a logical point of view there is nothing new in a validly inferred

---

[2] Moser, Paul K., Introduction, in: id. (ed.), A Priori Knowledge, Oxford: Oxford University Press 1987, p. 1.

[3] Cf. Cohen, Morris R., A Preface to Logic, New York: Henry Holt 1945, ch. 1.

[4] On this point, there are two opposing positions. One holds that the two meanings of truth are mutually independent; the other one sees only a gradual difference between them. For the first view, cf., e. g., Carnap, Rudolf, Introduction to Symbolic Logic and its Applications, New York: Dober 1958; id., Intellectual Autobiography, in: Paul Schilpp (ed.), The Philosophy of Rudolf Carnap, La Salle, Ill.: Open Court 1963; Lewis, C. I., An Analysis of Knowledge and Valuation, La Salle, Ill.: Open Court 1971. For the second, cf. Quine, W. V. O., Two Dogmas of Empiricism, in: id., From a Logical Point of View, Cambridge, Mass.: Harvard University Press 1953; Pap, Arthur, Semantics and Necessary Truth, New Haven, Conn.: Yale University Press 1958.

[5] Cf. on this subject, e. g., Whitehead, Alfred N., The Function of Reason, Princeton, N. J.: Princeton University Press 1966.

sentence, there *is* from an epistemic or psychological point of view.[6] That means that through reason we can acquire new knowledge of contingent sentences logically implied by presupposed premises.

Summing up what has been said so far about reason as a faculty, we can affirm that

– reason is a capacity for establishing formal relations following rules. The entities related by reason are always abstract entities, e. g., propositions;

– because of this capacity, reason is attributed a cognitive function. The kind of knowledge reason can provide is the one called *a priori* knowledge;

– the operation of reason is not restricted to analytic propositions. Through reason, we can also acquire knowledge of synthetic propositions. In all cases, however, the acquired knowledge will depend on the rules that were applied and the propositions that were presupposed. In other words, the knowledge provided by reason is always conditional. Generally, when reason is presented as a *theoretical* faculty, this epistemic function is alluded to.

Within this perspective, the opinion of those who hold that reason can also provide access to the unconditional truth of certain propositions deserves special mention.[7] On this view, the epistemic potential of reason is conceived in a much broader sense. Reason can thus not only establish truth relative to certain premises, but also provide direct knowledge of the truth of the ultimate premises.

Although this conception of reason is clearly different from the previous one, they both coincide in one fundamental aspect: The epistemic characterization of reason does not change when the substantial capacity is added to the formal one. In both cases, the function of reason is to discover and prove the truth of propositions. In contrast to this, there is an alternative way of understanding reason as a human capacity which does not refer to its epistemic potential. Let us examine this alternative view now.

4. Reason as a Practical Faculty

A) THE PRACTICAL AND THE THEORETICAL REALM

What does it mean to assert that reason is of a practical nature? What is acceptance or rejection of that quality based on? Just as from the epistemic point of view it is common to regard reason and experience as opposites, with respect to practical questions one usually finds that reason is opposed to the will or the passions. A first criterion of distinction between theory and practice is involved here. With its epistemic function reason enables us to respond to a typical theoretical concern, i. e., to questions of the kind 'What is the case?'. In that respect, reason is therefore seen as a theoretical faculty. In

[6] Cf. Bunge, Mario, La ciencia, su método y su filosofía, Buenos Aires: Siglo XXI 1985.

[7] For instance, the Kantian position that there are synthetic truths *a priori* in the physical as well as in the moral realm.

contrast, the typical practical question 'What ought one to do?' is thought to be answered not by an exercise of reason, but through the will or through passion.

Consequently, the possibility of attributing a practical nature to reason will depend on whether or not reason can, in fact, answer that practical question. Since reason is an epistemic capacity, the very idea of this makes sense only if such questions have an answer that can be *known*. In other words, if there *is* a true answer to the question of what one ought to do, then reason can discover it in the same way as it can come to know the truth or falsity of any other kind of proposition. If that is the test reason must pass in order to be regarded as a practical faculty, then this neither requires another conception of reason nor an extension of its capacities. All we need to do is accept that ought-expressions are knowable propositions. From this point of view, to say that reason has a practical quality presupposes that one regards practical discourse as belonging to the realm of theoretical knowledge and to accept the existence of normative facts that make practical propositions true or false. Reason can then link practical propositions to each other with the help of logical rules and in this sense lead to *knowledge*, as with any other kind of propositions. To deny the practical nature of reason, therefore, means to deny the assumptions that make the operation of the epistemic function in this realm possible, i. e., to deny that there are normative facts and that answers to the question of how one ought to act are true or false. Those who adopt that position argue, for instance, that practical sentences merely express emotions, or that they only attempt to influence others. To the extent that they are not descriptive, they are said to have no cognitive content.

If the matter is presented in these terms, it will depend on one's metaethical position which side in the discussion one takes. To say that reason is a practical faculty implies that one accepts a cognitivist metaethical conception according to which the truth of ought-statements can be known. This does not involve an extension of the functions of reason, but rather an extension of the ontology and the kinds of truths one is willing to accept. Practical reason, thus conceived, does not challenge the conception of reason as an epistemic faculty. It involves the exercise of the very same capacity, but applied to a particular kind of propositions. It is not reason itself, but the object of knowledge that is of a theoretical or practical nature; that means that the qualification of reason as theoretical or practical is only a reflection of the theoretical or practical nature of the *contents* or *sentences* it relates with each other.

This implies that there are two possibilities. The distinction between the theoretical and the practical can be grounded either in meanings or in sentences. In the latter case, if the issue is merely that descriptive *discourse* is regarded as theoretical and normative *discourse* as practical, the distinction is superficial, because every statement containing practical (deontic) expressions can be translated into the indicative mode, and *vice versa*. Even the practical question *par excellence* 'What ought one to do?' can be formulated as a formally non-normative matter: 'What *is* it that ought to be done?' Also, in the opposite direction, the theoretical concern represented in the question 'What *is* the case?' can be expressed through a practical question, as for example 'What *should* I believe to be the case?' – assuming that one ought to believe what is true. Consequently, according to the criterion based on sentence-type, we could say that reason is a practical or theoretical faculty, depending on the grammatical form of the respective sentence.

But then, that assertion would not express a real distinction between different capacities of reason at all.

In any case, even if the practical nature of reason is not grounded in sentences, but in the corresponding contents, those who deny the possibility that reason can be practical do not challenge the idea that reason has one single recognized function; instead, what they deny is the possibility that it can be exercised with respect to non-propositional contents. They think that if practical contents are not descriptive, they cannot be connected with the help of the logical rules applied by reason. In this context, we may remember the well-known dilemma originally formulated by Jørgensen: In standard logic, the notion of inference and all its connectives are defined in terms of truth or falsity. Therefore, either one acknowledges that logic cannot be applied to normative practical sentences, or one concedes that logic is applicable to them; but in that case, one will have to redefine the notion of 'inference' and all logical connectives. The dilemma only arises if one admits that normative language has no truth-values. Therefore, the position according to which answers to practical questions are true or false is not affected by Jørgensen's dilemma. It does not need to develop a new logic to be applied to prescriptive discourse, since that is essentially similar to the descriptive kind. If one accepts that both descriptive and normative formulations express propositions, then the logical relations unanimously accepted with respect to the former can also be applied to the latter.

As a corollary to what has been argued in this section, we can say that there are two important aspects that must not be confused. The first refers to the distinction between theoretical (propositional) contents, on the one hand, and practical (non-propositional) contents, on the other. The second refers to the functions reason can play with respect to each one of these two kinds of contents. There are, then, skeptical and optimistic positions concerning the question of whether or not reason can perform its epistemic function in both realms. A totally different matter is the question of whether or not in addition to its epistemic function reason also has a *practical* function. The distinction I have analysed so far does not say anything about that question; it calls reason practical or theoretical depending on whether the contents or sentences it links with each other are of a practical or a theoretical nature. In other words, what is merely a difference between the contents, or realms of knowledge or discourse on which reason can operate is presented linguistically as a difference within reason.

B) THE NORMATIVE AND THE MOTIVATIONAL FUNCTION OF REASON

But the practical nature of reason can also be defended in a different way. This second approach contrasts the theoretical function of reason, understood as an *epistemic* capacity, with its practical function, understood as a *normative* capacity. Here, to call reason 'practical' does not merely reflect a property of the contents reason operates on. On the contrary, it refers to the role reason plays with respect to action. Robert Audi has explained this in the context of his comparison of the positions of Aristotle and Kant:

„There are various ways in which reason may be normatively practical, and Kant differes from Aristotle here too. Reason may be *epistemically practical*, in the sense that it provides knowledge (or at least justified beliefs) of normative truths. It may be *legislatively practical*, in the sense that it lays down such truths as standards of conduct. And it may be *constitutively practical*, in the sense that its deliverances create normative standards."[8]

In each case, the practical nature of reason is given by an indirect relation to action, consisting in the knowledge, the adoption or the creation of the norms that ought to guide it. Of the three possibilities mentioned, the one referring to the knowledge of normative propositions can be regarded as a manifestation of the epistemic function discussed in the previous section. The other two, however, bring to light a new characteristic of reason. In the second case, reason not only discovers normative truths, but also chooses or points out which of them ought to be adopted as guidelines for behaviour. And in the third case, reason itself issues and constitutes the principles that ought to guide action. On all accounts, the practical virtue of reason is always linked to the possibility of answering the question of what ought to be done.

Now, besides this *normatively practical* conception, Robert Audi also points out the *motivationally practical* function of reason.[9] The latter refers to an empirical capacity, i. e., to the intervention of reason in the process that leads to action, by way of certain mental states. Although in both cases reason is qualified as 'practical', this predicate refers to different properties in each case. In the first case, the practical nature of reason is based on its epistemic and legislative capacity, that is, on the role it plays in the discovery and/or stipulation of normative principles (or truths). This is a matter of a moral kind and, as such, its discussion belongs to the field of ethics. In the second case, in contrast, the practical nature of reason is based on its causal relevance, i. e., on its capacity for affecting the conditions that lead to the performance of an action. That is clearly a topic for an empirical discussion that has to do mainly with psychological aspects. Investigation of the latter concerns action theory in general, regardless of its relevance from the moral point of view. In conclusion, we can say that the qualification of reason as having a practical nature means two things: that reason has an epistemic function in the practical realm, and that it has a causal function.

Usually, these two ways of understanding reason as a practical capacity are not considered independently of each other. In other words, it is generally taken for granted that reason has motivational effect only insofar as it provides a special class of insights, namely, that of moral norms or principles. That means that the *normatively practical* function is a necessary condition for the *motivationally practical* function. This does not hold for the other way around, though. To say that reason can stipulate or discover moral principles, i. e., that it can be *normatively practical*, does not imply that it also necessarily affects the performance of an action. The debate about how reason affects action shades into the discussion about the motivational force of mental states, regarded as products of reason. The greatest part of the inquiry into the practical nature of reason revolves around this point which will be analysed in detail in the next chapter.

So far, it looks as if we could distinguish three functions of reason: first, reason as a *theoretical or epistemic* faculty; second, reason as a *normatively practical* faculty; and finally, reason as a *motivationally practical* faculty. While the first and the last can

[8] Audi, Robert, Practical Reasoning, London: Routledge 1991, p. 71.

[9] Ibid., pp. 68-72.

be easily distinguished from each other; the difference between each one of these and the second is not yet very precise.

Going back to Robert Audi's observation, there are three ways in which reason can be *normatively practical*: by discovering normative truths, by stipulating such truths as standards of behaviour, or by constituting action principles. In this book, I will not analyse the possibility of a legislating reason issuing guidelines for behaviour. Now, the other two forms in which reason can be qualified as *normatively practical*, it should be remembered, can be explicated in terms of its *epistemic* or *motivationally practical* capacity. To say that reason is *normatively practical* (once the interpretation in the sense of a legislating reason is set aside) means to say either that reason can provide access to the knowledge of norms or normative propositions, or that the mental states produced by the exercise of reason have causal relevance for the production of action. In other words, to present reason as a normative faculty is ambiguous, since it denotes a set of epistemic and motivational functions. There is no specifically *normative* function besides these other two. But then, it is not advisable to refer to the practical nature of reason in terms of its 'normativity', if ambiguity is to be avoided. The different senses in which reason can be *normatively practical* belong to different universes of discourse. With the use of that label one therefore runs the risk of confounding the logical, moral and psychological questions underlying that characterization. One of the objectives of the present investigation is to show – and thus help avoid – the confusion of these aspects in the actual discussion about *normative* practical reason.

Reason understood as an epistemic faculty is the capacity to establish logical relations between abstract entities, i. e., between meaningful contents.[10] In contrast, reason conceived as a motivational practical faculty is a capacity that gives rise to empirical states of affairs that may be connected in a causal relationship.[11] It is assumed that such states of affairs are obtained, maintained and discarded rationally. On this approach to reason, a new kind of relation and a new kind of entities comes into play.[12] There is a classical philosophical controversy about the way in which such cognitive states affect the performance of actions. In this context, of course, one cannot fail to mention the controversy between two schools of thought divided on the question of whether or not reason has an active part in this. They are known as the 'rationalist' and the 'Humean' position, and their different viewpoints will be made explicit when we come to the analysis of the internal elements of action.

---

[10] This leaves open the possibility that such contents are of a propositional or a non-propositional kind. This subject will be treated in Chapter III, in the context of reasons understood as premises of practical arguments.

[11] Those who have written about this question usually identify rational states with beliefs. In this first part of the book, I will present several proposals, but will not question that conception. In the second part, when I come to the analysis of the concept of acceptance, I will consider an alternative way of unterstanding beliefs, in contrast to other kinds of mental attitudes.

[12] One could point out a number of problematic aspects concerning this factual function of reason. First of all, the interpretation according to which the relation between an individual's psychological states and its behaviour is of a causal nature is not unanimously accepted. Secondly, one can deny the existence of psychological entities and explain action directly on the basis of processes in the brain. These are points, however, that cannot be discussed in the confines of the present investigation.

5. Overview

The ideas just presented about the notion of 'reason' as a human faculty or capacity are intended to serve merely as an introduction to some distinctions the present study will be based on. First of all, the idea that reason can be motivationally practical provokes one to think about the starting point of this investigation: the concepts of *motive* and *human action*. There are different ways of understanding the meaning of these terms. Hence, there are also different ways of interpreting the assertion that reason *motivates* action. Very generally, we can distinguish two meanings of that statement. On the one hand, in a weak sense, reason plays a role in the conformation of cognitive states necessary for the process that leads to action. On the other hand, in a strong sense, the involvement of reason guarantees the conditions that are sufficient for producing action. The distinction is relevant because those who have traditionally rejected the practical nature of reason do not deny that it can provide motives, in the first sense. They would thus admit that the involvement of reason is necessary for the performance of an action. The disagreement concerns only the assertion that the cognitive states produced by reason can be sufficient conditions.

The cognitive states that will be at the center of attention in what follows are those related to normative contents. Some authors hold that the motivational force of reason arises whenever it operates on this kind of contents, regardless of whether they are of a moral or a strategic nature.[13] Others, in contrast, restrict that capacity exclusively to beliefs about contents of a moral nature.[14] Beliefs in descriptive contents are not regarded as problematic: They are recognized as part of the motivational factors in the weak sense; but there is also unanimous agreement that they cannot be sufficient conditions for the performance of an action. I will deal in more detail with these questions in Chapter I.

Reflection about the two functions attributed to reason leads to the second kind of contents that will be studied in the first part of the book: the distinction between different meanings of 'reason for action'. While the motivational capacity of reason is related to the psychological and explanatory sense of 'reason for action', its epistemic capacity is related to the normative and justificatory sense of that term. These distinctions will be analyzed in Chapter II.

Besides the question concerning the limits of the motivational capacity of reason in the production of action, one can also emphasize another one, concerning the limits of its epistemic capacity with respect to directives for correct behaviour. Again in very general terms, in this last respect two conceptions of reason can be pointed out. From the first perspective, the insights offered by reason are based on its capacity for drawing conclusions by way of linking contents with the help of logical rules. That means that the knowledge reason can bring about is always conditional on the premises and the

---

[13] Cf., e. g., Edgley, Roy, Reason in Theory and Practice, London: Hutchinson University Library 1969; also Nagel, Thomas, The Possibility of Altruism, Princeton, N. J.: Princeton University Press 1970.

[14] This is the opinion, e. g., of Frankena, William K., Obligation and Motivation in Recent Moral Philosophy, in: A. I. Melden (ed.), Essays in Moral Philosophy, Seattle, Wash.: University of Washington Press 1958.

applied rules of inference.[15] According to this idea, reason cannot establish the ultimate premises because, by assumption, they are not derived from other premises. Hence, they cannot be the object of an act of *rational* acquisition of knowledge. A broader perspective does not restrict reason's epistemic possibilities to its capacity of relating propositions formally. Rather, it regards reason as being capable of having direct access to certain categorical, i. e. unconditional truths. From this point of view, the epistemic capacity of reason is relevant not only for reaching conclusions, but also for determining the premises one must start from. As has already been pointed out, there is a serious problem with respect to the exercise of that epistemic faculty in the normative and justificatory realm. If such normative contents are not propositional entities, they cannot be rationally related to each other. Therefore, in that case we would be facing Jørgensen's dilemma.

So far, I have pointed out the close relationship between the notion of reason as a faculty and the different meanings of reason for action. But there are also some questions that bring to light a notorious difference between them. Usually, the logical concepts of reasoning and reason are confused with the psychological and moral notions which are related to the function of reason as a motivational and epistemic capacity. This will be analysed in Chapter III.

In conclusion, then, one of the primary objectives of the first part will be to draw up a clear distinction between empirical problems connected with the motivational notion of reason and reasons for action, and ethical problems related to an epistemic and justificatory notion of reason and reasons for action. The former is relevant in the descriptive realm of the explanation of action; the latter in the normative sphere of its justification. These observations point to the ambiguity of the notion of *rationality* which, when related to the concept of reason for action, also has two different meanings. On the one hand, it is a purely descriptive, on the other, a normative concept. In the first case, when an action is said to be rational, that means that the action is based on motives, i. e., on reasons in the motivational sense of the term. In the second case, to say that an action is rational is to say that it is justified by reasons. To act rationally, i. e., for a reason, in the explanatory sense of the term does not imply to act rationally, i. e., based on a reason, in the justificatory sense.

Finally, throughout the following I will attempt to draw a line between the problems just mentioned and the logical and linguistic aspects in relation with the notions of reason and practical reasoning. All these distinctions will serve the general objective of this first part: to give greater precision to a set of concepts used in legal theory, which will then be evaluated in the second part of this book.

---

[15] Cf. Klimovsky, Gregorio, El método hipotético-deductivo y la lógica, in: Jorge J. E. Gracia et al. (eds.), Análisis Filosófico en América Latina, Mexico-City: Fondo de Cultura Económica 1985, pp. 75-90.

PART I

REASONS FOR ACTION: CONCEPTUAL ISSUES

CHAPTER I

REASONS FOR ACTION – FIRST PART

1. Introduction

In this and the next chapter, the concept of reason for action will be discussed. Since the final objective is to use this notion for an analysis of other concepts, we will be moving on a metalinguistic level. I will undertake, first of all, a review of the different meanings the term has been given in philosophical discussions. It will then be possible to assess which of these uses can be helpful for a better understanding of the questions that will be taken on in the second part of the book, concerning the concept of legal norm, the notion of acceptance as a necessary condition for the existence of a legal system, and the justification of legal decisions.

For this task, we need to keep in mind the distinction between using and mentioning a term. When an expression is mentioned, the reference is the word itself, a fact usually indicated by putting it between inverted commas. In contrast, when a word is used, its reference are other objects, events, or relations which are designated by that name. In this first part, when speaking about 'reasons for action' and the meanings of that expression in different contexts, most of the time the term will only be mentioned. In the second part, however, the different concepts of reason will be used in the analysis of the questions indicated above.

In ordinary language, the expression 'a reason for doing *x*', where '*x*' is a variable that stands for the name of an action, is ambiguous and vague. Take, for instance, the fact that yesterday John went to Paris. One can say that among his *reasons* for travelling were the invitation he received from a friend as well as his wish to see Nôtre Dame, but that, in the last instance, neither one of them was *the reason* why he made that trip, because neither one would be regarded as a *good reason* for taking a leave of absence from his work. In each one of these phrases, the word 'reason' has a different meaning. First, it refers to events that are external to the agent, and then to psychological states. In one case, a reason is regarded as something that *explains* the action; then again, it is required for *justifying* it. In view of this plurality of meanings, we must carry out the metalinguistic task of reconstructing and fine-tuning the term before we can put it to theoretical use. For this purpose, in the field of practical philosophy different concepts have been proposed which can be understood as technical definitions of the expression 'reason for action'. Since the topic of these chapters is not the notion of reason in general, but that of *reason for action*, before starting the analysis it will be necessary to state more precisely what is meant by 'action'. What can be said about reasons for action depends in great part on what concept of action one adopts.

2. Action

In this section, I will try to give a sufficiently precise account of some ideas about human action, but only to the extent that they are necessary for understanding the concept of reason for action. The following discussion, therefore, does not pretend to be exhaustive.

The concept of action has a core meaning such that in certain cases there is no doubt about its applicability; but there are also marginal cases in which one can plausibly argue both for and against its applicability. Normally, the term 'action' refers to a specific result or change in the world that is brought about intentionally. Intention and result, thus, are the two elements constitutive of action. That means that all changes brought about unintentionally by an agent are not regarded as actions. Rather, they are usually called 'reflexes' or 'reactions'.[1] On the other hand, the notion of result must be interpreted in a broad sense. Generally, it designates the occurrence of a change that is external to the agent; but it is also not implausible to admit the possibility of results that are internal to the agent. That kind of actions is usually called 'mental acts' or 'internal acts'.[2] In other words, the notion of action that will be considered in this book always refers to intentional behaviour and, unless indicated otherwise, to external acts. For instance, the action of swimming consists not only of certain movements of an agent's arms and legs, but also of an internal psychological attitude of that agent with respect to those movements. Both elements are necessary for the identification of an action of swimming on a particular occasion. The internal aspect is what enables one to understand the external manifestation, i. e., the changes produced by an individual, as a particular intentional action of that person. Here, I will not enter into the controversy about what kind of relationship there is between the external and the internal aspects of action. I will assume that all action consists of an intention and a result, where the two are causally related.[3]

In order to identify an individual action, besides a concept of action in general, we also need two other notions, namely, those of an individual action (or act-individual) and of a generic action (or act-category).[4] A generic action or act-category – for instance, that of swimming – is a predicate that can be applied to different particular situations. It is the name of a class of individual actions. An individual action is a specific event, fixed in time and space, that is an instance of a generic action. Thus, the fact that John is gliding through the water right now in this swimming-pool can be identified as an individual action of swimming. On the other hand, the concept of swimming as a

[1] Since the main purpose of this study concerns the notion of intentional action, I will not analyse the notion of reaction. On this, cf. von Wright, Georg Henrik, Explanation and Understanding, Ithaca, N. Y.: Cornell University Press 1971, p. 87.

[2] A relevant case of an internal act, i. e., that of accepting a norm, will be analysed in Chapter V.

[3] Cf. Davidson, Donald, Actions, Reasons, and Causes, in: id., Essays on Actions and Events, Oxford: Clarendon 1982, pp. 3-19. Against this interpretation, cf. von Wright, Explanation and Understanding, op. cit.

[4] Cf. von Wright, Georg Henrik, Norm and Action. A Logical Enquiry, London: Routledge & Kegan Paul 1963, pp. 36 f. For a similar distinction between 'act types' and 'act tokens', cf. Goldman, Alvin, A Theory of Human Action, Princeton, N. J.: Princeton University Press 1970.

general predicate (act-category) can be applied not only to what John is doing just now, but also to many other events.

Now, one and the same individual action can be described in many different ways. In other words, it can be identified as an instance of more than one generic action. The agent's intention, however, may not cover all those act-categories. That is, he may not have meant to bring about the result defining some of those actions, and in that sense may not have intended to perform an action of that kind. On this, von Wright observes:

„Sometimes we do things 'by mistake'. We aim at something, but do something else instead. For example: I press a button to light the hotel-room, but it turns out that I have called the chambermaid. In cases like this, my mistake lies not in what I *immediately* did intentionally, e. g. pressed a button, but in the *remoter* consequence of what I did. A related case is when we speak of *negligence*. I reach out for the salt on the table and I topple over my neighbour's glass of wine. 'Look at what you did!', someone might say. The notion of negligence has a moral tinge. I ought to have taken care that the thing in question did not happen as an (unintended) consequence of what (intentionally) I did. I could, however, have done intentionally what I did without producing this undesired side-effect.“[5]

According to von Wright, that a generic action *can* be intentional, i. e., is possible to be intended, is a minimal and essential condition for the possibility of identifying individual actions of the corresponding class. For instance, one can breathe intentionally, although normally one does it without being aware of it; but one cannot intentionally make one's heart beat (although one can perhaps intentionally slow down or accelerate one's pulse rate). Therefore, an individual conduct could be identified as an action of breathing, but no behaviour could be identified as the action of making one's heart beat. With respect to individual actions, lack of intention, rather than making them *unintended* actions of the same category, makes it impossible to identify them as such actions. Behaviour without intention is not action; but, as von Wright himself observes, the borderline between intentional and unintentional behaviour is not very clear. How does one determine whether or not an agent acted intentionally? How does one identify the existence of a particular intention? In any case, to impute or attribute an action to someone is also to impute or attribute an intention to that agent, even if one has not been able to prove its existence, or if one is clearly mistaken about it. I will come back to this point later.

3. Rules Defining Generic Actions and the Identification of Individual Actions

The imputation of an individual action to a particular agent presupposes the existence of linguistic rules and rules of conduct that guide the formers' use. The linguistic rules in this case are semantic rules defining a word with the help of other words. In that sense, they delimit, or are constitutive of, its meaning. The identification of an individual action as a certain type of action presupposes, first of all, the use of rules that define the notion of action in general. Secondly, it also requires the use of rules that define the respective act-category attributed to the agent. Recognition of an individual event as an instance of a generic action – for example, of walking, voting, or killing someone – is

[5] Von Wright, Georg Henrik, Freedom and Determination, Acta Philosophica Fennica vol. XXXI, Amsterdam: North Holland 1980, p. 17.

always relative to, and presupposes knowledge of, linguistic sets of rules valid in some community. The distinction just made is important: One thing is the concept of action; quite another thing are the particular rules defining different generic actions. The semantic rules defining the notion of action are based on a theoretical reconstruction. Different theories can, of course, propose different semantic rules, that is, different concepts of action. In contrast, the rules defining the generic action, instead of being theoretical reconstructions, are usually stipulated spontaneously. Only exceptionally, this is not the case, as for instance when the purpose of prohibiting or requiring certain kinds of actions make a precise definition necessary.

With respect to the general notion of action, I will follow the definition proposed in the theory of von Wright. Thus, an 'action' will be an intentional interpretation of a segment of human conduct. According to this concept, as has already been pointed out, an action has two aspects: a result and an intention.[6] And with respect to the different generic actions, I will assume that the rules defining them are rooted in the linguistic uses of the respective communities. Generally, such concepts are not elaborated theoretically, except in those cases where the conceptual reconstruction of a certain kind of action is of special interest. For instance, the definitions of criminal actions are often precisely formulated by legal scholars working in the field of dogmatics, or by judges in their decisions. But even if they are not made explicit (or if the explicit formulations are rather vague), there are still semantic rules that define ordinary actions like walking, eating, or drinking. Generally, the greater the vagueness of the definition of a generic action, the greater the possibility of controversies about its application, and that also means: the more difficult the identification of an individual act of that type. One of these problematic aspects concerns the proof of the intention of an action. With respect to this point, the following three possibilities deserve to be mentioned:

(i) Under certain circumstances, actions may be imputed on the basis of the simple fact that certain results were produced by an agent. In these cases, the established practice for the application of the concepts of the respective act-categories rejects all inquiries in the existence of the corresponding intention. The intention is presumed, and therefore it becomes irrelevant whether or not it actually existed. An example of this would be the act of voting for a particular candidate in an election.[7] Once a voter has deposited her slip of paper in the ballot box, the act of voting for the person indicated on the ballot-paper will be imputed to her even if it could be shown that she made a mistake and actually meant to vote for someone else. The linguistic practice which in this case attributes an action without admitting any proof to the contrary regarding the agent's intention may be motivated by a number of different considerations. In the example given, it can probably be explained by the difficulties it would create if one were to permit discussions about an agent's intention in that kind of situation. Now, it may seem that this shows that the underlying concept of action is not that of intentional action; but that impression would be wrong. What is not required is a *proof* of the intention, precisely because the intention is presumed. In extreme cases, if it were obvious that the in-

---

[6] But remember that, in contrast to von Wright, I will admit that the psychological elements that make up the intention of an agent are causally related to the result of his actions.

[7] The example is taken from Blanke, Richard A., Objective Reasons and Practical Reasons, in: Metaphilosophy 17:1 (January 1986).

dividual in question was under the influence of drugs, or sleepwalking, the action would not be imputed because it would then be impossible to presume the intention.

(ii) Then, there are cases in which the rules regulating the imputation of individual actions stipulate exactly the opposite. The application of concepts of generic actions to particular situations then requires the proof of a specific intention and prohibits the imputation of an action if such proof is lacking. That is what happens in the case of murder or any other concept of a crime requiring premeditation. In order to be able to impute such actions, one must prove that the corresponding intent existed in the agent, i. e., they may not be imputed unless it has been shown that the resulting state of affairs was the object of his or her intention.

(iii) The rules regulating the application of most act-categories, it seems, do not say anything about the proof of intention. That is, they neither require nor reject it. In that case, the imputation of an action can either be based on prior proof of the intention or made directly on the basis of the observation of a certain behaviour. In that case, there may then be controversy about whether or not the individual act in question should really be attributed to the respective agent. For example, generic concepts like making fun of, insulting, or greeting someone are act-categories usually associated with certain external manifestations interpreted as characteristic results. For instance, it is questionable whether in order correctly to assert that someone has insulted someone else it is necessary to prove the presence of that intention or whether it is sufficient for the presumption of it that an offending result has been produced. There are arguments for as well as against direct imputation. In such cases, there is not one single correct use of the term in question. On some occasions, the concept is applied on presumption of the intention and without admitting proof to the contrary; on others, the production of a certain result is not considered sufficient, and proof of the intention to bring it about is required. These observations about the use or application of the rules defining different generic actions should not lead to confusion. The general notion of action is inseparably linked not only to the production of a result, but also to an internal psychological attitude. The fact that a conceptual reconstruction or an existing practice rejects the proof of intention for the identification of an individual action does not affect the theoretical notion of intentional action. The identification of an individual action involves the attribution of a result as well as the imputation of an intention.

4. Two Classes of Actions: Normative and Non-Normative Actions

The rules defining linguistic expressions are different from those that impose, prohibit, or permit certain conducts, linguistic or otherwise. Both kinds of rules can be taken as a basis for distinguishing two classes of actions. What similarities and differences are there between actions like eating, writing, or moving one's arms, on the one hand, and getting married, paying a bill, or signaling something, on the other? As generic actions, they are concepts depending upon a language. As individual actions, they are events the identification of which depends upon the rules regulating the use of those concepts. In other words, what they all have in common is that their identification presupposes the existence of semantic rules defining act-categories. But in contrast to the actions mentioned in the first place, actions like getting married, paying a bill or making a signal also have the following characteristics:

(i) They always presuppose the performance of an instance of another (or several other) generic act(s); and

(ii) they consist in actions that are defined (if they are generic) or identified (if they are individual) by normative results, i. e., they presuppose rules of conduct.

These characteristics enable us to specify a difference between non-normative and normative actions, or between what some authors have called 'brute facts' and 'institutional facts'.[8] The condition presented in *(i)* means that the actions satisfying it can never be basic actions since they always presuppose the performance of some other action. According to von Wright, whether or not an individual action is basic depends on how it is performed. It is basic if it is performed directly; and it is not basic if it is performed through the performance of some other action.[9]

The assertion of statement *(ii)* requires that one take into account the distinction between the *result* and the *consequences* of an action. The result is part of an action, i. e., it is intrinsically linked to the action itself. Consequences, in contrast, are effects of the result not conceptually related to the action.[10] The individual behaviour of an agent can be described in several ways. To ask what action a person performed is to ask relative to which of these descriptions that person's behaviour can be regarded as intentional.[11] That means that one and the same segment of behaviour may be regarded as intentional with respect to one description, but not with respect to another. Among all the states of affairs brought about by an agent's conduct, the result of his action is that which he intended to produce. The other ones can be understood either as causal antecedents or as consequences of his action. In this context, the following delimitation is important: The result and/or the consequences of an action need not be empirical effects.

---

[8] There are several definitions of 'institutional action'. The definition offered here is not exactly the same as that proposed by other authors. John Searle, for instance, distinguishes between brute and institutional facts on the basis of a classification of rules as regulative or constitutive. Institutional facts, then, are those which presuppose constitutive rules. Such rules define new kinds of conducts, but they also regulate behaviour. Cf. Searle, John, Speech Acts: An Essay in the Philosophy of Language, Cambridge: Cambridge University Press 1969, pp. 33-42 and 50-53. Even if the distinction between regulative and constitutive rules were made to coincide with the one indicated above between rules of conduct and semantic rules, the characterization of institutional acts based on them would not be the same. According to Searle, the aspect that belongs exclusively to institutional acts is their dependence on constitutive rules. In contrast, from the point of view adopted in this book, no action, whether institutional or not, is independent of a semantic rule constituting it as an act-category. On Searle's theory of institutional facts, cf., e. g., MacCormick, Neil and Ota Weinberger, An Institutional Theory of Law, Dordrecht: Reidel 1986, pp. 21-24. On the notion of constitutive rule, cf., e. g., González Lagier, Daniel, Clasificar acciones. Sobre la crítica de Raz a las reglas constitutivas de Searle, in: Doxa (Alicante) 13 (1993) pp. 265-276.

[9] Note that only individual actions can be classified in these terms; cf. von Wright, Georg Henrik, Norm and Action, op. cit., ch. III, sect. 3, and id., Explanation and Understanding, op. cit.,p. 199, n. 38. A different characterization from that of von Wright can be found in Danto, Arthur C., Basic actions, in: Alan R. White (ed.), Philosophy of Action, Oxford: Oxford University Press 1968, pp. 43-58. In the line of Danto, cf. also Moya, Carlos J., The Philosophy of Action. An Introduction, Cambridge: Polity Press 1990, pp. 14-17.

[10] Cf. von Wright, Explanation and Understanding, op. cit.,pp. 87 f.

[11] Cf. Anscombe, Elisabeth, Intention, Ithaca, N. Y.: Cornell University Press 1957, sects. 23-26.

An individual action can produce normative effects, i. e., it can *(i)* bring about the creation of a new norm of conduct, or *(ii)* make existing norms of conduct applicable. Norms of conduct are norms that regulate behaviour by stipulating obligations, prohibitions, or permissions. But the mere fact that an individual action may have normative effects does not yet make it a normative action. Eating, writing, or moving one's arms could be prohibited or obligatory and in that sense linked to the applicability of norms. All actions can have normative *consequences*, but they are not therefore normative actions. For a normative action to exist, there must be an act-category, i. e., a specific concept that singles out some segment of conduct and identifies it by its normative effect. That effect is then the *result* of that behaviour, that is, an integral part of the defined type of action.

A generic action is the name of a class of individual actions sharing certain properties which may be normative or empirical. Individual acts may have different kinds of properties. Not all of them refer to the (empirical or normative) effects the action brings about.[12] For instance, some may be given by the way in which the actions are performed, or by their deontic attributes. Such characteristics can be considered properties of an action too, although they are not among its effects. For example, the action of smoking in a particular place may have the property of being prohibited. Such a prohibition is neither the result nor a consequence of the action of smoking. It is the result of another action, namely, the action which prohibits smoking in that place. On the other hand, that same action of smoking may also have other normative properties that *are* based on its consequences, like bringing about the application of certain norms stipulating a sanction, such as the expulsion from that place or the imposition of a fine. The action may also have empirical properties, as for example that it produces a pulmonary disease. Taking into account all these properties, one could modify the description of the conduct of the agent in question, saying that *he* brings about a disease, or provokes his expulsion from that place, or the imposition of a fine.

All individual actions are described in terms of their properties or characteristics. In a description, one can distinguish the essential properties from those that are not essential. In von Wright's words:

„Which property of a given individual action is singled out as essentially belonging to it is to a large extent a matter of choice. The choice may depend on our *interest* in the action, on what is *important* about it."[13]

Suppose that a person driving a car comes to an intersection and holds her arm out of the window. In that situation, we can identify at least two different individual actions: the action of moving the arm, and the action of signaling. This is possible because of the existence of two different linguistic rules defining the two act-categories that individual event is an instance of. The characteristic effect of the action of raising one's arm is the arm being raised; and that is what in the technical sense von Wright calls its result. To identify an individual event as the action of raising one's arm means that one identifies

---

[12] I use the expressions 'bring about' or 'produce' in order to designate the relationship between the psychological states internal to the agent and the empirical or normative effects constituting either the result or the consequences of his action.

[13] Von Wright, Georg Henrik, On the Logic of Norms and Actions, in: id., Practical Reason, Philosophical Papers, Vol. I, Ithaca, N. Y.: Cornell University Press 1983, p. 113.

that characteristic as its essential property. The characteristic effect of the action of signaling, in the example given above, is to bring about the imposition of certain duties and/or the concession of certain rights. In other words, signaling makes certain existing norms applicable. In that sense, to identify an event as an action of signaling implies that one sees these normative effects as essential for the conduct in question, i. e., that one identifies them as its result. The difference between the two actions lies in their relationship to certain norms of conduct and, therefore, in their relationship to the rights and duties they give rise to. The action of moving one's arm is not necessarily linked to rights and duties, although it may, contingently, bring them about if performed under certain circumstances. Technically speaking, normative effects may be consequences of the action of moving one's arm, but they are not its result. In contrast, the result of an action of signaling is, by definition, that it brings about the application of certain norms imposing rights and duties. Such normative properties are essential to 'signaling', whereas they are not essential to 'moving one's arm'.

From this point of view, a generic action is normative if the semantic rules constituting it define it by its normative effects. And an individual action is normative if it is identified by its normative effects. As has already been said, that kind of effects is produced in two situations: either because the action creates a norm, or because it constitutes the condition of application of a norm. The identification of an event as an act of signaling (a normative or institutional act) and not merely as the movement of an arm (a natural, non-institutional act) means that what one is *interested* in with respect to that segment of conduct are its normative effects. That is why they are seen as essential, i. e., they are identified as the action's result, and are used as criteria for identifying such action. Now, the identification of an individual segment of conduct must not be confused with the imputation of an action. Imputation entails the attribution of an intention to an agent because it means that the respective segment of conduct is interpreted as an action of that agent. As we have seen, the possibility of imputing an action to an agent depends on existing conventions about the use of concepts. In some cases, imputation is admitted on the basis of a presumption of intention, without any proof; in others, the intention needs to be proved.

The distinction will become clearer with the following legal example: The action of getting married is performed by signing a document in front of a particular authority, provided a number of preconditions are satisfied. One and the same external event can be identified as an action of signing a paper or as an action of getting married. What is the difference between those two actions? In this particular case, the action of signing that paper makes certain norms become applicable. In other words, we can say that it has certain normative effects. But the action of signing a paper does not always have effects of that kind. They are not a defining or essential property of the act of signing a paper. The applicability of certain norms is only a *possible* consequence of it. In contrast, the action of getting married, *by definition*, has normative effects; that means that such effects are conceptually a part of that action and constitute its result. The result of getting married is being married. And that someone is married means that certain specific norms are applicable to that person, i. e., that (s)he has contracted certain rights and duties stipulated by those norms. In short, to sign a paper is not a normative or institutional act, because the creation or application of certain norms is is not its necessary result, but only a possible consequence. On the other hand, getting married is an institutional act. As such, it has the features indicated above: *(i)* it is always performed through another action, i. e., it cannot itself be a basic action; and *(ii)* it is defined by its normative effects. In the case of the example, by the fact that it brings about the applicability of certain norms.

The same can be said when we compare the action of signing a paper and the action of issuing a norm. To issue a norm is an institutional act because it is defined by a normative result, i. e., by the fact that a norm is created. Such an action is performed through other, non-institutional actions, for instance, through the signing of a paper by certain individuals. What such other actions must be depends, of course, on semantic rules, which may define the issuing of a norm in various ways.

Finally, it should be recalled that the normative properties constituting the result of an action of getting married or of issuing a norm must not be confused with the deontic qualification the respective behaviour may have in different circumstances, i. e., with the question of whether it is prohibited, permitted or obligatory. These qualifications may be regarded as properties, but not as effects of those actions (they are neither a result nor a consequence of them).

By way of conclusion, then, we can say that the identification of a particular action always singles out as the result of that action what is taken to be its essential property. In contrast, the properties identified as the consequences of an action are properties that are not taken to be essential of that action. With respect to normative or institutional actions, what is identified as their (by definition, normative) *result* is always the *consequence* of some natural action. Thus, an institutional action consists in a natural action that is identified by a subset of its normative consequences. In view of this, an ontological question arises: Are there two actions, or only one? According to Alvin Goldman, we have two actions. In the first example, under certain circumstances *(C)* the movement of the arm *(A)* conventionally generates the action of signaling *(A')*. The performance of that second action is guaranteed by a set of rules stipulating that to perform action *(A)* under circumstances *(C) counts as* another action *(A')*.[14]

If one follows von Wright's view, it seems plausible to say that in such situations there is only one event, which can be described in different ways, depending on the properties one takes into account. We do not need to multiply entities: it is perfectly comprehensible that one and the same individual conduct can be identified as two individual actions, i. e., as an instance of more than one generic act.[15]

What has been said so far about normative or institutional and non-normative or natural actions rests on the distinction between two kinds of rules: semantic rules and rules of conduct. The former are metalinguistic rules which determine, by convention, the relation between words and the things or properties they denote. They do not belong to the language we use to refer to reality, but to a meta-language.[16] Rules of conduct, in contrast, are expressed in a language meant to refer directly to reality. They prohibit, permit or make obligatory the performance of certain actions. Generally, only rules of

---

[14] Cf. Goldman, Alvin, A Theory of Human Action, op. cit., ch. 2.

[15] Cf. von Wright, Georg Henrik, On the Logic of Norms and Actions, op. cit., pp. 114 f.

[16] Cf. Alchourrón, Carlos and Eugenio Bulygin, Los límites de la lógica y el razonamiento jurídico, in: id., Análisis lógico y Derecho, Madrid: Centro de Estudios Constitucionales 1991, pp. 305 f.

conduct are regarded as norms. It could be objected that the distinction is inconvenient and that the two classes of rules can be reduced to only one.[17] The price for the greater elegance such a reduction perhaps permits would, however, be very high: We would lose sight of the clearly different functions fulfilled by those two kinds of rules.[18] And even if such a reduction were admitted, it would not dissolve the difference between actions identified by normative properties and actions identified by non-normative properties. For that distinction, we only need to admit the existence of these two classes of properties, regardless of whether or not normative properties are elucidated with the help of some special kind of rules.

5. The Structure of Actions

It has been said that the concept of action is a complex concept including, as its elements an intention, understood as a psychological state internal to an individual, on the one hand, and a result, which normally consists in an external conduct that can be observed, on the other. Usually, the elements of an action and its teleological structure are shown with the help of the schema of a so-called practical syllogism. Of course, this is not to be understood as an attempt to conceive of action as an example of logical reasoning.[19] From this perspective, the first element of action – i. e., the mental state directed to obtaining a certain end – is mentioned in a statement that constitutes the major premise of the syllogism. The second element, consisting in a belief about the necessary and/or sufficient means for obtaining that end, is mentioned in another statement that constitutes the minor premise. Finally, the third element, i. e., the result of the action, is mentioned in the statement serving as the conclusion of the argument. According to this interpretation, action has an instrumental, means-ends structure. Among the most controversial issues in that context is the characterization of each one of the mental states involved, the question of whether they are necessary or sufficient for the performance of an action, the kind of relationship they have to the result, etc.

Like many other kinds of internal states – for instance, being pleased, angry, ashamed, feeling regret, etc. – desires and beliefs are commonly regarded as mental states. Although this use of language does not necessarily imply the admission of special entities independent of the physical processes going on in the brain, it does imply a meaning that cannot be reduced to an explanation of such processes.[20] The intentionality

---

[17] For example, by extending the argument presented by von Wright in the analysis of the rules of a game. Thus, one could say that semantic rules define all the moves admitted in the game. Real moves would then be qualified as correct or incorrect, depending on whether or not they conform to what the rules stipulate. Furthermore: „It is understood that moves which are not correct are *prohibited* [...], and that a move which is the only correct move in a certain situation in the game is *obligatory* [...]" (von Wright, Georg Henrik, Norm and Action, op. cit., p. 6).

[18] Cf. Hart, H. L. A., The Concept of Law (1961), Oxford: Clarendon 2nd ed. 1994, ch. III, pp. 38 ff.

[19] In Chapter III, I will analyse different concepts and kinds of practical syllogism.

[20] The ontological status of the mental states constituting the internal aspect of action is controversial; and therefore, so is the way how they affect the process resulting in the change produced by an action. However, the controversy about the mind-body problem that comes into play here cannot be treated within the much narrower confines of this book.

of some mental states consists is the property of being directed at, or being about, objects and states of affairs in the world.[21] For example, the 'intentionality' of the belief that there is an international book-lending service at the university, or the desire that there be such a thing, consists in that both states refer to another state of affairs that is the object of intention, namely, the international book-lending service. Intentional states always consist of representative contents in some psychological mode. The representative *content* determines the set of conditions which satisfy the intentional state, and its psychological *mode* determines the propositional content's direction of fit.[22] These ideas deserve to be elucidated in somewhat more detail.

John Searle relies on speech-act theory, in the belief that a comparison between speech acts and intentional states is the best way for explaining the latter. When applying that method, he emphasizes four fundamental connections:

(i) First, just as, concerning speech acts, we distinguish between their propositional content and their illocutionary force, in intentional states we can also distinguish between their representative content (in the example: the existence of an international book-lending service) and the psychological mode in which this representative content is held (the belief, the hope or the wish that such a service exists). Every intentional state thus has a content which, in the cases we are interested in here, is always a proposition about some actual or possible state of the world.

(ii) Second, the notion of direction of fit usually applied to speech acts also serves for the characterization of intentional states.[23] For instance, certain kinds of speech acts – as, e. g., assertions – are defined by their claim of fitting or corresponding to the world. The same can be said of certain intentional states as, for example, beliefs. On the other hand, just as with speech acts like orders, requests or commands, there are intentional states defined by their objective to produce changes in the world so that the world is made to correspond to their representative content, as is the case, for instance, with desires. It is this difference that is meant to be captured by saying that those acts and intentional states have a specific direction of fit distinguishing them from each other.

Direction of fit is one of the features on which the difference between wishes and beliefs is thought to rest. A wish is a mental state the content of which the world should

---

[21] Searle, John R., Intentionality: An Essay in the Philosophy of Mind, Cambridge: Cambridge University Press 1983, pp. 1-4.

[22] These characteristics apply only to those intentional states the content of which is a complete proposition, i. e., to so-called propositional attitudes. Cf. ibid., pp. 6 f. This is the case of desires and beliefs, which will be the only intentional states considered here.

[23] The idea of what later came to be known as 'direction of fit' was first introduced by Elisabeth Anscombe in her *Intention*, op. cit., § 32. Later, the concept has been discussed by several authors: cf., e. g., Platts, Mark, The Ways of Meaning, London: Routledge & Kegan Paul 1979; Smith, Michael A., The Humean Theory of Motivation, in: Mind 96 (1987); Pettit, Philip, Humeans, Anti-Humeans, and Motivation, in: Mind 96 (1987); Smith, Michael, On Humeans, Anti-Humeans, and Motivation: A Reply to Pettit, in: Mind 97 (1988); Price, Huw, Defending Desire as Belief, in: Mind 98 (1989); Dancy, Jonathan, Moral Reasons, Oxford: Blackwell 1993. According to Humberstone, the expression was first used in Austin, John L., How to Talk – Some Simple Ways, in: Proceedings of the Aristotelian Society 53 (1953), pp. 227-246; cf. Humberstone, Lloyd, Direction of Fit, in: Mind 101 (1992).

correspond to, and a belief is a state the world is expected to correspond to. Michael Smith, for example, uses the concept of direction of fit, analyzing it as a dispositional property that is different and distinctive for each of these states.[24] These different dispositions are manifested in the different ways of counterfactual dependence of, for instance, a belief that *p* and a desire that *p* in view of the perception that not-*p*. The belief that *p* is a state with the tendency to disappear when confronted with the perception that not-*p*, whereas the desire that *p* is a state that tends to be reinforced in that same situation, disposing the subject who has it to bring about *p*.

„Thus, we may say, attributions of beliefs and desires require that different *kinds* of counterfactuals are true of the subject to whom they are attributed. We may say that this is what a difference in directions of fit *is*."[25]

Jonathan Dancy attempts to show with an example what the notion of direction of fit means. Suppose a man whose wife believes him to be unfaithful goes to the supermarket with a list of all the things he is supposed to buy. He is observed by a detective who is instructed to write down everything he buys. Afterwards, the two lists – the husband's and the detective's – are likely to have the same contents, but they do not have the same direction of fit. If the husband's list does not correspond to what is in his shopping cart, that means that he has made a mistake in his shopping, not that there is a mistake in the list; but if the detective's list does not coincide with the things the husband bought, that means that there is a mistake in the detective's list, not in what the husband bought.[26]

Generalizing this idea, the notion of direction of fit allows us to point to the following. On the one hand, there are intentional states aiming only at fitting to what the world is like. If correspondence is not reached, something seems to be wrong with such a mental state, and there is then a disposition to change that state rather than the world. In this case, one speaks of intentional states with a mind-to-world direction of fit. The paradigmatic example is belief. On the other hand, there are states with the opposite direction of fit; they aim at reaching some end. Here, in contrast to the former, if the mental state does not correspond to the world, there is a tendency to bring about the necessary changes in the world, so that it will in the end correspond to the content of that mental state. In this case, one says that the intentional state has a world-to-mind direction of fit. The typical example is desire.

The concept of direction of fit is one of the most controversial issues in the characterization of intentional states. Although its metaphorical nature has been criticized, it is generally mentioned as a plausible way of expressing an intuitive difference between mental states. Most of the scholars who reject this criterion do not argue for a more precise idea or a better formulation. On the contrary, they assert that the fact that it is impossible to state precisely what it means for two intentional states to have a different direction of fit indicates that there is no such difference; in other words, that the alleged

---

[24] Smith, Michael, The Humean Theory of Motivation, op. cit. (hereafter, THTM).

[25] Ibid., p. 54.

[26] Dancy, Jonathan, Moral Reasons, op. cit., p. 27; the example is taken from Anscombe, Elisabeth, Intention, op. cit.,p. 56. Note that Dancy, although he offers an analysis of the notion of 'direction of fit', does not think that it allows one to stipulate a difference between beliefs and desires, as the Humean conception claims.

distinction between desires and beliefs does not exist. That controversy is closely related to the discussion between Humeans and rationalists and their different positions on the internal conditions of action, the theory of motivation, and moral theory.

(iii) Third, another notion shared by speech acts and intentional states is that of their conditions of satisfaction.[27] Searle points out the process-product ambiguity of that expression. Just as we can distinguish between the requirement of something and the required thing, he distinguishes two aspects of the notion of 'conditions of satisfaction'. What is internal to speech acts and intentional states, and necessary for them, is the requirement or aspiration that they be satisfied, not their actual satisfaction as such. How an intentional state or a speech act is satisfied depends on its direction of fit. Which facts or states of affairs actually do satisfy them depends on their content. As Searle observes:

„So, we will say that a statement is satisfied if and only if it is true, an order is satisfied if and only if it is obeyed, a promise is satisfied if and only if it is kept, and so on. Now, this notion of satisfaction clearly applies to Intentional states as well. My belief will be satisfied if and only if things are as I believe them to be, my desires will be satisfied if and only if they are fulfilled, my intentions will be satisfied if and only if they are carried out."[28]

To say that the conditions of satisfaction are internal to intentional states means, for example, that to have the belief that there is an international book-lending service at the university partly means to be aware of the fact that the belief is satisfied if the service exists and not satisfied if it does not exist. What is internal to the belief in the example is the *claim* that there really is a service of such characteristics, not its actual existence. The former is a necessary requirement related to belief; the latter, i. e., the existence of the required thing, makes the propositional content of the belief true, without being part of it. A belief is not a belief if it is not accompanied by a claim of truth; but it can exist even if it is not true. Thus, we must keep in mind the distinction between the content of intentional states – i. e., propositions – and the objects or states of affairs those propositions refer to – a distinction which, according to Searle, is essential for his theory. If those objects or states of affairs exist, then the corresponding belief is satisfied, since their existence makes the proposition true.

(iv) Finally, all speech acts express or manifest a characteristic intentional state. For instance, to make an assertion is to state the belief in the asserted proposition.[29] But such an act can be performed with or without sincerity. That means that the expressed intentional state may or may not exist. Therefore, the *sincerity condition* of a speech act is the actual presence of the intentional state expressed by that act. In Searle's words:

---

[27] This link between speech acts and intentional states holds only if the act in question has some direction of fit. For instance, acts of excusing oneself and mental states of remorse are speech acts and mental states that have no direction of fit, although they presuppose other states that do.

[28] Searle, John, Intentionality: An Essay in the Philosophy of Mind, op. cit., p. 10.

[29] This may be controversial. For example, according to Jonathan Cohen, making an assertion commits the speaker to accepting, rather than to believing the propositional content. Cf. Cohen, Jonathan, Acceptance and Belief, in: Mind 98 (1989), pp. 374-378. In Chapter V, I will discuss the distinction between these two kinds of intentional states in more detail.

„[I]n the performance of each illocutionary act with a propositional content we express a certain Intentional state with that propositional content, and that Intentional state is the sincerity condition of that type of speech act. Thus, for example, if I make the statement that *p*, I express a belief that *p*. If I make a promise to do *A*, I express an intention to do *A*. If I give an order to you to do *A*, I express a wish or a desire that you should do *A*."[30]

Searle states that the conditions of intentional sincerity are internal to the performance of illocutionary acts. A speech act necessarily is an expression of the corresponding intentional state. To perform a speech act and, at the same time, to deny that the corresponding intentional state obtains is, if not self-contradictory, at least logically bizarre. Using a classical example, it would be unusual to say 'It is raining, but I don't believe it is'.[31] This relationship between speech acts and intentional states can be used to point out an asymmetry between them. According to Searle, every speech act necessarily has conditions of sincerity. But not every speech act is sincere. The distinction between sincere acts and acts that are not cannot be projected onto intentional states. It makes no sense to say that one 'unsincerely' has a belief or a desire. In such a case, what happens is that one simply does not have that belief or desire. When we come to the analysis of the speech acts the justification of legal decisions is associated with, we will come back to this connection between speech acts and intentional states.

In synthesis, in order to explain the elements and characteristics of intentional states it is useful to set them in relation to speech acts. The theory elaborated about the latter can serve to compare and better understand what intentional states consist in. According to this methodology proposed by Searle, intentional states are identified by a representative content, a direction of fit, and certain conditions of satisfaction. What the specific conditions of satisfaction are in each case depends on the representative content. How they are satisfied depends on the intentional states' direction of fit, that is, the psychological mode in which an individual holds certain representative contents. In what follows, on the basis of this characterization of the states constituting the internal aspect of action, I will present several conceptions of those states and their quality as action-motivating factors.

6. The Motivation of Action

Positions on the motives of action differ, depending on the meaning and the scope attributed to the word 'motive'. In what follows, I will discuss some cases that show the ambiguity of the term as well as the vagueness of some of its meanings. Generally, the concept of motive refers to the internal elements of action. It points to psychological states

---

30 Searle, John, Intentionality: An Essay in the Philosophy of Mind, op. cit., p. 9.

31 The paradoxical nature of the assertion is based on the thesis that in conversation all acts of assertion imply the belief in what is said. This idea is widely accepted in the field of legal theory. Furthermore, in a certain parallel to the case of assertions, it is also held that issuing of a norm commits the norm-giver to the belief in the moral correctness of the norm's content. One of the theses of the necessary connection between law and morality is based on this opinion. As will be seen in Chapter V, the paradox can be reformulated in terms that do not lead to that necessary connection with the belief in truth or correctness.

which are related to the behaviour of an agent and enable us either to identify it as an action or to explain it teleologically.

(i) First sense: One concept of motive refers to those intentional states which cause the result of an action.[32] Here, the notion of result must be understood in the technical sense, i. e., the result of an action is that state of the world that is brought about by the intervention of the agent and constitutes the final phase of his action. There is profound disagreement as to which of the psychological attitudes of an agent are the causal factors that are necessary and/or sufficient for bringing about such a change. Thus, the term, when used in this general sense, can have different extensions. In some cases, it is said only of that state which is regarded as decisive for the production of the action. This is, then, the notion of motive that is at stake in the debate about what kind of mental states can, in fact, *motivate* action, that is, when what is discussed is which of the intervening factors (desires and beliefs) plays an active role in the production of the corresponding behaviour. In general, in this version, the concept of motive is used to denote only one of the elements of the internal aspect of action, namely, that which has a world-to-mind direction of fit and is normally identified with a desire.

The same concept of motive as a causal factor of the result of an action is also often applied, indiscriminately, to the set of beliefs and desires that gave rise to the change brought about by the agent on a particular occasion. In that sense, what is identified as the motive of the action is what earlier had been called its internal aspect or intention. No distinction is made between the two psychological elements an intention consists of. If the concept of motive is interpreted with that extension – or with the one mentioned in the last paragraph –, then every intentional action has a motive. Motives are then a necessary phase, or part, of actions. In that case, the only criterion for knowing whether or not an agent had a motive is whether or not he performed an action. If no action was performed, that means that the agent was not really motivated, or that something external made him fail in his attempt. In that sense, motives enable us to recognize a particular behaviour as the intentional action of an agent.

(ii) Second sense: Another characterization associates motives with mental states that are not internal to an action, but teleologically linked to it. In contrast to the mental states constituting intention, on this interpretation motives are those purposes which enable us to give an instrumental explanation of an action as an adequate means for reaching some end. The mental states involved in this case are representations of states of affairs the agent hopes to bring about as a consequence of his action. Such motives we must be able to identify independently of the action, in the description of which they need not appear. From this perspective, not every action has a motive, since not every intentional action is necessarily aimed at the satisfaction of some ulterior purpose. In other words, some actions have no teleological or intentional explanation. This is the case, for instance, of actions which are 'ends in themselves' or which are performed 'for their own sake'.[33]

---

[32] The idea that intentional states compel action implies that they not only make an action rational or intelligible, but also have causal relevance for its result. This double role of internal attitudes can be found in Davidson, Donald, Actions, Reasons and Causes, op. cit., pp. 3-19.

[33] This happens when the action itself is the object of the agent's intention and not a means for reaching some other end. Cf. von Wright, Georg Henrik, Explanation and Understanding, op. cit., pp. 122-124.

(iii) Third sense: Finally, the notion of motive can also refer, generically and indiscriminately, to all those factors internal to an agent which potentially have the capacity to affect the performance of an action.[34] The difference between this concept and the previous ones can be explained by comparing it with the distinction between the actual sense and the dispositional sense of the term.[35] In the first case, motives are actual states of affairs which on a particular occasion cause an action. In the second case, they are dispositions one may or may not be aware of which explain why one comes to have the specific desires or beliefs that give rise to an action. Under that second perspective, we can speak of the motives of an agent independently of his behaviour. Every individual, whether acting or not, has a number of motivations, i. e., desires, fears, prejudices, beliefs, etc. On that conception, motives are mental states an agent can, to the extent that he is aware of them, weigh and assess, thus coming to generate or discard actual desires or beliefs on rational reflexion.

In summary, the meaning of the term 'motive' always denotes internal intentional states of an individual. Sometimes, it is used to refer only to the volitional aspect in which, from Hume's point of view, the moving force of action lies. On other occasions, the notion of 'motive' also encompasses the cognitive element that is equally necessary for a behaviour to materialize. In these two uses, motives are conceptually necessary elements of action, and they are causally related to its result.

Another concept is the one applied to those mental states representing ulterior ends to which the action in question is regarded as a means. In that case, motives are still internal states of an individual, but they are not internal to action. They are independent of action, and enable us to explain action teleologically. The first as well as the second sense of motive are relative to an individual action. In other words, those motives are always motives of a particular action, performed at a certain time and at a certain place.

Finally, in contrast to the previous two senses, the broadest meaning refers to the set of mental states an agent has, independently of his actions. That means that it applies to all the subjective attitudes of an individual, even when they are neither the intention nor the purpose of any specific action. From this point of view, we can speak of an agent's motivations even before we know whether or not he intends to act.

All those meanings will be used when we come to discuss reasons for action. An explanatory sense of that notion is directly related to the motives of an agent. Therefore, the ambiguity and lack of precision mentioned above may have been passed on to one of the meanings of 'reason for action'. An adequate reconstruction of the latter expression, thus, cannot proceed directly from the meaning of motive, without first elucidating what that term means and in what extension it is used.

A classical proposal for motives of action understood in the first sense is supported by David Hume's ideas. According to that proposal, a desire as well as a belief are necessary for action. The desire is the 'motor', it is what has the active force to

---

[34] Bernard Williams, e. g., uses the expression in this sense when he refers to the „agent's subjective motivational set'. Cf. Williams, Bernard, Internal and External Reasons, in: Moral Luck. Philosophical Papers 1973-1980, Cambridge: Cambridge University Press 1991, pp. 101-113.

[35] Falk, W. D., 'Ought' and Motivation, in: Proceedings of the Aristotelian Society (1947-48), pp. 116-118. This is the sense that is involved when the relationship between the recognition of a duty and the motives of an agent are discussed.

motivate, whereas beliefs, although necessary, are mental states which in themselves are inert. Characteristic of this interpretation is the stipulation of a clear difference between the two kinds of mental states in question. Desires are non-cognitive states the explanation of which may involve beliefs, but which, in the last instance, are always explained on the basis of other desires. In contrast, beliefs are purely cognitive states. Each one of these states has one single direction of fit. As will be seen later, if one accepts this conception of the factors motivating action, this affects the positions one can adopt with respect to the two main topics of this study: *(i)* the question what kind of entities reasons for action may be, and *(ii)* the question how the practical relevance of normative statements can be explained.[36]

There are several theories of action offering alternatives to the Humean account. One aspect they all share is that they admit at least two different forms of motivation. From their point of view, some actions are based on a special kind of beliefs or desires Hume's characterization does not fit to. According to those theories, some desires cannot be explained as states that are merely emotional, just as some beliefs cannot be understood as merely cognitive states. On that conception, beliefs, just as desires, may be sufficient conditions for action.

Thomas Nagel, for example, asserts that there are motivated desires, which he understands to be desires brought about by a decision following deliberation.[37] Similarly, Philip Pettit refers to desires that are implied by the presence of certain beliefs which he calls „desiderative".[38] In this case, the desire inherits the cognitive status of those beliefs. Joseph Raz, in turn, refers to beliefs the content of which is the existence of the duty to perform some action. Such beliefs lead to a kind of attitude that is at the same time epistemic and practical, i. e., on the one hand they represent the world, and on the other they aim at changing it.[39]

All these proposals agree in that desire is the typical motivating state, but they adopt a more complex psychological theory according to which there are beliefs and desires with a double direction of fit, whereas in the Humean conception such intentional states could have only one.[40] On this new approach, there are beliefs which dispositionally behave like desires: the agent is not willing to give them up, even if they are contradicted by his perception of the world. Prominent examples of this can be cited from the history of science. For instance, from Plato to Kepler everyone believed in the principle that all movements of celestial bodies were circular. For a long time, observations contradicting that belief did not lead to its being abandoned.[41] Similarly, there are desires

[36] For instance, Hume's theory is committed to an internalist position on the identification of reasons for action. Furthermore, from that perspective the practical relevance of normative statements presupposes an internalist conception of the relationship between the existence of a duty and the motivation of an agent. With respect to the first subject, cf. section 7.b) of this chapter; on the second, sections 2 and 3 of Chapter IV about legal norms and reasons for action.

[37] Nagel, Thomas, The Possibility of Altruism, op. cit., pp. 28-32.

[38] Pettit, Philip, Humeans, Anti-Humeans and Motivation, op. cit., p. 531.

[39] Raz, Joseph, Practical Reason and Norms, London: Hutchinson 1975, p. 32.

[40] Cf. Smith, Michael, THTM, op. cit., p. 56.

[41] Cf. Brown, Harold I., Perception Theory and Commitment. The New Philosophy of Science, Chicago, Ill.: Precedent 1977, ch. VII.

which, since they depend entirely on beliefs, an agent would be willing to give up if the evidence taken from reality would suggest it. David Lewis speaks of an agent who desires things only insofar as he believes them to be good.[42] Huw Price uses a real example: his wish that his aunt Ana had died in 1989, only because in that case he would have inherited a fortune.[43]

For these conceptions, action does not lose its teleological nature; it can still be interpreted as a conduct directed towards some end. Intentional states aimed at reaching some goal can not only be spontaneous desires, but also desire-like beliefs, motivated desires, or other practical critical attitudes.[44] Besides, beliefs about the necessary means for reaching the goal pursued by an action are still needed. And that kind of beliefs always is of a strictly epistemic nature.

It is difficult to derive a simple classification of the positions that admit beliefs as a source for the motivation of action. There are several controversial aspects, and some authors agree on some of them while disagreeing on others. Among them, we can name, e. g., the phenomenological and the ascriptive conception of desire, the characterization of states with more than one direction of fit, the kinds of relationships possible between beliefs and desires, etc. In some cases, it is accepted that desires are necessary for motivation to exist, but they are not considered to be comprehensible independently of the beliefs that bring them about. In others, to say that an agent *desires* to do what he does is only a way of speaking, something attributed to an individual adequately motivated by the corresponding beliefs. In any case, beliefs are regarded to be sufficient for explaining action.[45]

Although they are presented as a critique of the Humean conception of motivation, those theories presuppose (in accordance with Hume) that states of a purely cognitive nature are insufficient for motivating action. The proof is that when they say that beliefs can be motivating, they introduce a non-epistemic component into beliefs that Hume would only have associated with desires. Although it is not said explicitly, there is agreement that for an action to be performed, there must be an intentional state with a world-to-mind direction of fit. That is so because an action is a teleological event, and the aim of bringing about a change in order to reach a goal is internal to it. But such an aim cannot be characterized as a merely cognitive state.

By way of conclusion, we can say that the concept of direction of fit allows us to preserve, and at the same time to enrich, the central idea of Hume's proposal. For an action to be performed, there must be an intentional state aimed at some end; a cognitive state alone is not sufficient. Intentional states aimed only at representing the world can-

---

[42] Lewis, David, Desire as Belief, in: Mind 97 (1988), pp. 323-332. Lewis argues that one cannot regard desires as beliefs. Throughout his essay, he attempts to prove that a thesis that admits desires as beliefs would contradict standard theories of rational decision.

[43] Price, Huw, Defending Desire as Belief, op. cit., pp. 123-125. Price argues in favour of a position that is opposed to that of David Lewis.

[44] It must be pointed out that the idea of desires motivated by beliefs is not incompatible with Hume's conception. The disagreement lies in the fact that for Hume such a motivation is also based on some ulterior desire. In this way, we come to basic desires that are not motivated, i. e., that do not depend on nor can be explained through other beliefs or desires.

[45] Cf. Dancy, Jonathan, Moral Reasons, op. cit., ch. 2.

not by themselves provoke action.[46] Now, it seems plausible to say that not only desires, as conceived by Hume, can have the appropriate direction of fit for mobilizing action. The agreement on the necessity of that kind of states for the production of action does not end the controversy between rationalists and Humeans about the origin of those states. The former hold that they can be totally rational products, whereas the latter say that in order to have the required direction of fit, we must have a state implying some volitional or emotional attitude.

This disagreement is, to a great extent, related to the wish to defend different conceptions of moral discourse and its practical relevance. A moral cognitivist must show how moral beliefs, that is, allegedly cognitive states, can motivate action. But it is important to note that that debate does not affect Hume's theory of the structure of human action and the elements it consists of. On the contrary, to the extent that they want to give practical relevance to moral knowledge, even cognitivist positions confirm Hume's theory of the structure of action, although they disagree about the consequences Hume arrives at. Each one of these philosophical proposals, at some point of the process of the acquisition of moral knowledge, introduces an element that is not merely cognitive and which explains the appeal to the action that is typical for that knowledge. Metaphysical realism, for instance, when applied to the ethical sphere, puts it into the very nature of moral facts, characterizing them as something essentially practical. Thus, belief in them is not a purely epistemic state. The very content of a value-judgment – for example, '*x* is good' – involves an appeal to action.[47] In a different way, a certain kind of internalism holds that the disposition to an action arises at the moment when a moral statement is accepted or agreed with.[48] To recognize something as correct implies a favourable attitude towards acting accordingly. This idea can be found, for instance, in Kant's theory according to which this practical inclination intrinsically linked to moral belief must exist in every human being in order to be considered rational.

7. Reasons for Action

With these basic ideas about action in mind, we can now go on to the presentation of a first approach to reasons for action. Two paradigmatic questions can be said to mark the two main axes of the philosophical discussion of this topic: What are reasons for action? And: Do reasons for action exist? Obviously, the answer to the second question depends on the answer given to the first. To say that there are reasons for action does not make

---

46 The idea that for an action to be performed there must be a mental state with the adequate direction of fit is compatible with the conception of Hume as well as with that of his critics. On this point, there is agreement, e. g., in Michael Smith, who attempts to defend Hume's conception, and in Jonathan Dancy, who criticizes Hume and attempts to show how mental states other than desires are also capable of bringing about action. In conclusion, it does not matter what kind of states one favours. What matters is their direction of fit.

47 This is the conception of Plato and Aristotle. It is also the one adopted by Mackie, although with the purpose of rejecting the existence of such entities. Cf. Mackie, John L, Ethics. Inventing Right and Wrong, London: Penguin 1977. For the characterization of metaphysical realism, cf. Moore, Michael S., Moral Realism as the Best Explanation of Moral Experience, Paper presented at the Saturday Discussion Group of Southern California Legal and Political Philosophers, January 21, 1989, mimeo.

48 Nagel, Thomas, The Possibility of Altruism, op. cit., p. 7.

any sense as long as it is not clear what it means that something is a reason for action. That is, the conceptual question must be answered before the ontological one. Besides, the different meanings of the notion of existence must be kept in mind.[49] The assertion of existential statements about reasons commits to different, not necessarily metaphysical kinds of entities.[50] In order to stipulate the truth-conditions of this kind of statements as precisely as possible, I will review three lines of discussion about reasons for action. The first concerns the different kinds of internal states that can be reasons for action. The second is about the question of whether reasons can also be entities external to an agent. And the third questions the possibility that reasons refer to different classes of entities, depending on their function, i. e., on whether they are to explain or to justify action.

A) REASONS: DESIRES OR BELIEFS?

In his 'Internal and External Reasons', Bernard Williams points out two properties a state of affairs must have in order to be regarded as a reason for action.[51] In this section, I will refer only to the first.

For Williams, if something is to be a reason for action, it must be able to motivate. That means that it must be possible that someone act *because of* that kind of entity. In that case, it must be possible for that entity to appear in some correct explanation of the action in question, although not necessarily in all correct explanations of it. This proposal links the notion of reasons for action with the concept of motive. As we have seen above, one of the classical ways of understanding the motivation of action is based on Hume's theory of action. The enormous influence of Hume's ideas in that matter make them an obligatory starting point for any analysis of reasons for action. This also explains why all alternative theories are in fact presented as a discussion of those ideas. According to Hume's theory, only desires can provoke action. Desires are the only specifically motivating kind of intentional states. A belief in itself cannot motivate. Therefore, a belief cannot by itself be a reason. It can at best be a reason in a secondary or derivative sense, namely, insofar as it is relevant for a desire.

On the contrary, if one adopts a theory according to which beliefs can have the right direction of fit for giving rise to action, the conclusion is different. From that point of view, not only desires can be reasons, because they are not the only things that can motivate action. A certain kind of beliefs by themselves can also be reasons. That is the position, e. g., of Bernard Williams who explicitly admits beliefs in the set of intentional states with the capacity to motivate action.

If presented in this way, the controversy seems to refer exclusively to a disagreement about the motivating power of different intentional states. Because of what has

---

49 Cf. Hare, Richard M., Ontology in Ethics, in: id., Essays in Ethical Theory, Oxford: Clarendon 1989, pp. 82-89. I will come back to the ontological question in Chapter V.

50 To the extent that the truth-conditions of such statements are fully established within a theory, an existential statement only commits to theoretical entities internal to that theory. Cf. Carnap, Rudolph, Empiricism, Semantics, and Ontology, in: L. Linsky (ed.), Semantics and the Philosophy of Language, Urbana, Ill.: University of Illinois Press 1952, pp. 208-228.

51 Williams, Bernard, Internal and External Reasons, op. cit., pp. 101-113.

already been said, a controversy in these terms about reasons for action would have to be regarded as settled. There is general agreement that an action cannot come about without some intentional state of a practical nature, i. e., a state defined by being directed towards obtaining some end. This characteristic is typical of desires, but it can also be present in other internal attitudes of a partially cognitive nature. Beliefs can be reasons if they presuppose or imply a practical attitude. And that is the factor that may not be absent if an action is to be performed.[52]

But there is also another way of opposing Hume's view as a basis for a theory of reasons for action. This critical position suggests that there are facts external to the agent which also pass the test of all reasons for action, that is, they have the capacity to motivate. In this case, what is questioned is the thesis that only elements internal to an agent can be reasons of action for him. One relevant meaning of the expression 'reason for action' refers to external facts. Thus, the criticism is that the application of Hume's ideas makes one unable to account for an important sense of that notion.

B) REASONS: INTERNAL OR EXTERNAL?

Common expressions like 'There is a reason for *A* to do *x*' the truth-conditions of which do not seem to require the presence of any internal element suggest that factors external to the agent can also constitute reasons for action. Bernard Williams denies this and presents an argument against the existence of external reasons: if it is true that a fact that is external to an individual can be a reason for his action, then it must have motivational capacity, independently of any internal factor. It must somehow be connected with the individual in order to be able to promote his action, and the appropriate link seems to be the belief in or the desire for that external fact. Williams admits that if an agent *believes* that some external fact is a reason for him to act, i. e., if he believes in a statement about the existence of an external reason, he is motivated in the right way. But in his view that happens because the *belief* (not the external fact the agent believes in) is an adequate factor for motivating an agent. The belief is a psychological fact internal to the agent which enables one to give a teleological explanation of his action. In other words, to say '*A* believes that there is a reason *R* for doing *x*' is an assertion of belief about an *external* reason which states the motivation of the agent and at the same time explains his action. But an agent who has such a belief in an external reason is an individual about whom one can always make a true statement of an *internal* reason: '*A* has a reason *R'* for doing x'.

According to Williams's argument, reasons for action are always internal to an agent. For something to be a reason, it must be able to be a motive, and a motive is an internal state of an agent. This suggests that the concept of reason for action varies with the interpretation of the notion of motive. Williams's thesis is that the interpretation of statements about reasons is relative to the respective agent's subjective motivational set (set *S*). From this point of view, reasons only potentially have a motivating nature. A mental state of an agent must not necessarily be the effective cause of an action (a motive in the first interpretation), nor the purpose that is to be reached by some parti-

---

[52] That means that the entire discussion about motives is projected onto the sphere of reasons for action. On this point, see above the discussion of the different theories of the motivation of action.

cular action (a motive in the second interpretation) in order to be able to be understood as a reason for action. In Williams's version, reasons are 'motives' in the third sense indicated earlier, that is, internal states that can become 'motives' of an action in the two previous senses. According to this conception, only elements internal to an agent, i. e., belonging to set *S*, can motivate action. The alleged external reasons thus do not satisfy the requirement that they must be able to motivate. A person's movement provoked exclusively by external factors without the participation of any subjective element seems to be what von Wright calls a 'reaction', where the person in question is not an agent and what he does is not an action. If reasons for action must satisfy the condition required by Williams, the very concepts of action and intentional explanation imply that reasons must be internal. Williams must conclude that there can only be internal reasons because that is presupposed by the concepts he uses.[53] But, then, what about statements that refer to external events as the reasons of an action? Must we say, as a result of Williams's analysis, that they are false or incoherent?[54] What kind of argument must one bring forward if one wants to broaden the concept in a way that admits the existence of external reasons independently of internal ones? Take for example:

(i) 'John went to see Mary because she was sick.'

The statement asserts an external fact (Mary being sick) which would usually be interpreted as the reason for the action in question (John's visit). Now, according to Williams, one would need to show that the agent's motivational set can be determined (i. e., extended or restricted) as a causal result of the existence of external factors. In other words, one would have to show that at least in certain cases external events do give rise to the internal reasons of an agent. In this way, those external factors would acquire indirect motivational relevance and enable us to broaden the explanation of actions. If that could be shown, it would become possible to distinguish two different meanings of 'reason for action': on the one hand, internal reasons – among them those which form part of the action and those which enable us to explain it teleologically; on the other, external reasons which causally determine the emergence of internal reasons and can be part of the explanation of an action too.

Two points should be noted about that proposal. First, the explanation of an action on the basis of external reasons, besides making use of the notion of reason for action in a sense that is different from the one used so far, is also a different kind of explanation than the one grounded on internal reasons. It is not a teleological explanation, but is rather based on probabilistic hypotheses or statements.[55] The fact given as a reason in this kind of explanations is an event that does not constitute a motive in any of the meanings normally attributed to that term. This way of interpreting statements about reasons which mention external events could not be admitted by Bernard Williams, since it requires the acceptance of a meaning of 'reason' that does not satisfy any of the

53 Cf. Cohon, Rachel, Are External Reasons Impossible?, in: Ethics 96 (1986), pp. 545-556.

54 Williams, Bernard, Internal and External Reasons, op. cit., p. 111.

55 In the following chapter, I will present different kinds of action explanations and the different concepts of reason they are grounded on.

criteria he proposes. As we will see shortly, the second one of these criteria also constitutes a constraint in favour of the internality of reasons.

According to Williams, the second property any reason must have is that it must rationalize the action. A person acting for a reason acts rationally in the following sense: if the agent were to deliberate on it consciously, she would be able to recognize that she has that reason. Such a rational deliberation is the process by which the subjective motivational set is changed, by discarding or incorporating reasons. Reasons are always elements arrived at by way of an exercise of deliberation. And just as the first one, this requisite shows that reasons can only be internal because the starting point as well as the result of all rational deliberation is always a subjective element of set *S*. What the agent takes into account in the deliberation process by which he comes to acquire new reasons and to discard others are not external factors, but his own beliefs, desires, fears, etc. Summing up, then, there is no way of forming set *S* on the basis of external elements. The generation, disappearance or correction of the factors belonging to that set is always the result of evaluation or deliberation, starting from other elements of that same set. Therefore, a statement of reason of the kind 'There is a reason for doing *x*' can plausibly understood only as the assertion that any rational agent who believes in that statement would be motivated to act.

In view of that last requisite, the possibility of being recognized as such in rational deliberation is a necessary characteristic of reasons. Hence, to say that '*x* is a reason for *A*'s action' is an ambiguous statement. It may mean merely that *x* is an internal factor which is in fact capable of motivating action, or that it is the factor which ought to motivate it if *A* would think about it rationally. This shows how the debate about reasons is moved from the strictly descriptive to a normative level where what is called reasons are those factors which ought to be taken into account by anyone wanting to be rational. In that case, an action is not rational simply because it can be reconstructed as an adequate means for the satisfaction of some motive of the agent in question. This new notion of reason and rationality presupposes some directive or principle of conduct. An agent acts for a reason, i. e., is rational, if the motivation that determines his action is the product of a deliberation in which the best reason is chosen. Note that in this context, the idea of best reason does not have a moral sense. In order to act rationally, what is implicitly required is that one must evaluate one's set of motivations and act in such a way that one's own purposes, rather than being frustrated, are promoted. An agent can make a mistake in the evaluation, thus choosing an action that is not really appropriate for his ends. Nevertheless, as J. L. Mackie has maintained, it makes no difference whether the general instruction of rationality is conceived as the requirement to do that which one *believes* to satisfy one's objectives or as the requirement to do that which *really* promotes them. Both principles, according to Mackie, will direct the agent to the same choice.[56]

The second condition a reason for action must satisfy, in Williams's view, tacitly presupposes that individuals do follow that general instruction of rationality. It is important to note, however, that once that is assumed as unproblematic the notion of reason for action acquires a new meaning. To act rationally implies to act for what so far has been called a reason, but to act for a reason does not imply to act rationally. For in-

---

56 Mackie, John L., Ethics. Inventing Right and Wrong, op. cit., p. 77.

stance, among the elements of the subjective motivational set there may be desires or goals that cannot be satisfied all at once. A principle of rationality then requires a hierarchical order, or some other criterion for the choice between such incompatible reasons. In that case, not just any action would be rational simply for being grounded on one of the elements of that subjective motivational set.[57]

Williams's second criterion imposes a substantial restriction on the use of the term 'reason'. The condition referring to the capacity to motivate is necessary, but not sufficient. Besides, on that account, reasons always rationalize an action, thus implying that the action is chosen by the agent following some criterion of rationality. Williams seems to identify *by definition* the elements of an agent's motivational set with the elements produced by a rationally guided choice. Otherwise, if one admitted that among an agent's motives there can be elements that are not voluntarily chosen, there would clearly be two senses of reason. Both refer to an agent's motives, and both explain his action. But while in one case they are the result of a rational *choice*, i. e., a choice guided by some principle of rationality, in the other case they are *causally* determined by the agent's environment and have come to be internalized by him in a non-deliberate way, i. e., without his rational decision.[58] Here, linguistic usage is far from clear: we can speak of two senses of reasons, or discriminate between motives and reasons, or between mental causes and motives. But it is important to note that all refer to entities that either produce or teleologically explain, but in no case justify an action. That notion of reason, however, which presupposes that one follow a principle of rationality usually leads to an inadvertent step from a notion of reasons as explaining actions to a notion of reasons as justifying actions. When an agent acts for a rationally chosen reason, he *believes* the action to be justified, relative to the principle of rationality he follows. But that, of course, is independent of whether the action actually *is* justified. The belief that something is justified is still a motivational element which explains, but does not justify the agent's action.

The step from a merely descriptive conception of reasons to a notion that presupposes normative principles has not always been clearly seen. On this point, see, for instance, Michael Smith's paper where he explicitly states that the notion of rationality provides a normative criterion and that therefore the concept of reason also acquires a normative nature.[59] Above, reasons for action have been regarded as empirical entities characterized by verifiable properties, as for example their capacity to produce action or their being internal or external to the agent. The fact that they may have been chosen following certain principles of rationality does not mean that those principles *explain* the action. In any case, such standards are reasons in a different sense, namely, *justificatory* reasons.[60]

---

[57] Cf. Caracciolo, Ricardo, Autoridad sin normas y normas sin autoridad, unpublished manuscript, 1994, p. 18.

[58] This distinction between voluntary and involuntary intentional states will be seen in more detail in Chapter VI. There, different kinds of mental states will be characterized in order to give more precision to the notion of acceptance.

[59] Cf. Smith, Michael, THTM, pp. 42 f.

[60] An example of that inadvertent step from one to the other type of reason can be found in Jay Wallace when he characterizes the rationalist conception in contrast to the Humean position. Wallace asserts that rational-

This distinction between explanatory reasons and justificatory reasons brings us to another way of presenting the controversy about this topic.

C) REASONS: EXPLANATORY OR JUSTIFICATORY?

The insight that the concept of reason for action appears indiscriminately in descriptive and in normative contexts raises a question about the differences and similarities between explanatory and justificatory reasons. Obviously, they presuppose the notions of explanation and justification. These concepts will not be analysed in detail here. I will only advance a pre-analytic idea in the sense that to explain or to justify an action is to respond to the questions of why that action *was* performed or why it *should* be performed, respectively. The relationship between the meanings of 'explanatory reason' and 'justificatory reason' can be conceived in different ways. One can define explanatory reasons in terms of justificatory reasons, or *vice versa*, or one can understand the two notions as independent concepts. The first two positions have to od with the idea of the priority of the normative-justificatory or of the explanatory-motivational, respectively. Here, then, we have one of the points of contention between rationalists and Humeans about the characteristics of moral discourse and its motivating force.

As an example of the position advocating the priority of the explanatory notion of reason one can mention all those meta-ethical proposals which reduce the meaning of normative terms to projections of people's individual or shared desires or beliefs.[61] Such a semantic conception also implies a reductionist position on the ontological level. In other words, the meaning of 'justificatory reason' is not independent of the meaning of 'explanatory reason', because there are no such things as the first concept refers to that could be identified independently of such things as the second concept refers to. According to that view, then, reasons in a justificatory or normative sense must be analysed in terms of reasons in the explanatory sense. Therefore, one must understand what the latter consist in, in order to be able to show how the former are constituted. Later we will see that it is possible to separate the ontological from the semantic questions and to hold a reductionist ontological thesis without being committed to a semantic thesis of that same kind.[62]

The opposite conception is that which gives priority to the idea of reason as a normative element that justifies action. According to Thomas Nagel,

---

ism advocates two theses: a stipulative one about the motivations a rational agent would have to have; and an explanatory one according to which the motivations of a rational agent can be explained in terms of norms or principles of correct reasoning. The Humean position, in contrast, is said to deny that the principles of rationality can explain motivation if no desire is involved. In that sense, the two conceptions are said to be opposed. Cf. Wallace, R. Jay, How to Argue About Practical Reason, in: Mind 99 (1990), pp. 358-360. According to the point of view adopted in the present work, to say that the principles of rationality can explain motivation or action, i. e., that they can be explanatory reasons, implies the confusion of two different and independent senses of reason.

61 Among them, all classical theories – the emotivist (non-descriptivist) as well as the naturalist subjectivist (descriptivist) ones. As a contemporary example, one can see Sen, Amartya, Rights as Goals, in: Guest, S. et al. (eds.), Equality and Discrimination: Essays in Freedom and Justice, ARSP Beiheft 21 (1985); cf. also Harman, Gilbert, The Nature of Morality. An Introduction to Ethics, New York: Oxford University Press 1977.

62 The argument in favour of that possibility will be presented in Chapter II, sect. 5.

„To understand the motivation we must understand how the ethical principle governs us. [...] This solution may seem to involve an illegitimate conflation of explanatory and normative inquiries. But a close connection between the two is already embodied in the ordinary concept of a reason, for we can adduce reasons either to explain or to justify action. [...] But though the explanatory and normative claims can diverge, this does not mean that we are faced with two disparate concepts finding refuge in a single word. When action is explained by reasons, it is brought under the control of normative principles. A consideration can operate as a motivating reason only if it has, or is thought to have, the status of a reason in the system of normative principles by which individuals govern their conduct."[63]

For Nagel, the concept of explanatory reason is subordinate to the concept of justificatory reason. Generally, one can say that this is the position adopted by all those whose thinking has a Kantian origin. The idea is formulated clearly by David Richards when he asserts that the justificatory notion of reason stands in an analytical relationship to the existence of principles of rationality or morality, and that the concept of explanatory reason is logically dependent on the notion of justificatory reason.[64] This dependence becomes obvious when one notes the difference between explaining an action in terms of mental causes and explaining it in terms of reasons for action (regardless of whether they are insufficient, sufficient, or conclusive). While the first kind of explanation says nothing about the agent's rationality, the second always implies some reference to principles of rationality or morality which constitute justificatory reasons. That does not mean that each and every action involves a process of deliberation about justificatory reasons. Richards distinguishes between *thought* and *belief* and holds that an action based on reasons is an action that requires, on the one hand, the *belief* in the validity of certain principles of rationality and morality and, on the other, the desire and the capacity to act in accordance with them. But it does not require that the individual must explicitly *think* about all that before acting. On this view, the *reasoning* involved in all action is a process that can be regarded as the logical structure of a belief of which the agent in question thinks that it justifies his action when he performs it.[65] Richards insists that this reasoning is not a psychological process. It is a characteristic that exists whenever an action is performed intentionally, even if it is carried out habitually and without thinking about it.

On this conception, only what justifies an action is really a reason, and the existence of reasons is independent of the agent's disposition to accept them. The conceptual relationship between justificatory and explanatory reasons, while necessary, is not immediate. Not always when an agent has a reason that explains his action does he accept or feel committed to a justificatory reason. The relation of dependence between the two concepts of reason is based on the fact that it is impossible to understand what an action carried out for an (explanatory) reason consists in if one does not previously, on a metatheoretical level, have the notion of justification and, with it, the notion of justificatory reason. According to Richards, whoever acts for an (explanatory) reason has a concept of what a rational choice is. And that means that such a person is aware of certain prin-

---

63 Nagel, Thomas, The Possibility of Altruism, op. cit., pp. 14 f.

64 Richards, David A. J., A Theory of Reasons for Action, Oxford: Clarendon 1971, p. 54.

65 Ibid., p. 58.

ciples that justify action – even if she herself rejects them and prefers to act without adapting her action to what they prescribe.[66]

That way of seeing the relationship between the two concepts of reason must be distinguished from the one where the link is made directly. An example of that position can be found in Joseph Raz.[67] Raz holds that an explication of the concept of reason for action must show three things: *(i)* how the notion serves different purposes, i. e., explains, justifies and guides conduct; *(ii)* how those purposes are interrelated, and *(iii)* why one and the same concept can serve all three objectives. For Raz, reasons are those facts „in virtue of which true or justified statements are true or justified".[68] If it were admitted, a purely explanatory notion of reason would be a secondary notion presupposing the notion of justificatory reason. Strictly speaking, it could be eliminated in favour of belief in justificatory reasons;[69] because explanations of actions in terms of reasons

> „explain the agent's behaviour in terms of his beliefs as to what he should do, in terms of his own assessment of the relevant reasons (in the primary, normative, sense) which apply to him".[70]

Raz understands the concept of reason to be just one, and he thinks that this single concept is all that is needed to account for the meaning of the different reason-sentences. As he himself admits, however, that proposal inevitably implies a certain degree of regimentation of the notion in question. And it seems very important to underline how that regimentation shapes the concept of reason for action. So far, following a line of work taken mainly from the theory of human action, the notion of reason, according to the different positions, had referred to those (epistemic or volitional, external or internal) factors (mediately or immediately related with an action) which are capable of motivating behaviour. But seen from this new approach, the main sense of reason is a normative one. The term thus no longer refers to the internal determinants capable of producing a behaviour. Still, Raz admits that the expression can be used in both senses:

> „We should admit that we use reasons in both ways. We could even distinguish between two notions of reason. But they should not be regarded as of equal significance. Only reasons understood as facts are normatively significant; only they determine what ought to be done."[71]

The question about reasons then is no longer the one formulated by Bernard Williams, about the factors that can give rise to action. What we are interested in now is which facts indicate what ought to be done. Such facts are reasons for action, independently of whether they come to be known or desired and, therefore, whether they lead to action.

This point of view suggests the distinction between mental causes, motives, and reasons. What until now had been called 'reasons internal to an agent' should be trans-

---

66 Ibid., p. 54.

67 Raz, Joseph, The Authority of Law. Essays on Law and Morality, Oxford: Clarendon 1979; id., Practical Reason and Norms, op. cit. (hereafter, PRN); id., The Morality of Freedom, Oxford: Oxford University Press 1986.

68 Raz, Joseph, PRN, p. 17.

69 Ibid., p. 19.

70 Ibid.

71 Ibid., p. 18.

lated either in terms of mental causes[72] or in terms of motives,[73] and they are not to be confused with reasons for action. That concept refers to something objective and external to the individual, the primary function of which is not to give rise to and explain, but to guide and justify action. If one accepts this regimentation of the concept, one must also accept an important terminological consequence. There is, for example, a certain kind of desires that can lead to action although they do not consist in beliefs about justificatory reasons. *Ex hypothesi*, such desires, then, are not justificatory reasons, i. e., they are not facts that are relevant in determining what ought to be done. And they are also not explanatory reasons, i. e., they are not beliefs in justificatory reasons. Therefore, an explanation of the action in question on the basis of those desires would not be an explanation in terms of reasons or motives. It can perhaps only be considered an explanation in terms of mental causes. This general idea of reducing the meaning of reason to normative or justificatory considerations, as opposed to mental causes or motives of action, is accepted by several authors; not so the idea that reasons should be regarded as facts.[74] In any case, if one adopts that point of view, in order to avoid confusion one should give up the explanatory notion of reason, because then the only existing reasons are justificatory. Technically speaking, what is usually said to be a reason that *explains* an action is nothing but the belief in a fact that *justifies* that action. If such a fact does not exist, that is, if the belief is false, then there simply was no reason for the action.[75]

Finally, it should be noted that there is a still stronger way of uniting the two concepts of reason. This becomes apparent, for instance, in von Wright's example:

> „I did A. Someone challenges me 'Why did I do this?'. I may *justify* my conduct by reference to what I was after and that I thought my doing of A a practical necessity for me (this, however, is not the only sense in which a man is said to 'justify' his actions)."[76]

In this case, that which from the perspective of an observer explains the action is exactly what for the agent himself is its justification. From the ontological point of view, the explanatory reason is the same as the justificatory reason. It is the same event, seen in one case by a third person and in the other case from the perspective of the agent him-

---

[72] The distinction between mental causes and motives can be found, e. g., in Anscombe, Elisabeth, Intention, op. cit., pp. 15 ff.; cf. also Anscombe, Elisabeth, Intention, in: White, Alan (ed.), The Philosophy of Action, Oxford: Oxford University Press 1968, pp. 144-152, esp. pp. 145-148.

[73] On this, cf. Grice, G. R., Motive and Reason, in: Raz, Joseph (ed.), Practical Reasoning, Oxford: Oxford University Press 1975, pp. 168-177.

[74] Cf. Nino, Carlos S., Introducción a la filosofía de la acción humana, Buenos Aires: Eudeba 1987, p. 83.

[75] On this question, see Ricardo Caracciolo's critique, pointing out the consequences following from that relation of dependence between the concepts of reason. Caracciolo observes that if one adopts Raz's thesis only true beliefs can be considered reasons that explain an action. If the belief is false, that is, if the fact that makes it true (the justificatory reason) does not exist, then that belief is no reason, since explanatory reasons depend on justificatory reasons. If a false belief were an explanatory reason, then one would have to admit that justificatory reasons are irrelevant, in other words, that beliefs are explanatory reasons independently of the existence of justificatory reasons. Cf. Caracciolo, Ricardo, Autoridad sin normas y normas sin autoridad, op. cit., pp. 34 f.

[76] Von Wright, Georg Henrik, On so-called practical inference, in: id., Practical Reason, op. cit., p. 30. I will come back to this concept of justification in Chapter V in the context of the discussion of the notion of acceptance in relation to justificatory reasons.

self. Even so, the qualification as a justificatory reason is primary, since in giving the reasons that explain an action what one intends to do is to spell out what the agent's justification was. What reason explains an action depends on what reason justifies the action for the agent.

It is important to note that the last one of the three positions just presented presupposes a radically different concept of justification and of justificatory reason than the other two. In the first two approaches, the concept of explanatory reason presupposes the concept of justificatory reason by way of the agent's belief in certain principles that justify an action or in the existence of justificatory facts. But, of course, it is never said that beliefs justify an action. The action is justified only if it does in fact conform to the adequate principles or facts, regardless of whether or not the agent believes in them or accepts them. The notion of justification appeals to principles of action or to normative facts, not to an individual's subjective states. In the third case, in contrast, the notion of justification refers to what the agent in question intends, desires, or believes to be the right thing to pursue. The distinction between the belief that an action is justified and its actually being justified, which is essential in the first two positions, disappears in the third one. The disagreement between those positions derives from the fact that the former see justification, and therefore also justificatory reasons, from a normative point of view that is external to the individual, e. g., a religious, moral, or legal point of view, whereas the latter understands justification, and with it justificatory reasons, from a psychological point of view that is internal to the agent.[77]

The approaches to the notion of reason for action presented here are not mutually unrelated. In general terms, we can say that those who tend to defend the priority of the justificatory concept of reason are those who also hold that external reasons exist and that one can regard beliefs as sufficient motives for action. On the other hand, those who defend the priority of the explanatory concept of reason must admit only the existence of internal reasons and the thesis that desires are the only motivating factors. The greatest difficulty with this topic is not that there are several opposed positions, because that could very well help foster the understanding of what is disputed. The problem is that the apparent agreement that supports all those currents is based on the ambiguity of the term 'reason'. It is not very helpful for the elucidation of the concept to say, for instance, that a justificatory interpretation is primary to an explanatory one, or *vice versa*, without first saying precisely what the two notions are supposed to mean. And it also seems not very convincing to identify the explanatory and the justificatory senses of reason *a priori* with subjective or objective elements, respectively.[78] Such equations are problematic. On the one hand, starting from the assumption that explanatory reasons can only be factors internal to an agent means to discard without any argument the possibility that external states of affairs can also be a kind of explanatory reason. On the other, to identify the notion of justificatory reason from the very beginning with external objective data

---

[77] On the different concepts of justification cf. Schueler, G. F., The Idea of a Reason for Acting. A Philosophical Argument, Lewiston: Edwin Mellen 1989, pp. 25-63.

[78] Carlos Nino, for example, directly commits himself to that identification which makes it impossible to speak of objective or external 'explanatory' reasons and of subjective 'justificatory' reasons; cf. Nino, Carlos S., La validez del derecho, Buenos Aires: Astrea 1985, p. 126.

makes it impossible even to suggest that that kind of reasons could also be a product of beliefs or other subjective attitudes of people.

In view of these controversies about the meaning of reason for action, it does not seem promising to look for, or to stipulate, one single sense. That means that methodologically it is not advisable to begin this investigation with an attempt to establish the necessary conditions for something to be a reason for action, e. g., whether or not reasons must be internal or external, or explanatory or justificatory. That would amount to a regimentation of the use of the term from the very start.

In what follows, the strategy will be another one. I will analyse different kinds of meaningful statements related to the notion of reason for action. To the extent that we can determine the truth-conditions of such statements, we will be able to see one of the meanings of 'reason for action'. With this purpose in mind, I will now go back and start the analysis all over from another point of view that will show that there are different, mutually independent concepts.

CHAPTER II

REASONS FOR ACTION – SECOND PART

1. Introduction

Earlier, I have distinguished between the ordinary and the technical use of the expression 'reason for action'. A clear case of the latter is the use of that notion in the analysis of other concepts – for instance, that of a legal norm, or that of the acceptance or justification of a decision. The technical use presupposes a precise meaning of 'reason for action' since otherwise statements containing the expression cannot fulfil the cognitive function assigned to them.

Let me begin with a clarification: It is assumed that the meaning of words depends on their use, rather than that it consists in that use. Thus, the meaning of the word 'meaning', insofar as it also depends on a use, is variable. On the theoretical level, one of the most common proposals alludes to the set of generic properties serving as criteria for the use of a word. Such criteria enable us to identify the scope of a term, i. e., they determine the class of objects it refers to.

According to this point of view, the expression 'reason for action' does not have just one single meaning. Different uses take different properties to be relevant, and in that sense constitute different meanings. The pragmatic aspects connected with the use of statements of, or about, reasons for action are not independent of the problem of meaning; but they deserve some consideration of their own. For this purpose, the properties taken into account as the criteria of usage, i. e., what has been called 'meaning', will be distinguished from an act of speaking or writing performed on a particular occasion. Context, including, among other aspects, the ends and interests pursued by a speaker, is what indicates what is done, or what is intended to be done, in speaking. For example, in legal theory the use of the notion of reason for action in the analysis of different problems puts the expression into different contexts. In each one of them, it has a specific function. Thus, we can mention three different purposes the concept can be used for:

(i) explanation,
(ii) justification, and
(iii) analysis.

As we have seen above, even proposals intended to stipulate one single meaning of the expression 'reason for action' recognize that there are two uses that can be distinguished: a *descriptive* one, when the expression is used for the purpose of giving an explanation, and a *normative* one, when the purpose is to offer a justification. This ambiguity is normally dissolved by the context. Generally, within a context in which a behaviour is explained or justified, the use of the word 'reason', even when it is not accompanied by any further specification, does not give rise to any difficulties of understanding, besides and above those genuinely connected with the purpose of explaining or justifying an action. However, this does not extend to the use of the notion of reason for action as an instrument in the semantic analysis of other concepts. There, the term is not used with a new meaning, but with one of those it already has in its explanatory or justificatory function. Therefore, if the sense in which it is used in analysis is not specified, ambiguity can lead to problems other than those we always encounter in the understanding and analysis of concepts. In the remainder of this chapter, I will consider only the notion of reason for action and its relation to the notions of explanation and justification. Against positions that attempt to unify the concept, I will defend the thesis that the ambiguity cannot be eliminated since the meanings involved are mutually independent. Once the different concepts have been sorted out, in the following chapters I will examine their use in contexts of semantic analysis.

2. Explanation and Justification

To state or give a reason why something was done amounts either to an explanation or to a justification. Therefore, in order to understand the sense of the word 'reason' in each one of these situations, we need a clear definition of what 'explaining' and 'justifying' mean.

First of all, it must be noted that these terms suffer from process-product ambiguity. On the one hand, they denote the *act* of expressing a set of grounds, causes or reasons supporting an explanation or justification; on the other, they also refer to the *result* of such an act.[1] The first sense (referring to the act of explaining or justifying) would perhaps be conveyed better by the expression 'giving an explanation' or 'giving a justification'. The locutions 'explaining' and 'justifying' could then be reserved for their respective results. In any case, the ambiguity indicates that these notions can be analysed from both perspectives.

As with all acts that can be performed through language, some typical distinctions can be drawn with respect to acts of explanation or justification. We can, for instance, distinguish three aspects. First, there is the act of uttering some words or sentences. Then, there are different actions performed through such locutions. And, finally, there are states of affairs brought about as consequences of such actions. In other words, we can distinguish between so-called locutionary, illocutionary, and perlocutionary acts involved in speech-acts.[2] In the following sections, the discussion will mainly concentrate on illocutionary acts. I will analyse what it is that is done when certain statements said to be an explanation or a justification of an action are made. The question can be answered in different ways. Here, I propose an answer that requires only a minimum of concessions which can easily be agreed to: Acts of explaining or of justifying an action are illocutionary acts answering to questions about why the action was performed or why

---

[1] Cf. Caracciolo, Ricardo A., Justificación y pertenencia, in: Análisis Filosófico 2 (1988).

[2] Austin, John L., How to Do Things With Words, The William James Lectures 1955, eds. J. O. Urmson and Marina Sbisà, 2nd ed. Oxford and New York: Oxford University Press 1990.

it should have been performed, respectively. Since explaining and justifying are not basic acts, they are always performed through some other act, for instance, through the act of making certain sounds, of writing certain letters, of uttering a series of statements in speaking or in writing, etc. Such acts are a means of performing an action of explanation or justification. And an act of explanation or justification, in turn, can be performed as a means of performing some other action which would then have to be regarded as a kind of *effect* of the former.[3] For example, one can explain or justify an action in order to compare it to another action, to convince a judge, to mislead someone, etc. Which action can be imputed to an agent on a particular occasion will depend on the rules regulating the use of those terms.[4]

The factors that are relevant for an explanation or justification are determined by each context. That means that an explanation or a justification of one and the same action may be different, depending on the context in which it is given. For the explanation of an action from a historical point of view, for instance, attention must focus on other aspects than those relevant for a psychological investigation. The same applies to justification. For example, the justification of the duty to take care of one's children, when given by a judge in a civil court, will invoke other principles than the ones that will be prominent in the justification given by a priest intending to utter a religious reproach. What does not change from one context to another with the content of an explanation or a justification is the kind of relationship established by it. What the contextual variation shows is only that explanations or justifications are never absolute. They are always relative to some sphere of interest, and what is relevant for one context may not be relevant for another.[5]

Before I begin with the analysis of the notion of reasons for action with respect to explanation and justification, remember that there is also another notion of reason, called a 'premise-reason', and this too is connected with the idea of explanation and justification. As I said before, acts of explanation and justification are performed through other actions. An uncontroversial requirement is the spoken or written formulation of a number of statements. What is controversial, however, is whether or not that sequence of statements must be a valid argument in the logical sense. In any case, the presentation of a set of statements, normally in the form of an argument, is one phase to be distinguished in that kind of acts. Understood very generally as speech-acts, they are not *one* of the forms in which explanations or justifications are performed, but *the* only way in which they can be carried out. The locutionary action of uttering or writing a sentence or, if you wish, the action of unfolding an argument in speech or in writing, is the action by

---

[3] It should be recalled that, according to the proposed approach, actions can have effects, which are not necessarily causal. Cf. Chapter I, sect. 4.

[4] There are cases in which such rules authorize one to attribute an action to someone only if one has shown the existence of the corresponding intention. In other situations, the production of the result is sufficient, and the rules require the imputation of the action without admitting any proof to the contrary. Finally, when the rules neither require nor reject a proof of intention, the imputation may be controversial, depending on whether or not a proof of intention is thought to be necessary. On this, see Chapter I, sect. 3.

[5] As far as the justification of actions is concerned, contextual relativity is a very controversial matter. However, it should not be confused with the relativity of justificatory principles. The latter is involved in the controversy about the principle of the unity of practical reasoning which will be discussed in Chapter V.

which an explanation or a justification is given. On this description, then, the assumption is that there is one and only one action: that of explaining or of justifying, for which the formulation of an argument is an instrumentally indispensable activity.

But we can also identify the act of formulating a sequence of sentences as an independent action. In that way, two actions are distinguished: an action of explanation or justification in the formal sense, and another one of explanation or justification in the substantive sense. Both are externally manifested in the same way: through the uttering of a number of statements. But they have different intentions and results. The intention of a formal justification is merely the correct articulation of a sequence of statements. For this purpose, one only needs to assume a number of propositions or norms from which a conclusion is drawn. In order to explain or justify something in the formal sense, neither the intention of making the action comprehensible (when explanatory reasons are mentioned) nor that of assenting to it and endorsing it (when justificatory reasons are given) is required. Acts of explanation or justification in the substantive sense, in contrast, presuppose those further intentions; therefore, for them, mere logical assumption of the (propositional or normative) content is not enough: it must also be accepted.[6]

Thus, for instance, an agent may only want to bring forward an explanatory or justificatory argument in order to test whether he has learned the rules of inference, or in order to compare the conclusion with that of another argument. In other words, the intention of the agent may be only the articulation of a sequence of statements. In such a case, one possible description is to say that the agent presented an argument, but did not intend to explain or justify an action. That implies that one single concept of explanation and justification is admitted. The description will be different if two notions are distinguished: a formal one and a substantive one. In that case, one could say that the agent neither explained nor justified the action in the *substantive* sense of the term, but that *formally* he did indeed give an explanation or a justification of the action. The words 'explanation' and 'justification' are normally used in both these senses. In what follows, I will adopt the second way of describing the situation, i. e., I will assume that there are two concepts of explanation and justification.

Regardless of the position one adopts, note that there are, if not two altogether different actions, at least two aspects of the action. This is important because they involve different notions of reason. From the formal point of view, through the sequence of the argument in which a substantive explanation or justification is presented, a formal relationship between sentences is established even in those cases where the final purpose is an explanation or justification in the substantive sense. A formal justification is a number of statements from which a conclusion is drawn. Here, the reasons are the (propositional or normative) contents which play the role of premises.[7] This notion of reason as a premise of an argument should not be confused with the substantive notion of reason for action, just as the formal notion of justification should not be confused with the substantive notion of that term. Formal justification is linked to the notion of premise-

[6] On the distinction between assuming and accepting a content, cf. Chapter V.

[7] The logical cogency of such sequences of statements is one of the controversial aspects of this topic. On this point, see the next chapter.

reason; substantive justification involves the substantive concept of reason for action. Whether a premise-reason really expresses a reason for action is a contingent matter. And whether something is a premise-reason depends on its role in an argument; and arguments can be about very different matters. Only some of them are intended to explain or justify actions. Hence, only some premise-reasons are linked to reasons for action. Besides, a premise-reason that mentions a reason for action may be false. In that case, it fails to provide a reason for action, but that does not affect its condition of being a premise-reason. For a content to be a premise and, in that sense, a reason which supports a conclusion, it must neither be nor refer to a reason for action. The fact that premise-reasons sometimes *mention* and sometimes *constitute* reasons for action has caused confusion about these two senses of the word 'reason'. And the confusion is made even worse by the additional fact that reasons for action as well as premise-reasons are said to be *justificatory*. But as we have seen, that predicate means different things in the different cases.

The conditions something must satisfy in order to be a premise-reason capable of formally justifying a conclusion are determined by the theory of arguments, i. e., by logic. In that sense, the essential condition is that it must be a statement or proposition.[8] On the other hand, the conditions for something to be regarded as a reason capable of explaining an action depend on what theory of action and of explanation one adopts. Similarly, the conditions for something to be regarded as a reason that justifies an action in the substantive sense depends on what normative conception (religious, political, legal, moral, etc.) one chooses. These last two ideas of reason linked to the substantive concept of explanation or justification, respectively, are the ones I will be concerned with in this chapter. A reason in the substantive sense does not need to be uttered, nor must it be part of an argument. The notion of reason as a premise of an argument will be examined in the next chapter.

3. Explanation and Justification as Illocutionary Acts

In this section, I will analyse the acts of explaining and justifying from the perspective of their content, i. e., as acts intended to answer the questions, already mentioned above, of why some action was performed or why it should have been performed. Seen as generic illocutionary acts, explanation and justification, as all actions, are defined by an internal aspect and a characteristic result. Explaining and justifying are different actions insofar as they are guided by different purposes and also conclude in different results. Explanation always has a descriptive purpose, whereas the purpose of justification is evaluative or normative. The internal aspect, i. e., the intention of explaining, presupposes a *cognitive* interest in making the action in question comprehensible. In contrast, the intention of justifying an action presupposes a *practical* interest in evaluating or endorsing it. The respective results consist in the satisfaction of these intentions. The statements through which such actions are performed establish a specific relationship between the action

[8] In this chapter, I will use the words 'statement' and 'proposition' interchangeably, in the sense of 'meaningful linguistic expression'. In the next chapter, it will be necessary to establish their precise meaning.

that is explained or justified and the reasons for it. Generally, an explanation or justification is not given by uttering one single statement, although in a very simple case this may be possible. Therefore, it would perhaps be better to reconstruct explanation and justification as an activity involving a process, rather than as an act.[9] But that activity too would be identified by an internal aspect and its result.

A) THE INTERNAL ASPECT

The descriptive interest assumed in explanation and the evaluative attitude assumed in justification indicate that these acts have different directions of fit. The direction of fit of a speech-act is manifested in the speaker's disposition to stick to his statements or to take them back when confronted with opposing evidence. As a verbal act defined by a descriptive interest, an explanation has the word-to-world direction of fit typical of all assertive acts. The statements constituting its external manifestation are defined by their claim to correspond with reality. Justification, in contrast, has the world-to-word direction of fit generally found in directive acts;[10] i. e., it is characterized by the purpose of making reality correspond with what is said.

The direction of fit the generic acts of explanation and justification in the substantive sense are necessarily committed to must be distinguished from the sincerity or insincerity they may be performed with on a particular occasion. The generic act of explaining an action by giving the reasons for its performance is, by definition, the assertion that the reasons mentioned are in fact the answer to the question of why that action was performed. An individual act of explanation conveys the impression that the speaker really believes what he is saying; that is, it presupposes the *acceptance* of the propositions the explanation is based on. That is why it is characterized by a word-to-world direction of fit. The same can be said with respect to the act of justifying an action in terms of reasons in its favour. The generic act of justification analysed in this book consists in grounding the duty or permission to perform the action in question. Such an act conveys the impression that the speaker *accepts* the normative standards a justification is based on. Hence, the perplexity which, from a pragmatic point of view, results from saying things like 'John returned the book to Peter because he wanted to keep his promise, but actually what I'm saying is wrong' or 'You should accompany John, because we should all help those in need, but I think that norm is wrong'. Such attempts must fail: the former, because immediately after stating the motive it denies that this really was the motive; and the latter because it appeals to a standard of justification and at the same time denies the adequacy of that standard for justifying the action in question. On the other hand, these observations should not lead to rash conclusions about the intentional states a speaker actually is in when he explains or justifies something. The existence of those intentional states on a particular occasion is the condition for the sincerity of those acts. The conditions of sincerity are internal to the act, in the sense that they define it. Therefore, whenever someone is said to have given an explanation or justification, he or she is also necessarily attributed the corresponding intentional state. But whether or not

[9] Cf. von Wright, Georg Henrik, Norm and Action, op. cit., ch. II, sect. 5, and ch. III, sect. 6.

[10] Searle, John R., Intentionality: An Essay in the Philosophy of Mind, op. cit., pp. 4-9.

the speaker was actually in that state is another question. Perhaps, as some authors say, the expressions mentioned above are pragmatically contradictory. But neither an explanation nor a justification is pragmatically contradictory if the speaker, *without revealing it*, does not have the internal attitude characterizing one or the other. In that case, strictly speaking, the agent has not performed the imputed action. But the linguistic rules governing the use of those concepts may permit one to attribute the action to an agent even when there is no evidence of the corresponding intention. The action will then be imputed to the agent without prior knowledge of his internal attitudes, unless the speaker is explicit about them. The idea that the act must be sincere is linked to the thesis that all speech-acts imply a claim of correctness. On this point, we can refer, for instance, to Philip Soper who in his analysis of the relationship between claims of justice and the law takes the case of promises as an example:

„It is usually agreed that part of the very meaning of promise is the idea that one commits oneself to act in the future in a way in which one would not otherwise be obligated to act [...] Thus, one can imagine people who do not in fact intend to commit themselves nevertheless making promises. Those people, one would say, are forced to pretense. Indeed, the whole point of the pretense lies in taking advantage of what the pretender knows is understood within society whenever the language of promise is used [...] What one cannot do is make a promise and simultaneously deny any intention of keeping the promise or any belief in an obligation to keep promises. In that case, the promisee understands that no promise has been made, but at most only a statement of future intent."[11]

In contrast to intentional states, linguistic acts can be insincere, but that does not affect the possibility of attributing an individual action to someone. When it is hidden, the absence of the corresponding internal state not only does not impede the imputation, it is also a symptom of the speaker having the generic skill necessary for performing that kind of act. The agent knows that if he revealed that he does not have the attitude defining that act he would commit a pragmatic contradiction and would not reach his goal, namely, to convey the impression that he is explaining or justifying the action. To impute an individual action of explaining or justifying in terms of reasons for action means to impute an intention and a characteristic result. The rules governing the usage of the terms are variable. In some contexts, a proof of the existence of the respective intentional states may be required before it can be admitted that someone has explained or justified an action. In other contexts, one may be able to impute such actions without having to discuss the existence of those internal attitudes.

In conclusion, then, one cannot claim to perform an explanation or a justification in the substantive sense without conveying the impression that one accepts the correctness of what one is saying. But a situation may adequately be described as an act of explanation or justification without the speaker actually *having* such an intentional state.

---

[11] Soper, Philip, A Theory of Law, Cambridge, Mass. and London: Harvard University Press 1984, p. 36 f. Here, we could distinguish between belief and acceptance as different attitudes. Cf. Cohen, Jonathan, Acceptance and Belief, op. cit.; Bratman, Michael E., Practical Reasoning and Acceptance in a Context, in: Mind 101 (1992); Williams, Bernard, Deciding to Believe, in: id., Problems of the Self. Philosophical Papers, 1956-1972, Cambridge: Cambridge University Press 1973, pp. 136-151. Here, I will not discuss the kind of internal attitude involved in the performance of assertive and directive acts. According to Soper's text, that attitude is the belief in truth or in correctness, respectively. That conception, however, is controversial. The arguments on this point will be presented in Chapter V.

Otherwise the discourse, i. e., the speech-act, would be identified with the intentional states, without taking into account the possibility of hypocrisy and simulation.[12]

I insist on this difference because some authors suggest that attributing an individual act to someone (as, for example, the justification of a verdict) implies that the agent (in the example: the judge) has a certain intentional state – i. e., a belief in the justice or correctness of the invoked norm.[13] This thesis is based on a mistaken identification of the concepts of justification in the formal and justification in the substantive sense, and on a confusion between the definition of a generic act and the imputation of an individual act. It is true that a generic act is defined by a specific intention and a result. That means that the intention is conceptually necessary. And therefore it is also true that someone who performs a corresponding individual act on a particular occasion is committed to that intentional state, or conveys the impression of its existence. But that is a far cry from saying anything about the truth of the assertion that the attribution of an individual act to someone presupposes the existence of that intention; because that is an empirical and, thus, a contingent question. Lack of evidence about the psychological states of an agent need not affect the imputation of an action to that agent. It depends on whether or not the rules governing the application of the respective terms require such evidence.[14]

B) THE EXTERNAL ASPECT

Statements containing the result of the action of explaining or justifying an action establish a relation between two terms. One of them, the one sustaining the explanation or justification, is a reason for action. The other one is the explained or justified action itself. Thus, we can say that both the explanation and the justification of an action assume a relation between that action and some reasons; and this seems to suggest that we are dealing with a kind of relation common to both cases. In other words, one could think that both in explaining and in justifying, a relation of 'being a reason for' is mentioned. However, were one to choose this way of approaching the concepts of explanation and justification, two difficulties would arise.

On the one hand, note that the notion of reason for action itself already presupposes a relation. Something is a reason for an action only because it stands in a specific relation to that action. But the *relation* 'being a reason for' is one thing, and *being* a 'reason for action' quite another. A reason for action is just one of the terms of such a relation. Although the concepts are not completely unrelated, that relation is something of a very different nature than the entities that can come into play as one of the arguments of the relation, i. e., the nature of the entities that can be reasons for action.

On the other hand, it must be emphasized that the relation apparently common to explanation and justification is, in fact, ambiguous. As we will see later, a relation be-

---

[12] Cf. Rescher, Nicholas, An Introduction to the Theory of Values, Englewood Cliffs, N. J.: Prentice Hall 1969, p. 3.

[13] Cf., for example, Alexy, Robert, On Necessary Relations Between Law and Morality, in: Ratio Juris 2:2 (1989); also Raz, Joseph, RPN; Nino, Carlos S., The Ethics of Human Rights, Oxford: Clarendon 1991; Ruiz Manero, Juan, Jurisdicción y normas, Madrid: Centro de Estudios Constitucionales 1990.

[14] Cf. Chapter I, sect. 3.

tween a reason and an action, when mentioned in an explanation, is different and independent from such a relation when mentioned in a justification. Paradoxically, what in the beginning looked like a common element of explanations and justifications, i. e., that they both mention a relation of 'being a reason for', turns out to be only a terminological coincidence. Explanations and justifications only share a certain vocabulary, but the relations established in each case are different. To say that there is one generic type of a relation of 'being a reason for' and then distinguish different kinds of it either leads to confusion between the different kinds of links, or is itself a sign of such confusion.

In what follows, I will analyse explanation and justification as sets of statements grounded on two independent kinds of relations. Such statements are the means by which an action is explained or justified. They will now be examined under the assumption that behind them we will find the relations we want to understand. We will thus be able to specify with respect to each of the two cases what it means that something is a reason for action.

4. Statements Explaining an Action

'*A* did *X* because she wanted *R*' or '*B* did *Y* because he believed that *P*' are reason-giving statements intended to inform about why a certain action took place or how it was possible. I will call this kind of statements 'explanatory reason-statements'. There are different ways of making an action understandable. Hence, we can say that there is more than one kind of explanation and, therefore, also more than one kind of explanatory relation. Here, I am interested only in the kind of teleological explanation given through reason-statements. In the abundant literature on this subject, there is disagreement about how the relationships established by such explanatory statements are to be interpreted.[15]

In view of what has been discussed above, a teleological explanation, by definition, is subject to certain limitations. To begin with, as all explanation, it looks towards the past, that is, it assumes that the event it attempts to make comprehensible has already taken place. In that case, the action is explained by setting it into a framework of purposes the agent believes to be able to reach by performing that action. That is why it has a teleological nature. On the other hand, because of the nature of the states that can be explanatory reasons, such an explanation must always refer to certain events taking place within the agent. These mental states are those characterized as 'motives' in the second sense of the term.[16] It is assumed that the means-ends relation an explanation is

---

[15] There is a long discussion about the nature of the link between an action and an agent's intentional states. Those who hold that the independence typically existing between cause and effect does not exist between reasons and actions see a conceptual relationship between the latter. Cf. von Wright, Georg Henrik, Explanation and Unterstanding, op. cit. The contrary position is maintained by those who hold that while a reason-statement does not link the description of an event to a general law, it is a special kind of causal statement linking individual events. Donald Davidson, for instance, defends this position. Cf. Moya, Carlos, Introducción a la filosofía de Davidson: mente, mundo y acción, in: Davidson, Donald, Mente, mundo y acción, Barcelona: Paidós, ICE - UAB 1992, pp. 18 f.

[16] Mental states, that is, which represent the states of affairs the agent means to bring about by a particular action. Cf. Chapter I, sect. 3.

based on is a relationship of a causal nature.[17] It is important to take note of the restrictions implied by that definition. If, for the purpose of a teleological or intentional explanation, something is mentioned in the *explanans* that cannot be a motive of the agent, then the attempt to give such an explanation will have failed completely.

Quite another question is whether or not the motives suggested in an explanation actually *were* the motives which determined the action. On that point, it should be noted that giving an explanation is perfectly compatible with that explanation being false or inadequate, and also with the fact that some explanations are more plausible than others. One can invoke different criteria for evaluating an explanation, but undoubtedly 'truth' is the most important. The truth of reason-based explanation statements depends on whether or not the intentional states mentioned in those statements actually were those pursued by the agent in acting. The psychological states on which explanations are based are those called 'explanatory reasons'. An explanation grounded on explanatory reasons explicitly shows the teleological structure and the intentional character of an action. There is, however, another way of explaining an action which proceeds in the same language, but does not refer to an agent's intentional states. That kind of explanation involves another meaning of 'reason', without affecting what has been said here. I will refer to that kind of explanatory reasons in section 6 of this chapter.

In order to analyse the content of a teleological explanation, we must remember some consequences of what has been said in Chapter I about the internal elements of an action. As was pointed out there, the presence of certain intentional states is a necessary prerequisite for the performance of an action. Among these, a state characterized by its direction towards the reaching of some end is indispensable (a world-to-mind direction of fit).

A teleological explanation makes an action intelligible in the light of what the agent wanted to achieve and the information he had. These two kinds of data do not need to be desires or believes of the agent. An individual can adopt certain objectives even against his own wishes.[18] Similarly, a person can accept certain propositions even

---

[17] The causal relationship between what is going on inside of an agent and his external movements must not be confused with the union of these elements necessary under the concept of action. The former shows the nature of the physical process by which an action comes about. The latter shows a conceptual decision to restrict the meaning of 'action' to 'intentional action'. In the present study, I have adopted the intentional concept of action. That means that the concept of action is necessarily linked to intentional states. The fact that mental states and body movements are necessarily connected under the concept of action and, in that sense, logically connected, does not imply that there can be no causal relationship between them. On this point, von Wright's *Explanation and Understanding* confounds the necessary relationship implied by the conceptual choice with the nature of the connection between the events necessarily linked by the concept. In any case, it is advisable to maintain von Wright's distinction between the explanation of the external manifestation of an action and that of the action as such. From the point of view defended in the present investigation, both can be given in terms of reasons, and both are causal. The explanation of an individual's conduct on the basis of its immediate internal determinants ('motives' in the first sense of the term) enables us to understand that conduct as an action. The explanation of that action makes it comprehensible in the light of other intentional states representing states of affairs which the agent believes to be instrumentally linked to its result ('motives' in the second sense of the term).

[18] This statement would not be admissible under some reconstructions of the concept of desire. For instance, when that notion is used in a wide sense, such that it denotes any intentional state with a world-to-mind direction of fit. Cf. Smith, Michael, THTM.

against her own beliefs. The adoption of policies and ends, as well as the acceptance or rejection of propositions, are brought about by voluntary internal decisions. This enables us to distinguish them from other attitudes, as for example the beliefs and desires an individual may involuntarily have.[19] Therefore, there are different intentional states a teleological explanation can be based on. Some of them, in turn, can be adopted voluntarily, i. e., deliberately (for instance, the acceptance of or the search for some ends, and the acceptance of certain propositions), whereas others cannot (for example, desires and beliefs). As Jonathan Cohen points out, taking this into account, explanations of human actions should be classified into at least four main categories referring to the appropriate relations between *(i)* beliefs and desires, *(ii)* beliefs and the search for ends, *(iii)* accepted propositions and desires, and *(iv)* accepted propositions and the search for ends.[20]

The paradigm generally used for teleological explanations of actions is based on the desires and beliefs of the agent. According to the distinctions presented before, this possibility is the least interesting of all, since it is based on an agent's involuntary dispositions. It does not show the agent as responsible for what he does, since it explains his action on the basis of attitudes he has not consciously adopted. In contrast, explanations based on intentionally chosen objectives and policies and on accepted propositions presuppose some degree of conscious reasoning on the part of the acting individual. Such explanations enable us to see the agent as responsible for his action. They show his behaviour as a means the individual deliberately sets in motion in order to satisfy rationally chosen ends. The distinction between these kinds of mental states will be useful when we come to the analysis of the acceptance of norms as a kind of internal attitude of an agent which can explain his actions.

5. Statements Justifying an Action

Acts of justification are performed through justificatory statements expressed orally or in writing. A statement justifying an action is a statement qualifying that action as obligatory or permitted. 'Peter ought to return the book to Mary', for instance, is an individual deontic statement.[21] Since one of the main purposes of the present investigation is the analysis of ought-statements, the following will refer only to these and not to permissive statements.

Taken out of context, the statement 'Peter ought to return the book to Mary' is ambiguous. It can be understood, first of all, as the *assertion* that there is an individual norm according to which that act of Peter's is obligatory. In that case, the stătement is purely descriptive. But it can also be understood as an individual *norm* which qualifies Peter's action as obligatory. Only in that last case, the statement is normative. In the first case, we simply have a descriptive statement informing about the existence of a norm

[19] Cf. Cohen, L. Jonathan, Acceptance and Belief, op. cit.; also id., An Essay on Belief and Acceptance, Oxford: Clarendon 1992. Below, in Chapter V, I will analyse these attitudes in detail.

[20] Cohen, L. Jonathan, Acceptance and Belief, op. cit., pp. 378-384.

[21] A deontic statement will be any statement containing words of that nature, like 'ought', 'permitted'., 'prohibited', etc., regardless of whether its meaning is normative or descriptive.

prescribing the action. As such, it can be judged to be true or false, whereas a normative statement does not have a truth-value.

The two possible meanings of a deontic statement are analysed with the help of the concept of reason for action. When such a statement has a descriptive meaning, it is the result of a speech-act asserting something *about* reasons.[22] Its truth-value is determined by the existence or inexistence of those reasons. The condition for the sincerity of such an act, as with all assertive acts, is the acceptance of what is asserted, i. e., the acceptance of the existence of a norm qualifying the action as obligatory. In the second case, the statement is part of an act of justification and constitutes an individual norm. It does not consist in a description, but in the qualification of an action as obligatory.[23] Such an individual norm can, in turn, be grounded as a specific case of a general norm calling for the action in question. The condition for the sincerity of such an act of justification is the acceptance of the general norm invoked as a reason for the duty to perform that kind of action. Whether or not a given norm can be said to be a reason for acting depends on the normative conception or theory one holds.[24] Acceptance of the duty to perform the action stipulated in a norm presupposes acceptance of a normative theory according to which that norm is an adequate standard of conduct.

The process of justification consists of two steps. The first is the formulation of an individual statement qualifying an act as obligatory; the second consists in showing the reason which justifies that individual normative statement. Linguistic usage on this point is not clear. It should be noted that the mere fact of qualifying an individual action as obligatory, that is, the formulation of an individual norm, is not sufficient for justifying an action. One must also show a general principle from which the duty to perform the individual act derives. That kind of universalization is usually considered a minimum requirement of a substantive concept of justification and seems to be accepted by all those who do not adopt a situational ethics.[25] From that point of view, statements qualifying a particular action as obligatory without presenting the general foundations on which they rest are only part of a justification. They constitute the conclusion of a general norm to which all justifications must be committed. To say that Peter ought to return the book to Mary is only part of what is required for justifying that action. It must also be shown *why* this ought to be done. Therefore, taken in isolation, what has been called 'justificatory statements' – whether referring to individual or to generic acts (i. e., whether individual or generic norms) – are just one of several elements of the set of statements by which an act is justified. Such a set of statements normally has the structure of an argument. One of the premises of such an argument is a general normative statement justifying (in the formal sense) an individual normative statement. Taken together, these statements are the answer to the question of why the action in question ought to be performed.

---

[22] Cf. Schueler, G. F., The Idea of a Reason for Acting. A Philosophical Argument, op. cit.; also Raz, Joseph, RPN, pp. 33-37.

[23] Cf. Alchourrón, C. and Bulygin, E., Normative Systems, New York and Vienna: Springer 1971, pp. 168 ff.

[24] Cf. Pap, Arthur, The Verifiability of Value Judgments, in: Ethics 60 (1949); also Mackie, John L., Obligations to Obey the Law, in: Virginia Law Review 67 (1981).

[25] Cf. Mackie, John L, Ethics. Inventing Right and Wrong, op. cit., ch. IV.

Suppose, for instance, that the parliament of some country decides that 'We ought to send an observer to the upcoming elections in state *x* because we ought to help citizens take autonomous decisions whenever we can'. For analysis, that complex statement can be disected into several simpler ones: 'Individuals ought to be helped to take autonomous decisions. The mechanism of the democratic election of public officials is one of the forms in which individuals autonomously decide about who should govern their community. State *x* is about to hold its first democratic elections. In this case, the process must be supervised in order to guarantee that the mechanism works. Therefore, we ought to contribute to the supervision of these elections. Sending observers is one way how that supervision can be achieved. *Ergo*, we ought to send an observer to the upcoming elections in state *x*.'

The relationship underlying that set of statements is based on general norms. These norms may or may not be accepted. If they are accepted, a duty to act in accordance with them is assumed. On that hypothesis, norms are not only used as premises, as is the case in formal justification, but are admitted as substantive reasons in favour of some act-type. Thus, particular normative statements founded on general norms also are reasons, but reasons for an individual action. From a formal point of view, a justification is an argument in which the description of a particular action is subsumed under a general norm. The argument's premises, that is, the statements expressing the reason or the foundation of the duty to perform the individual action in question, are always norms.

What distinguishes justification in the formal sense from justification in the substantive sense is the internal aspect. When something is justified in the formal sense, certain norms are used (assumed) as the foundation of the argument presented without necessarily being accepted. When something is justified in the substantive sense, the principles invoked are accepted. Acceptance presupposes an internal act of decision, the adoption of a commitment to be coherent with the accepted content.[26] The external aspect of the formal and the substantive justification of an action is the same. It consists in the expression of a set of statements linked together in an argument. From the point of view of the person performing that act, the norms may or may not be accepted as reasons for the action. That does not mean that the norms are reasons for the action simply *because* they are accepted by some speaker. The status of a reason for an action depends on a normative theory which has the function of providing a set of behavioural standards. Reasons for action cannot be identified outside of the context of some normative theory. To be a reason for acting (in the justificatory and substantive sense) is to be a behavioural standard proposed by a normative theory. In other words, just as an act of justification in the formal sense can be evaluated and qualified as correct or incorrect on the basis of a logical theory, an act of justification in the substantive sense can be judged, from an objective point of view, on the grounds of some normative theory. The standards accepted as reasons for action by some agent may not be reasons for action from another normative conception. And, *vice versa*, an agent may refuse to accept the norms which from the standpoint of some specific theory are reasons for action.

---

[26] Cf. Cohen, Jonathan, Acceptance and Belief, op. cit. Chapter V will be dedicated exclusively to the discussion of that topic.

The distinctions just drawn explain why the notion of substantive justification is used, sometimes inadvertently, in two different senses. In the subjective sense, it is the justification given by an individual on the basis of norms accepted as reasons for acting by that individual. And in the objective sense, it is a formal or substantive relationship stipulated in some theory. Whether or not something is a substantive justification in the objective sense depends on the conditions imposed by a normative theory, and not on what an individual accepts. Similarly, whether or not something is a formal justification in the objective sense depends on the conditions stipulated by logic, and not on what the person making the argument believes. An agent can perform the action of justifying an action by invoking reasons that may be criticized and rejected from an objective standpoint, i. e., from the standpoint of some theory. In that case, the agent in question has accepted as premise-reasons or as reasons for acting statements which according to some logical or normative theory, respectively, should not be considered reasons at all. For the purpose of the present investigation, I am primarily interested in the objective concepts of justification and reason for acting.

According to that classification, a substantively justified individual normative statement expresses a *relative* duty.[27] Its justification is relative to a norm which is a *prima facie* reason. This kind of justification is normally distinguished from that other kind which grounds conclusive ought-statements and which is justified not relative to one single reason for an action, but relative to the evaluation of all the reasons applicable to the situation in question.[28] The pattern of justification of that kind of conclusive duties will be analysed later.

Concerning justificatory reason-statements, there is a controversy similar to that about explanatory statements. The meaning of the justificatory relationship is discussed, as well as the extension of the notion of reason. There is disagreement on whether the relationship involved in the justification of an action is necessarily a normative one or whether it can be reduced to an empirical relationship, i. e., whether a justification must always be supported by a normative entity or whether it can also consist in facts.

So far, I have said that to justify an action is to offer general foundations for a particular normative statement. The so-called principle of Hume asserts that a normative statement cannot be derived from another kind of statement.[29] If one concedes that at least in some of its senses the notion of 'ought' is normative, then it is a fallacy to ground the corresponding ought-statements in other, non-normative statements. The implication is that not just any kind of entity can be invoked for supporting a justification, i. e., as a justificatory reason. From statements asserting that something *is* the case, even if they refer to the belief in or the acceptance of some duty, it does not follow that an action is justified, i. e., that it *ought to be* performed. That does not necessarily mean that there are two ontological realms, that of 'is' and that of 'ought'; rather, it implies the recognition of two kinds of meanings: normative meaning and descriptive meaning. If the conclusion of an argument has a normative meaning, then among its premises there must also be a statement with a normative meaning. I will not discuss the nature of those

---

[27] Raz, Joseph, Introduction, in: id., Practical Reasoning, op. cit.

[28] Richards, David, A Theory of Reasons for Action, op. cit.; see also Raz, Joseph, PRN.

[29] Hume, David, A Treatise of Human Nature, London: John Noon 1739-40.

abstract entities. To say that there are normative meanings does not imply that there is an objective realm of 'ought' or of moral facts, nor does it imply that there is no such realm, or that those who believe in such facts are wrong.[30] In any case, even under the hypothesis of the error theory (that is, even conceding the ontological division between 'is' and 'ought') it is still true that there are terms which are used in a normative sense and that their meanings cannot be reduced to empirical concepts. This semantic division resulting from the usage of terms is independent of whether or not there are two different ontological realms. This shows that the thesis of semantic independence is compatible with the idea of ontological reduction or dependence.

Another question is whether the invoked norms are in fact adequate reasons for action. A number of criteria for identifying the set of norms that are relevant for a substantive justification can be suggested. For a utilitarian, for instance, a norm will be an appropriate justificatory reason if compliance with it furthers general happiness. For an extremely positivist ideological conception, it is sufficient for judging a norm to be an adequate reason for action if it belongs to a certain legal system. According to Michael Smith, it is an acceptable criterion to regard as reasons the norms we would choose under certain idealized conditions of deliberation.[31] Thus, every normative theory offers its own criteria for the identification of reasons that justify action. In Chapter VI, I will discuss whether there is only one or a plurality of admissible justificatory frameworks.

Substantive soundness (in the light of some normative theory) is a necessary prerequisite for justification in the substantive sense. A justificatory norm is an adequate standard of conduct, according to some theory. However, this does not imply that a justification is always absolutely or definitely correct, since in that case it would be impossible to explain some widely accepted uses of the term. For instance, it would make no sense to say that a justification is wrong. But that sentence is perfectly comprehensible and implies, above all, that there is a sense of 'justification' which does not require it to be definitely adequate. Besides, such a restriction of the meaning of this word would not only exclude a great part of common usage; it would also require a reformulation practically of the entire debate in normative ethics about more or less plausible justifications. That seems to be sufficient reason for admitting a concept of justification that is relative to the norms invoked as reasons for action. The notion of justification then becomes compatible with its being performed in a good or in a bad way, and with

---

[30] Mackie, John L, Ethics. Inventing Right and Wrong, op. cit. Mackie holds that those who believe in the existence of moral facts are wrong. But note that this thesis presupposes that there is some absolute point of view from which to judge whether or not certain facts objectively exist. If one accepts that all existential statements are made from some point of view, one can understand why what can be admitted to be a fact from one perspective may not be admissible from another. Thus, it is the error theory itself which commits the error of not recognizing that its perspective is just another point of view, and that it is just as partial as the one asserting that there are moral facts. It is not an external and neutral parameter for judging whether or not the assertions made from other perspectives are right or wrong. Cf. Strawson, P. F., Skepticism and Naturalism, London: Methuen 1985.

[31] Cf. Smith, Michael, Realism, in: Peter Singer (ed.), Ethics, Oxford and New York: Oxford University Press 1994, pp. 170-176. This proposal is similar to Rawls' idea for the choice of the principles of justice. Cf. Rawls, John, A Theory of Justice, Cambridge, Mass.: Harvard University Press 1971.

the fact that (in the light of some normative theory) some justifications are more plausible than others.

In summary, then, Hume's principle functions as a formal constraint on the *meaning* of 'justification': one can only justify something on the basis of norms. On a parallel level, the ethical theory one adopts functions as a constraint on the *content* of justifications: only norms that are reasons for action can justify something. If someone wanting to give a justification relies exclusively on the assertion of non-normative events or states of affairs, he will have tried, but completely failed to give a justification. Similarly, an agent who justifies an action by invoking norms he accepts but which are not reasons for acting (according to some normative theory) has not justified that action in an objective sense (according to that same theory).

What has just been said about explanatory and justificatory statements clearly reveals the ambiguity of the expression 'reason for action'. A reason for action is something which provides support for explanatory relationships (in which case it is an empirical entity) or for justificatory relationships (in which case it is a normative entity). The meaning of each of these relationships determines the extension as well as the intension of 'reason for action'. Of course, at the root of that fundamental ambiguity is the admission that explanation and justification are independent concepts. Therefore, those who wish to recover the unity of the concept of reason for action must deny that independence. Thus, to say that explanation and justification are connected is one of the ways how one can show that there are no independent meanings of 'reason for action'.

6. A Special Kind of Reason-Giving Statements?

A) NON-TELEOLOGICAL EXPLANATORY STATEMENTS

Until now, the two kinds of reasons for action we have analysed were either motives explaining an action (empirical entities internal to an individual) or norms qualifying it as obligatory (abstract non-propositional entities). Therefore, all statements *about* the existence of reasons must refer either to psychological aspects concerning an agent or to normative principles. But there are reason-giving statements which do not refer to either of the two kinds of entities. Rather, they invoke as reasons for action facts that are external to the individual and which are neither mental states nor norms of conduct.

Returning to our earlier example of John who visited Mary because she was sick, we can say:

(i) 'The reason why John visited Mary is that she was sick.'

That kind of statement is used and works adequately in the explanation as well as in the justification of an action. If one were to hold that the concept of reason refers only to intentional states (explanatory reasons) or norms (justificatory reasons), the statement would be incomprehensible. The reason for this is that the statement is incomplete because it presupposes certain informations. Depending on what information is presupposed, the statement can be part of an explanation or of a justification of the action in question. In most cases, the speaker explicitly says whether he intends to explain or to justify an action. And if he doesn't, the context usually reveals what it is he wants to do. For instance, the statement is part of an explanation if it is complemented by the information that John wanted to be nice to Mary and that he thought that visiting her while she was sick was one way of being nice to her. But it would be regarded as part of a justification if the speaker would add that John acted as he should because it is everyone's duty to keep the sick company. In the first case, the reason explaining John's action is his wish or objective to be nice, together with his belief or acceptance of the proposition that visiting someone is an adequate means to satisfy that objective. In the second case, the justificatory reason is the norm stipulating the duty to keep the sick company. On that account, the fact that Mary is sick can be regarded as a reason in a secondary or subsidiary sense, since it is a fact that is relevant for the actual reasons, which are intentional states or norms.

Now, the same statement expressed in *(i)* can be interpreted as part of an explanation that is not based on the objectives or ends pursued by the agent, but on a generalization about behaviour. That is the kind of interpretation which must be given by those who say that there are *external reasons* that can be invoked in the explanation of an action.[32] The possibility of formulating behavioural generalizations is based on the existence of a practice. When there is a behavioural practice, whether or not it constitutes a social rule, expectations about established behaviour arise.[33] Given appropriate circumstances, where a practice is established individuals can be expected to behave in accordance with it. For example, if a social rule requires queuing in order for some service to be administered in the order of arrival, it can be expected that on arrival at the place where the service is provided, people will either take their place behind the last person in the line or ask who is last. Similarly, it can be expected that those who impart the service will always attend the person standing in front of the line first. The existing practice supports a generalization which links the fact that someone is last in the line with the action of stepping behind that person, or the fact that someone is first in the line with the action of attending him or her first. Habits or social rules of obligation enable us to explain actions on another basis than that of intentional explanation. One can say:

(ii) 'The clerk attended *A* before *B* because *A* was the first in line.'

Although that statement presupposes that the employee's action is intentional, it is not an intentional explanation of his conduct. It is not based on the agent's objectives and in that sense does not constitute an explanation in terms of internal reasons. Neither is it a causal explanation of the result of the action. The statement can be understood as an explanatory statement only because a practice is presupposed. The same interpretation could be given to the statement expressed in *(i)* provided it is presupposed that in

---

[32] In the previous chapter, I have mentioned the possibility to make sense of statements about external reasons. According to Bernard Williams, they should be discarded as false or incoherent. Cf. Chapter I, sect. 7.c.

[33] What matters for the possibility of such an explanation is simply that there is continual repetition of the same conduct. Participants need neither be aware of that convergence nor approve of it. Therefore, the existence of a habit is sufficient. As for the difference between habits and social rules, I follow H. L. A. Hart, The Concept of Law, op. cit., pp. 55-60.

the group John belongs to there is a practice of visiting people who are sick. In that context, to say that 'John visited Mary because she was sick' is an explanation based on a generalization which may be drawn because of the existence of that practice. The fact that Mary is sick *causes* John's action, in the sense that it is a condition to which John is used to react intentionally in a certain way. His intention arises when he finds out about that fact, and it would not exist without that fact.[34]

If statements as expressed in *(i)* and *(ii)* can be complemented with the description of a practice – for instance, 'Most individuals of this group resort to behaviour *M* in situation *S*' – plus the assertion that the agent in question participates in that practice, the answer to the question of why the respective action was performed is complete, i. e., no further data will be needed. This is a kind of explanation, though not a teleological one. There may also be a teleological or intentional explanation for the behaviour involved; but that must not necessarily be the case. The subject may have internalized the a behavioural pattern in such a way as to have learned to react to certain events without thinking about the ends which are satisfied by that means. This normally happens as the result of a process of socialization of an individual into a group. Only in two cases is such a situation, where the agent acts by following a rule, compatible with an intentional explanation of his conduct. First, when the agent knows and adopts the ends or states of affairs instrumentally connected with compliance. And second, when by complying the agent pursues some personal end which is independent of the ends supported by the practice. If the agent does not act in order to pursue some end which has been autonomously or heteronomously imposed on him, his action has no teleological explanation; but that does not mean that it is not intentional.[35] In such a case, the only possible explanation is the one based on the agent's participation in some practice. Whether or not such an explanation is trustworthy depends on how strongly and deeply the practice is rooted in the group in question.[36] The probability estimate sustaining such an explanation is always relative to the conduct of a group. Therefore, the explanation can be admitted only relative to the group in which the practice is in force and to which the generalization is applicable.

---

[34] In Bernard Williams's terminology, this means that the wish to visit Mary, i. e., the element of set S which motivated the action, is causally determined by an external fact, i. e., the fact that Mary is sick. Williams, of course, would not accept that description. From his point of view, the elements of S only arise or are discarded by rational deliberation on the basis of other elements of S. In the present investigation, it will be maintained that among the elements of an individual's subjective motivational set there are voluntary and involuntary states. The latter do not arise by decision and can be causally explained from external states. This is the basis for the distinction between the internalization and the acceptance of norms. Cf. Gibbard, Allan, Moral Judgement and the Acceptance of Norms, in: Ethics 96 (1985). I will come back to this in Chapter V.

In any case, the admission of that kind of 'external reasons' which may explain an agent's motivational states and, therefore, his actions does not contradict Williams's general conception. It assumes that an individual always acts for internal reasons and that something is considered a reason precisely because it is related to the capacity to motivate action.

[35] Cf. von Wright, Georg Henrik, Explanation and Understanding, op. cit., pp. 122-124.

[36] Cf. von Wright, Georg Henrik, Determinism and the Study of Man, in: id., Practical Reason, op. cit., pp. 35-52.

B) STATEMENTS GIVING REASONS FOR FUTURE ACTION

There is a kind of statements which are different from those treated in the previous section but which can be understood on the basis of the same assumptions. These statements mention facts that are external to the individual and assert that they are reasons for an action *before* that action has been performed. For instance, the fact that Mary is sick is a reason for John to visit her. The fact that someone is first in line is a reason for attending her first. And in the example chosen by Bernard Williams, the fact that all male members of the Wingrave family have been soldiers is a reason for Owen Wingrave to enlist in the army.[37] As in the previous cases, we can ask what purpose such statements are intended to serve and what kind of relation between reason and action they imply. Since they do not refer to an action of the past, we can discard the idea that they are part of an explanation. But they do qualify some fact as a reason for some action. That means that they are descriptive statements resulting from assertive acts. Again, the denomination 'reason for action' points to a subsidiary or secondary sense of that expression. Such reasons either presuppose a *norm* (in this case, they are reasons in the justificatory sense), or they presuppose a *desire* to perform the action in question, or the *acceptance* of a norm which prescribes it (in which case they are reasons in the explanatory sense). The former is necessary if the purpose is to give a justification; the latter is needed if the statements are intended to guide behaviour.

Such statements describing something as a reason for an action that has not yet been performed may also be uttered without any further purpose. That is, they may simply be an information about some fact being a reason for some action. In that case, without a context it is impossible to know what kind of reasons – explanatory or justificatory – they refer to. Just as in the situation treated in the last paragraph, such statements presuppose some information and, in that sense, are incomplete. The fact that, although they are descriptive, they can be relevant for guiding as well as for justifying behaviour is due to the assumed existence of rules of conduct. The descriptive nature of a statement mentioning a reason that can guide an individual's conduct is ensured by the existence of a social rule, i. e., by the efficacy of a norm. To say that a social rule exists is to say that there exists a certain practice in some group. This, in turn, supports the probability that the members of the group have the appropriate motivations for performing the required action.[38] Of course, that probability does not guarantee that every individual of the group necessarily has the adequate internal dispositions for acting. Being a male member of the Wingrave family is a relevant fact for guiding Owen Wingrave's action only if he accepts, or has internalized, the social or family rule which in that case stipulates the obligation to enlist in the army. The assertion, then, that an external fact is a reason that can guide the behaviour of the members of some group depends on a practice accepted by the majority, or by a relevant set, of the group's members. The existence of a rule of conduct confers predictive value on the occurrence of

---

[37] Williams, Bernard, Internal and External Reasons, op. cit., p. 106.

[38] Here, the notion of motive must be understood in the third sense mentioned earlier, that is, as an element of the set of mental states an individual has. They are not related to any particular action, although they can give rise to an action.

the states of affairs which are the conditions for the behaviour required by the corresponding standard.[39]

The standard itself, independently of its acceptance or efficacy, is a foundation for justifying the action. The *fact* indicated as a reason for the action is always a condition for the applicability of a norm. That is, it is the fact in view of which the standard stipulates the duty to perform a certain action. The assertion that a fact is a reason in the justificatory sense (where facts can be either states of affairs or processes or events)[40] can be explained analogously to our earlier explanation of so-called normative or institutional acts.[41] An institutional act is nothing but a natural event the normative effects of which are taken to be essential. These effects are that certain norms become applicable. That means that certain actions are now deontically qualified as prohibited, obligatory, or permitted. Any fact can have normative effects, and in some contexts these may be regarded as their essential properties. From this point of view, when a *fact* is invoked as a reason for an action in the justificatory sense, this is because in identifying that fact, its normative effects have been considered essential. To some extent, it is a matter of decision whether or not relevance is attributed to the normative properties of a fact. To do this means to presuppose and to use the rule which stipulates these normative effects. In order to identify a fact as a reason for action, one must at least assume a normative theory. But *assuming* a normative conception does not mean *accepting* it. It does not imply a commitment to the duty of doing what it stipulates. For instance, one can affirm that according to a particular moral conception, being a woman is a reason for covering one's face; but that does not imply that one accepts that conception.

This interpretation raises the same question that was formulated with respect to institutional acts: Are there two kinds of facts, one natural and the other institutional? For example, on the one hand, there is the fact that all male members of the Wingrave

---

[39] Such reason-statements may form part of a prediction as well as a justification of some conduct. In order to account for their predictive relevance, we only need to presuppose the existence of a habit. Their relevance for justification, in contrast, can only be explained by the existence of a social rule which implies that the participants accept a certain standard of behaviour.

That a norm 'exists' may mean several things. Eugenio Bulygin distinguishes four possible senses of the 'existence' of a norm. First, it can be a normative concept related to the obligatoriness or binding character of a norm (existence as validity). Second, there is a sense generally attributed to a norm when it has been issued by a competent authority and has not been derogated (existence as belonging). Third, there is a formal sense; from this point of view, norms exist to the extent that they have been formulated by someone or are logical consequences of norms that have been formulated; they need not have been enacted, nor must they be accepted, or effective, or regarded as obligatory. Finally, Bulygin refers to a notion of factual existence denoting the fact that a directive is in force within a certain group. Cf. Bulygin, Eugenio, An Antinomy in Kelsen's Pure Theory of Law, in: Ratio Juris 3:1 (1990) pp. 29-45.

The first three meanings of existence are independent of the probability that an agent is actually motivated to act when the facts conditioning the application of a norm come about. In contrast, that probability is part of the necessary conditions for the factual existence of a norm. That last sense of existence thus coincides with the efficacy of a norm in Kelsen's sense and the existence of a social rule in Hart's.

In the case under scrutiny, the existence of the presupposed rule must be understood in Bulygin's sense of factual existence.

[40] Cf. von Wright, Georg Henrik, Norm and Action, op. cit., pp. 25-27.

[41] Cf. Chapter I, sect. 4.

family have enlisted in the army, and the fact that Owen Wingrave is a male. On the other hand, there is an external reason for enlisting in the army. If the notion of 'existence' is interpreted in the empirical sense, then it can only be predicated of facts which are located in time and space. Institutional facts do not exist in that sense and, therefore, neither do justificatory reasons for action. However, it makes perfect sense to assert of the latter that they exist, and such an assertion can be analysed. To say that a fact is a reason for some action means that the circumstances under which, in accordance with some norm, that action *prima facie* ought to be performed obtain. One may not accept the norm; but even in that case one can still recognize the conditioning facts as reasons relative to that norm. As has already been pointed out, without some norm it is impossible to identify a fact as a reason for an action in the justificatory sense. But that one identifies a fact as a reason does not mean that one accepts the norm making that identification possible, just as the acceptance of a norm does not mean that it really is a reason for action. Acceptance is not constitutive of reasons. It is one thing that something is believed to be, or is accepted as, a reason for action, and quite another that it really is such a reason.[42] One can identify something as a substantive reason even if one does not accept it; and one can accept something as a substantive reason without believing that it is one.

Statements mentioning facts as justificatory reasons can be uttered even with respect to persons who do not belong to the group in which the corresponding rule is accepted. Suppose individual *A* does not belong to the group in which rule *N* is accepted. Then, to say that *R* is a reason for *A* to do *X* means to apply rule *N*, according to which *X* ought to be done in circumstances *R*, to *A*. This is perfectly possible, because a rule may apply to a group that is not necessarily coextensive with the group of individuals who accept it. But such a reason-statement referring to someone who does not belong to the group in which the rule is in force is purely normative and loses all explanatory or predictive capacity. This is so because the agent in question does not take part in the corresponding practice and, therefore, does not belong to the sphere where the probabilistic generalization is valid.

In summary, then, we can underscore the following:

(i) The notion of reason for action always refers to one side of a relation. The other side of that relation is always an intentional action. There are different kinds of relations between reasons and actions. First, there is a relation of an empirical nature, on which explanatory statements are based. Concerning this case, a teleological and a probabilistic relation have been mentioned. Second, there is a normative or deontological relation, on which justifications of action are based. It should be noted that the notion of reason for action refers to different kinds of entities in these cases.

---

[42] This distinction is similar, but not exactly identical to Hart's distinction between 'being obliged' and 'having an obligation'. The feeling of obligatoriness an individual may have is not an interesting category. The contrast proposed in the present study is that between accepting an obligation, on the one hand, and actually having an obligation, on the other. Accepting an obligation implies voluntarily adopting an attitude of commitment to the standard. This subjective decision may, but need not, be grounded on a feeling of obligatoriness. In contrast, that one 'has an obligation' is an objective assertion which is independent from acceptance and presupposes that one has a normative theory which justifies the standard requiring the action.

(ii) The word 'reason' can appear in explanatory and in justificatory contexts. In the first case, 'reason' refers to mental states which are teleologically linked to the action, or to external facts linked to it by probabilistic generalization. In the second case, 'reason' refers either to normative standards stipulating the *(prima facie)* duty to perform some action, or to normative or institutional facts.

(iii) The classification of reasons as 'explanatory' and 'justificatory' can be complemented by another one distinguishing reasons in the 'formal' sense from reasons in the 'substantive' sense. We can say that explanations and justifications in the substantive sense are expressed through arguments which are justificatory in the formal sense. The statements in which such arguments are expressed are also called reasons, namely, premise-reasons.

(iv) Finally, we must distinguish two different levels on which the notions of justification and reason can be analysed. From a subjective point of view, a justification is an action performed by an agent. The agent performing that action assumes or accepts some norm as a reason for an action. From an objective point of view, whether or not something can be qualified as a justification or a reason does not depend on the attitudes of some individual, but on a logical (in the case of formal justification) or normative (in the case of substantive justification) theory.

Throughout this chapter, I have emphasized the distinction between explanatory reasons and justificatory reasons in the substantive sense. In the following chapter, the distinction between the formal and the substantive sense of a reason will be treated in more detail.

CHAPTER III

PRACTICAL ARGUMENTS. REASONS AS PREMISES

1. Introduction

This chapter will be dedicated to the discussion of the notion of reason understood as a premise of an argument. In the analysis of some problems in legal philosophy, this meaning of 'reason' is just as relevant as the meanings treated in the previous chapter.

The concept of reason as a foundation for an assertion is sometimes obscured by the special relationship it has to the concept of reason for action in practical contexts. Above all, note that in the former understanding the term 'reason' is a metalinguistic expression referring to statements or propositions uttered in the context of an argument. As we will see, that notion of reason only occasionally has something to do with that of a 'reason for action'. From this point of view, then, the study of 'reasons' is a subject of interest for logic, as the discipline concerned with the proposal and investigation of valid types of arguments. The distinction between a correct and an incorrect argument is the central problem of that field.

An argument is a sequence of propositions or statements, one of which follows from the others by way of the application of certain rules of inference. In a logical sense, reasons are the elements of an argument of inference. For the present purpose, I will use the words 'argument' and 'inference', on which the definition of the notion of reason as a premise or reason in the logical sense is based, as synonyms. Traditionally, to say that an argument is correct means to hold that the truth of the premises guarantees the truth of the conclusion. This is to say that the rules on which correctness is grounded are truth-preserving rules.

Since the present study revolves mainly around practical arguments, it will be necessary, first of all, to review some criteria for the distinction between practical and theoretical arguments. Once this is done, three different meanings of the notion of practical inference, their possible applications and the different concepts of reason involved will be presented. The purpose of that review is mainly to find an adequate model for justificatory judicial arguments.

2. Theoretical and Practical Arguments

Every logically valid structure constitutes a correct form of presenting an argument and justifying (in the formal sense) a proposition, regardless of its content. Compliance with the rules which define proper relations between propositions guarantees the validity of an argument, that is, it ensures that if the premises are true, then the conclusion will also be true.

With such a definition, the elements arguments consist of must always be linguistic or semantic elements. This interpretation clearly constrains the range of possible proposals for the distinction between practical and theoretical arguments. For once, it implies rejecting the distinction based on the alleged fact that the conclusion of a theoretical argument is a statement whereas the conclusion of a practical argument is an action, the formation of an intention, or the taking of a decision. The classification may, of course, turn on the kind of conclusion resulting from an argument, but only within the confines of what, by the definition of 'argument', a conclusion may consist in. This first approach serves to reflect on whether the suggested criteria point to a classification within one and the same concept of argument, or whether they actually indicate different meanings of that term. Normally, practical arguments are characterized as a subgroup within a more encompassing group, i. e., that of arguments in general. But in that case, all practical arguments must conform to the restriction that they must consist in a sequence of statements. With this idea in mind, I will now briefly examine some of the criteria that have been proposed to indicate the differences between arguments of a theoretical and arguments of a practical nature.

A) THE CRITERION OF THE CONCLUSION

An argument is theoretical if it grounds a statement with a theoretical content, and it is practical if it grounds a statement with a practical content. Obviously, this criterion presupposes that one can distinguish kinds of statements that are typical for practical and theoretical discourse, respectively. The question about the criterion of distinction between arguments thus becomes a question about a criterion of distinction between statements. Several typical ways of drawing the line of distinction can be pointed out. Here, I will consider four options arising from the application of the following two parameters: *(i)* the dichotomy between statements of 'is' and statements of 'ought'; and *(ii)* the distinction between statements in general and statements referring to action in particular. The resulting classifications overlap with two other ways of distinguishing theoretical from practical statements. The first understands theoretical statements to be statements expressing propositions, whereas practical statements are conceived as non-propositional, i. e., as neither true nor false. From this point of view, the predicate 'theoretical' is equivalent to 'cognitive'; and practical discourse, by definition, lacks that characteristic of theoretical discourse. The second way holds that practical statements can also be cognitive; the difference with theoretical statements here is the kind of facts that makes them true or false. This perspective implies that there are normative facts which make it possible to verify or falsify practical discourse, and empirical facts which enable us to corroborate theoretical discourse. I will now look somewhat closer at all these possibilities.

(i) Practical statements as ought-statements: When we take as our starting point the distinction between is-statements and ought-statements, a theoretical argument is an argument the conclusion of which is always a statement of the former kind, i. e., a statement about what is the case. In contrast, the conclusion of a practical argument is always a statement about what ought to be the case or what ought to be done. This proposal

calls for the following objection: One and the same proposition can be expressed through an ought-statement as well as through an is-statement.[1] It may make no difference whether one says that it *is* the case that something ought to be done or whether one states directly that something *ought* to be done. We must therefore concede the possibility that two arguments which, looked at superficially, ground different kinds of statements – one an is-statement, the other one an ought-statement – are actually identical with respect to their significant content. If we use the grammatical form of a statement as the criterion of distinction, any argument can be presented either as theoretical or as practical.

Despite these difficulties, this criterion of classification is widely used. It is used, for instance, when practical arguments are characterized as arguments justifying deontic statements, where it is acknowledged that their meaning is ambiguous: their deontic premises as well as their deontic conclusion can either be norms or propositions informing about the existence of norms.

(ii) Practical statements as action-statements: The distinction between theoretical and practical statements can also be based on the discrimination between statements in general, and action-statements in particular. From this point of view, the characteristic aspect of a practical argument is that its conclusion is an action-statement. According to this classification, among practical statements one must count statements expressing *(i)* the duty to perform some action, for instance: 'I ought to do *x*'; *(ii)* the performance of an action: 'I am doing (did, will do) *x*'; *(iii)* the intention of performing an action: 'I intend (intended) to do *x*'; *(iv)* the choice of an action: 'I choose (chose, will choose) to do *x*'.

Following this criterion, the class of practical arguments is larger than that derived from the application of the previous criterion. It includes the arguments which justify deontic statements, but also all those which ground factual statements about actions. To the extent that it overlaps with the first criterion, the same criticism applies.

All proposals according to which a practical argument is an argument that culminates in an action, an intention, the taking of a decision, or a choice can be reconstructed with the help of this criterion.[2] In this case, a practical argument is a linguistic sequence culminating in a *statement* about an action, an intention, the taking of a decision, or a choice.

(iii) Practical statements as non-cognitive statements: We can distinguish between propositional (i. e., cognitive) and non-propositional (i. e., non-cognitive) meanings. A statement is theoretical if it has a propositional meaning, and it is practical if it has a non-propositional meaning. The grammatical form of the statement is irrelevant. In that sense, a deontic sentence is ambiguous. On the one hand, it can be interpreted as the assertion that some norm exists. In that case, it has a descriptive meaning (it can be true

---

[1] The possibility of such a 'translation' was already mentioned in the context of the analysis of reason as a practical or theoretical faculty. There, I pointed out that a merely formal criterion trivializes the distinction between the theoretical and the practical.

[2] Cf. Edgley, Roy, Reason in Theory and Practice, op. cit.; also Aune, Bruce, Reason and Action, Dordrecht: Reidel 1977.

or false) and is a theoretical argument. But it can also be interpreted as a norm. On that hypothesis, the statement has a normative meaning (it cannot be true or false) and is a practical statement. If one accepts this idea, then some arguments founding is-statements may be practical, and some arguments justifying ought-statements would have to be considered theoretical. The classification of an argument as theoretical or practical will depend on the meaningful content of its conclusion, regardless of its grammatical form.[3] This criterion becomes inapplicable, of course, if meaning is said to be always propositional. And that is what happens in the following case.

(iv) Practical statements as expressions of normative facts: There is a conception according to which practical as well as theoretical statements have cognitive meaning, that means that even the language of norms can be true or false. From this point of view, their propositional nature is no longer a criterion of distinction between statements, since they are all of that kind. For those who adopt that position, the relevant difference rather lies in the truth-conditions. Practical statements are statements expressing a proposition the truth of which is based on the existence of moral or normative facts which cannot be reduced to empirical facts. A deontic statement may have two different meanings, but both of them are cognitive. Take the following example: 'Professors must permit the review of exam papers.' On the one hand, this can be understood to be true because of the existence of an individual empirical fact or a social practice[4] – for instance, because an authority issued a command in that sense, or because there is a custom to that effect. In this case, the statement expresses an empirical proposition and could be replaced by a description of the fact that makes it true. It would, thus, be equivalent to 'The rector ordered all professors to permit the review of exam papers' or 'There is a practice according to which all professors permit the review of exam papers, and they consider it obligatory to do so'. On the other hand, the deontic statement could also be judged to be true because it expresses or represents a normative or moral fact. Only on that condition is it considered a practical, or genuinely normative, statement. Note that such normative or moral facts are necessarily primitive, in the sense that they do not depend on the prior existence of any norm or empirical fact. If they depended on norms, we would have a vicious circle since something is a genuine norm because it represents a normative fact. And if they depended on empirical facts, all deontic statements could be reduced to empirical statements. In summary, this criterion of distinction presupposes metaphysical realism in the moral realm: only statements referring to normative facts that are independent of human attitudes or behaviours are practical statements. Its application singles out as practical the same arguments as the previous criterion, but on different grounds.

---

[3] Cf. Edgley, Roy, Practical Reason, in: Joseph Raz (ed.), Practical Reasoning, op. cit., pp. 18-32.

[4] For Carlos Nino, for instance, there are deontic statements the truth of which is relative to the existence of a contingent empirical fact (for example, a social practice). But such statements are not automatically normative; a genuinely normative statement is relative to a moral fact. Note that according to this conception, while normative statements are not ambiguous, deontic statements are, precisely because they can be normative (based on some moral fact) or empirical (based on contingent empirical facts).

B) THE PRAGMATIC CRITERION

In view of this new insight, as a linguistic structure an argument can never be regarded as practical or theoretical in its own right. Rather, that characterization depends on the function if fulfils, or the purpose it is supposed to serve. From this point of view, two arguments are different, even if they have the same propositional content, when they presuppose different practical attitudes on the part of the speaker. Such different attitudes are usually reflected in the course of a justificatory argument. This position seems to get support from Robert Audi, e. g., when he says:

„[...] but the arguments, *as* abstract structures, are not intrinsically practical: they can be used for theoretical purposes. To be sure, this is a functional (and in some sense pragmatic) contrast; but it commonly marks the difference we seek to characterize".[5]

Similarly, when he analyses the distinction between arguments that ground statements like 'I ought to do *A*' and 'It is true that I ought to do *A*', he asserts:

„Equivalent propositions need not be identical; and that the two in question are apparently not identical is suggested by the clear difference between the reasoning undertaken in order to determine *what to do* (or even what I should do) and reasoning undertaken in order to determine *what it is true that I should do*. The latter phrase suggests the detachment of people who want to determine what their duties are *and then* if there is any reason why they should fulfill them [...]"[6]

Audi's distinction is based partly on the fact that with each one of these arguments different kinds of questions are intended to be answered.[7] To discover the pragmatic attitude through the kind of question that is intended to be answered poses some problems. As has been said before, a cognitive interest may be expressed through questions formulated in practical terms, such as 'What should I believe?', 'What should I understand?'. Similarly, a practical interest could hide behind apparently theoretical questions such as 'Which one of the propositions about what I ought to do is true?' or 'Is „I should not lie" true?'.[8] If the criterion is pragmatic, then the grammatical type of the questions should be just as irrelevant as that of the assertions answering them. What is relevant is the intention of the person actually developing the argument, and the function the latter serves. But according to Audi, the grounding of an assertion as, for instance, 'I ought to work every day' is thought to reveal a practical interest and the commitment to act accordingly. In contrast, a grounding of an assertion like 'It is true that I ought to work every day' must be regarded as an expression of an intellectual interest in the knowledge of existing duties, and not as an indicator that the agent has some reason (motive) for acting accordingly.

---

[5] Audi, Robert, Practical Reasoning, op. cit., p. 103.

[6] Ibid.

[7] Ibid., pp. 90 f. Again, it should be noted that the distinction between the theoretical and the practical is drawn on the basis of the formulation of the questions 'What is the case?' and 'What ought to be done?'. On this, see above, sect. 4 of the Presentation.

[8] Edgley, Roy, Reason in Theory and Practice, op. cit., pp. 17-20.

In that sense, it can be objected against Audi that, although in the passage quoted he presents a pragmatic criterion of distinction, he seems to think that all statements of *is* necessarily imply a cognitive attitude, and all statements of *ought* a practical interest. The grammatical type of the statement thus turns out to be sufficient for determining the pragmatic attitude. The linear correlation between the use of a specific kind of statement and the presence of a certain internal attitude is, however, highly questionable. It is not sure that the assertion 'I ought to do *A*' is always the expression of a practical attitude whereas that of 'It is true that I ought to do *A*' never is.

C) THE CRITERION OF THE TYPE OF RELATION

Can we perhaps distinguish theoretical and practical arguments on the basis of the type of relation established between the premises of such arguments? According to this proposal, practical arguments constitute specific reasoning patterns in which a substantive relationship between the considered contents is established. One example for this is the teleological practical argument. Here, we have a pattern which represents, through verbal statements, a relationship between certain states of affairs or actions regarded as means, and other states of affairs or actions regarded as ends. The relation alluded to in a teleological argument is a causal relationship between the respective events. Understood in this way, a practical argument is generally used in the intentional explanation of an action (as a means for reaching some end), and in the understanding of a body movement as an action (as a change that is intentionally directed towards the realization of a result). It must also be emphasized that this notion of practical argument is often accepted as a pattern of justification too. This is then a kind of 'instrumental' or 'rational' justification 'relative to an end'.[9] Within this conception, there is controversy about whether or not the premises stating the end justify only what is necessary or also what is sufficient for bringing it about. Later, I will briefly come back to that distinction.

If this criterion is used as the basis for classification, then all deductive arguments, whatever their conclusion or purpose, must be regarded as theoretical arguments. But taking the kind of relation established between the premises as the backbone of the distinction enables one to point out an important aspect. All deductive arguments are verbal structures establishing a relationship of a *logical* kind. It makes no difference what kind of statement they ground and with what purpose.

Another kind of practical argument, according to this criterion of classification, consists in the verbal representation of a comparison and assessment of reasons. As an example, we can use the pattern proposed by Joseph Raz in *Practical Reason and Norms*. There, he says:

„There are other forms of practical inferences. For example, p is a reason for x to ϕ; q is an overriding reason for x not to ϕ; therefore x has a reason not to ϕ."[10]

---

[9] Cf., for instance, Hans Kelsen, What is Justice? Justice, Law and Politics in the Mirror of Science, Berkeley: University of California Press 1971; also von Wright, G. H., On So-Called Practical Inference, op. cit., p. 30.

[10] Raz, Joseph, PRN, p. 29, n.

This 'practical inference' consists in a balancing of considerations in which reasons are compared with respect to their force or weight. In this case, as in the teleological argument, the proposed relationship between premises and conclusion is not of a logical kind. Rather, it is a substantive relationship (force, weight, or importance) between the facts in question (in this case, reasons for action).

Although teleological and evaluative arguments are expressed in a sequence of statements, they are not based on a formal linguistic relationship. A teleological argument alludes to an empirical relationship, and a comparative argument to a normative or valuational relationship. The conclusion can then be drawn because of these relationships. In a teleological argument, the conclusion states an empirically necessary or sufficient condition for the content of the major premise. In an evaluative argument, the conclusion is a conclusive ought-statement depending on the weight of the reasons considered in the premises. These patterns are usually presented as 'inferences' or 'arguments'. However, the correctness or validity of the statement serving as the conclusion obviously does not depend on a formal relationship with the statements serving as premises. Thus, one of the defining elements of the notions of inference or argument is neglected, and this fact is often overlooked. What is called 'practical argument' in these cases is not a sub-type of what has been defined as the class of arguments or inferences in general. Therefore, although I will later present some more reflections about these possible argument structures, this criterion will not be taken as a starting point for the distinction between theoretical and practical arguments. This does not mean that it is wrong to call teleological or evaluative reasoning patterns as presented above 'practical arguments' or 'inferences'. But it should be noted that these terms then acquire a completely different meaning. The fact that such patterns of statements are called 'arguments' too shows the ambiguity of that word.

The relationships between the members of a set of statements are precisely what defines the set's structure.[11] An argument or inference in the logical sense is a sequence of statements linked to each other through a deductive relationship. Whether the conclusion of such an argument is correct depends on the satisfaction of the rules constituting that relationship, with respect to a set of premises, regardless of their force or weight or the empirical relationships existing between the facts mentioned in those premises. If one admits that the distinction between practical and theoretical arguments is a classification to be made within that notion of argument, then the criterion presented here is unacceptable.

Since it is the most useful criterion for the purposes of this book, in what follows practical arguments will be understood as arguments which justify an ought-conclusion. In other words, I will adopt a strictly linguistic criterion based on the dichotomy between statements of 'is' and statements of 'ought'. Also, since the existence of propositional (cognitive) as well as non-propositional (non-cognitive) meanings is assumed, the practical nature of an argument says nothing about the meaning of the conclusion. The ought-statement that is founded may be a proposition or a norm. That is, it may be a propositional meaning that can be true or false, or a non-propositional meaning without a

---

[11] Cf. Caracciolo, Ricardo, El sistema jurídico. Problemas actuales, Madrid: Centro de Estudios Constitucionales 1988, p. 12.

truth-value. This criterion of classification enables us to identify a set of practical arguments within the general class of logical arguments. But there are other meanings of the expression 'practical argument' which do not fit that classification. I will now turn to such non-logical meanings of the term.

3. Practical Arguments: Different Meanings and Uses

A) FIRST DISTINCTION

So far, we have focused on a logical sense of the expression 'practical argument' which alludes to a deductive argument justifying a practical statement, i. e., an ought-statement. There is another way of understanding practical arguments which, in turn, is used with different purposes in philosophy of action and in legal philosophy. One of the main purposes is of a theoretical kind. As typical examples, one may think of the so-called 'patterns of practical argument' applied in the representation of the internal structure of action, in the teleological explanation of conduct, in the reconstruction of certain concepts, etc. On this interpretation, a practical argument is a model, an abstract pattern of statements, which claims to represent a relationship (between objects which may be empirical or ideal entities) that is independent of the statements the pattern is filled with.[12] The validity or correctness of the model (where this does not mean the logical validity or correctness) depends on whether it is able to account in the best possible way for the relationship it attempts to reconstruct or explain. Such argument patterns are also advanced and justified as the content of rules of conduct by some theories of normative ethics. In that case, the model is proposed in a normative sense. Generally, it is regarded as a standard to be followed in order to found the rationality or morality of a duty to perform some action.

In view of this, there are two clearly separable concepts of 'practical argument'. Only one of them is of a logical kind, although both are linguistic structures. In a practical argument in the logical sense, a deductive relationship between the statements it consists in is established. In the non-logical sense, the relationship between the statements of the argument pattern is not an implication. It can be a connection of an empirical, a moral or a conceptual nature, depending on the kind of entities the relationship between which is modelized in the linguistic structure. From the functional or pragmatic point of view, practical arguments in the logical sense are typically used as standards for assessing the validity of real reasonings. Non-logical models of practical arguments are basically used for explanatory or reconstructive, but also for normative and ethical purposes. Their form or structure is a matter of controversy and depends on the ends to which they are to be applied.

---

[12] The way in which the notion of a model is used here is common in the social sciences, but different from how it is more often used in physics. For example, when one says 'The solar system is a model of classical particle mechanics', the model is the real system, to which the theory can be applied. From this perspective, different models of one and the same theory all have the same structure, as characterized by the theory. Cf. Mosterín, Jesús, Sobre el concepto de modelo, in: id., Conceptos y teorías de la ciencia, Madrid: Alianza Universidad 1984, pp. 147-156.

The teleological structure is generally accepted as a theoretical model for the reconstruction of the means-ends relationship existing between the elements that are internal to action. Independently of this application, some authors also think that the teleological pattern can be regarded as a specific form of a practical argument in the logical sense.[13] Perhaps for that reason, the statements about teleological practical arguments in the literature on this topic can be confusing. In many cases, there is no clear distinction between a practical argument as a structure of a logical nature and a practical argument as a theoretical, reconstructive model. An example of this confusion is von Wright's first proposal in *Explanation and Understanding*, where he attempts to show the deductive nature of the relationship between statements about the internal and the external elements of action.[14] In the same vein, we can find expressions giving rise to that confusion in the work of legal philosophers. David Richards, for instance, trying to elucidate the internal structure of action, refers to it as the 'logical process' underlying all action.[15] The same applies to Joseph Raz when he qualifies comparative arguments as a kind of 'inference'.[16] This use of language leads to confusion between the different meanings of 'practical argument' and the different functions of the proposed patterns. I seek to avoid such confusion with the following first distinction: The pattern of a practical argument does not yield an argument in the logical sense – neither when proposed as a theoretical model (for explanation or reconstruction) nor when it is seen as an ideal model for the foundation of conclusive ought-statements.

B) SECOND DISTINCTION

The different notions of practical arguments as structured sets of statements must be distinguished from the respective mental processes or verbal acts in which they are used. In the first place, the abstract logical relation which is one of the meanings of the term 'inference' must not be confused with the actual realization of an argument, i. e., with the steps an individual performs, from the assumption or acceptance of some premises to the explicit formulation of the implied statements. The mental or verbal activity of drawing a conclusion from given statements which serve as premises is one thing, and the deductive relationship between the statements a very different one. Whether or not a given statement follows from certain other statements is entirely independent of whether or not anyone actually infers it (correctly or wrongly) from those other statements as a conclusion. As Morris Cohen and Ernest Nagel unequivocally observe:

---

[13] Cf. below, in sect. 4. b) of this chapter, the conceptions attributed to the logic of satisfaction and of satisfactoriness.

[14] Von Wright, Georg Henrik, Explanation and Understanding, op. cit., pp. 95-117. Meanwhile, von Wright has abandoned this position which was a confusion of a logical notion of practical reasoning and a conception of it as a theoretical model for the reconstruction of action. Cf. von Wright, Georg Henrik, On So-Called Practical Inference, op. cit., pp. 18-34.

[15] Richards, David A. J., A Theory of Reasons for Action, op. cit., p. 58.

[16] Raz, Joseph, PRN, op. cit., p. 29, n.

„We *infer* one proposition from another *validly* only if there is an objective relation of *implication* between the first proposition and the second. Hence, it is essential to distinguish *inference*, which is a temporal process, from *implication*, which is an objective relation between propositions."[17]

A similar distinction can be made between the model of a practical argument understood as a theoretical pattern, and the actual mental process intended to be represented or reconstructed by that model. As has often been asserted in the theory of human action, the process underlying all agents' rational acting consists in a causal connection between certain internal states of affairs (mental states) and other, external states of affairs (bodily movements). This *empirical process* often referred to as a process of 'practical reasoning' must not be confused with the *model* of a practical argument which serves to reconstruct that process.

Finally, the distinction becomes even more apparent when it is applied to the different conceptions of practical arguments as normative models. The reasoning patterns one should follow according to different moral theories are something completely different from the actual processes of moral justification and conflict resolution these theories attempt to regulate.

The way how mental or verbal reasoning processes are related to the corresponding abstract models varies in each case. An argument, understood as a logical structure, can be taken as a standard of evaluation for the procedure a person follows in her reasoning. For example, if a judge, in founding a decision, does not follow a deductive structure, his justification must be considered invalid and discarded as a logical argument. On the other hand, the abstract pattern of a practical argument used in the reconstruction of action must be discarded if it turns out that it does not enable us to understand as actions what an intuitive idea would identify as such, or if it is of no use for the formulation of adequate hypotheses or predictions. Finally, in the case of an argument in the normative sense, when argument patterns do not conform to real reasoning processes it is not the models that must be discarded; rather, it is the behaviour that can justifiably be regarded as incorrect.

To sum up, then, according to the first distinction there are three typical uses of the notion of 'practical argument' (as a linguistic structure), only one of which corresponds to the logical meaning of the term. The other two refer to sets of statements representing relationships other than the logical relations that can exist between the elements of the linguistic structure. According to the second distinction, each of these kinds of 'practical arguments' is linked to real mental processes also called 'practical arguments', and the two must not be confused. Besides, the different mental processes themselves also should not be confused. One process begins with the acceptance of some premises and ends with the acceptance of a conclusion; another one starts with the acceptance of a conclusion and concludes with the actual performance of an action.

In the literature on practical reasoning, what is usually emphasized is only the need for the distinction between the logical and the psychological notion of argument.[18]

---

[17] Cohen, Morris R. and Nagel, Ernest, An Introduction to Logic and Scientific Method, New York: Harcourt, Brace 1934, pp. 7 f.

This distinction is of fundamental importance in legal theory. Among other things, it facilitated the detection of the mistake at the root of one of the critiques legal *realism* has presented against *normativism*.[19] However, the distinctions drawn above indicate that there is also more than one mental process at work, and that, therefore, there is more than one sense in which confusion can set in. As has been pointed out, one thing is the mental process that culminates in the drawing of a conclusion, and quite another the process which leads to an external manifestation in action. Both are practical arguments in the psychological, rather than in the logical sense. This distinction too is relevant for legal theory, because it will enable us to see the mistake on which one of the critiques contemporary legal theory has directed against legal positivism is based.[20]

In what follows, when speaking of practical arguments, I will not refer to a person's mental processes unless I explicitly say so. In the present chapter, I am mainly interested in the concept of practical argument as a model of speech and in the notion of premise-reason as an integral element of such a model. For this purpose, I will briefly consider the three uses of 'practical argument' mentioned above. I will analyse how they are applied and how the reasons taken as premises for such arguments are related to reasons for action.

4. Practical Arguments in the Logical Sense

A) DEDUCTIVE PATTERNS

There are numerous interpretations of the Aristotelian idea of the distinction between deductive and practical syllogisms.[21] According to von Wright, the structure of Aristotle's practical syllogism is such that an individual state of affairs is subsumed under a general rule of action.[22] Anscombe, for her part, emphasizes the condition the major premise must satisfy: It must be a universal proposition, although according to the examples given by Aristotle it may have many different contents; i. e., it must be a general statement about the duty, the expediency, or the desirability of a given action or state of

---

[18] Cf. Gauthier, David, Practical Reasoning, Oxford: Clarendon 1963, p. 26; Schueler, G. F., The Idea of Reason for Acting. A Philosophical Argument, op. cit., p. 31; Alchourrón, Carlos E. and Bulygin, Eugenio, Limits of Logic and Legal Reasoning, in: A. A. Martino (ed.), Preproceedings of the III International Conference on Logica - Informatica - Diritto, vol. II, Florence 1989.

[19] In Chapter VI, when I come specifically to the topic of reasoning in judicial justifications, I will have to say more about this.

[20] One of the theses of contemporary legal theory is that it is a mistake of positivism not to have seen that the justification of a judicial decision necessarily presupposes the existence of moral norms. As will be shown, this assertion is based on a confusion between a 'practical argument' as a mental process and a 'practical argument' as a linguistic pattern relating statements to each other. In other words, it rests on a confusion of justification in the subjective sense and in the objective sense. The former is an action, whereas the latter is a relationship between reasons, namely, between premise-reasons in formal justification and substantive reasons in substantive justification. This question will be discussed in Chapter VI.

[21] Aristotle, Nichomachean Ethics, 1112b, 1113a, 1147a.

[22] von Wright, Georg Henrik, Practical Inference, in: Practical Reason, op. cit., p. 1.

affairs.[23] The minor premise is a particular statement in which the universal term of the major premise is predicated of a particular thing. The conclusion states the duty or intention to perform a certain action, or directly its performance. Without entering into the discussion about the status of the conclusion, it will be assumed that it is also a statement.[24] The logical validity of an argument with these characteristics is highly controversial. Still, from Aristotle's examples one can reconstruct a model of a practical argument that is similar to one of the classical deductive structures. For instance:

- All men ought to eat dry food.
- John is a man.
- John ought to eat dry food.

The conclusion that a certain action ought to be performed follows logically from what is asserted in the major premise about a generic act.

(i) Application of the model

This kind of practical argument is of special interest for legal theory, since it is used in one of the main tasks of legal scholars, i. e., in presenting different sectors of a legal system and showing the consequences to be drawn from a given set of norms.[25] That same task must also be carried out by anyone wishing to find out what norms derive from a given set of explicitly formulated norms.[26]

Besides, the pattern of a deductive argument is also useful in the application of law. Judges must resolve conflicts by judicial decision. It is assumed that a judicial sentence must be a decision founded on general norms. Thus, it must be possible to reconstruct it by following some valid pattern of reasoning. General legal ought-statements (norms or principles) constitute the major premise, the description of the facts constitutes the minor premise, and the content of the judge's particular decision takes the place of the conclusion.[27]

---

[23] Anscombe, G. E. M., Intention, op. cit., pp. 63 ff.

[24] Cf., for example, Aune, Bruce, Reason and Action, op. cit., pp. 112 and 113.

[25] Cf. Caracciolo, Ricardo, Entrevista a Eugenio Bulygin, in: Doxa (Alicante) 14 (1993), p. 504.

[26] A derived norm is a norm that is implicitly prescribed because its content follows logically from a set of explicitly enacted norms in some legal system. Cf. Alchourrón, Carlos E. and Eugenio Bulygin, Sobre el concepto de orden jurídico, in: Crítica (Mexico-City) VIII:23 (1976) p. 396; also by the same authors, Sobre la existencia de las normas jurídicas, Valencia, Ven.: Universidad de Carabobo, CLIJS 1979, p. 54.

[27] The applicability of the deductive model in the justification of judicial decisions is a very controversial topic. Cf., e. g., Aarnio, Aulis, On Legal Reasoning, Turku: University of Turku 1977, pp. 53-70; MacCormick, Neil, Legal Reasoning and Legal Theory, Oxford: Clarendon 1978, pp. 53-71; Wellman, Vincent, Practical Reasoning and Judicial Justification: Towards an Adequate Theory, University of Colorado Law Review 57:1 (1985); Atienza, Manuel, Las razones del Derecho. Teoría de la argumentación jurídica, Madrid: Centro de Estudios Constitucionales 1991, pp. 39-48. At this point, however, I do not need to analyse the different positions adopted in the controversy. I only wish to point out that within legal theory, the application of this model as a standard for the reconstruction of judicial sentences is a usual practice. Cf. Bulygin, Eugenio, Sentencia judicial y creación de Derecho, in: *La Ley* 124 (1966).

A problem for the application of the model of a practical argument in the logical sense is the ambiguity of the word 'ought'. Depending on the criterion one chooses for the distinction between practical and theoretical arguments, the major premise of a practical argument could be either the description of the existence of a principle or norm, or directly a principle or norm. In the latter case, the standard notion of inference is inapplicable.[28] From the point of view of classical logic, one cannot say, strictly speaking, that the content of a judicial decision is *deduced* from the norms invoked, or that a derived norm is a *logical consequence* of an explicitly formulated norm. This difficulty has given rise to numerous investigations attempting to develop a logic that is not founded on truth-values. Independently of the progress made in this field, most reconstructions of judicial justificatory arguments in the general theory of law accept the deductive syllogism of classical predicate logic as a model. The same holds for other fields of practical philosophy where the justification of (not necessarily legal) norms and duties is discussed.[29]

(ii) Validity

Practical arguments in the logical sense are deductive arguments the major premise of which, just as the conclusion, is an ought-statement. Therefore, all argument structures of classical logic are valid with respect to them, i. e., it is possible to develop practical arguments by applying any of the rules of inference admitted by logic. For instance, following the method of natural deduction, from a given set of deontic statements one can infer others by double negation, by introducing or eliminating conjunctions or disjunctions, by *reductio ad absurdum*, or by introducing conditionals.[30]

A first difficulty with this arises in applying the logical notion of practical argument directly to norms. This problem is usually expressed through the so-called 'Jørgensen dilemma' which has given rise to prolonged controversy. It has been shown that one can design rules for a syntactical calculus relating statements that have no truth-value.[31] The problem is the semantic interpretation of such a calculus. On the assumption that there are no truth-values in normative language, there have been attempts to show that the connectives operating in prescriptive language can be defined with the help of the same value-tables used in propositional logic. The only difference is that the basic connectives are interpreted by reference not to truth or falsity, but to some other pair of values. Thus, a deontic logic is constructed as a new interpretation of the old formal system of traditional calculus.[32] The obstacle encountered in this enterprise is, of course, the identification of those values. Several proposals have been tried, none of which has given satisfactory results. So far, it has not been possible to develop a set of rules of in-

---

[28] Provided norms are not interpreted as true or false statements.

[29] See, for instance, David A. Richards when he justifies the content of normative statements from principles of rational choice and moral principles of action. Cf. Richards, David A., A Theory of Reason for Action, op. cit., pp. 49-52 and 214-226.

[30] According to Genzen's method; cf., e. g., Lemmon, John, Beginning Logic, London: Thomas Nelson 1965; Garrido, Manuel, Lógica simbólica, 2nd ed. Madrid: Tecnos 1983.

[31] Cf., e. g., Alchourrón, C. and Martino, A., Logic without truth, in: Ratio Juris 3:1 (1990), pp. 46-67.

[32] Cf. Ross, Alf, Directives and Norms, New York: Humanities Press 1968, pp. 174 f.

ference as rigorous as those of propositional logic that would define a notion of validity not based on the notion of truth.[33] And if, for the sake of the argument, one accepts the rules of inference of classical logic for normative discourse, a second problem arises: Their unrestricted application leads to highly counterintuitive conclusions.[34] It may seem that these inconveniences are serious enough to warrant discarding the logical notion of practical argument for normative discourse. The notion is, however, widely used; and therefore, it will be admitted that it is possible to speak of 'practical arguments' in the logical sense, constructed on the basis of the rules of predicate logic, but relating non-propositional sentences, i. e., norms.[35]

(iii) Reasons as premises

In practical arguments in the logical sense, there are two kinds of premise-reasons which justify the conclusion. The major premise can consist in a normative proposition or a norm, whereas the minor premise is a statement of fact describing a state of affairs or an action. It is instructive to compare this notion of premise-reason with the notions of reason for action presented in the previous chapter.

When the content of the major premise-reason is a *norm*, it may be a reason in the substantive sense, from the point of view of some theory. That means that it may be justified as a reason for action, regardless of whether or not it is recognized or accepted. The possibility that one and the same content is at the same time a premise-reason and a substantive reason is based on the concepts of 'norm' and 'substantive reason'. Norms can be premises, first of all, because they are regarded as meanings that can be expressed through language; secondly, because, despite of all the difficulties mentioned above, the application of logic to such entities, which have a meaning but no truth-value, has

---

[33] One proposal, for instance, replaces the values 'true' and 'false' with 'valid' and 'invalid', where the latter are interpreted psychologically. The validity of a directive, thus, consists in a mental state an individual is in. Cf. Ross, Alf, Imperatives and logic, in: Theoria 7 (1941). Another suggestion has been to take 'satisfaction' and 'non-satisfaction' as the logical values of directives. Cf. Hofstadter, A. and J. C. McKinsey, On the logic of imperatives, in: Philosophy of Science 6 (1939); Sosa, E., The logic of imperatives, in: Theoria (1966), pp. 224 ff. Based on a critique of that last approach, the values of 'satisfactoriness' and 'non-satisfactoriness' have been proposed as an alternative. Cf. Kenny, A. J., Practical inference, in: Analysis 26 (1965-66), pp. 65 ff. Other conceptions do not claim to identify or define the value of 'validity' usually associated with normative language; instead, using specific rules of calculus, they attempt to show its logical properties. Cf. Ross, Alf, Directives and Norms, op. cit., p. 177.

[34] Take, for example, the norm 'You should do military service'. Introducing disjunction, from this norm we can infer 'You should do military service or blow up the army base'; or, introducing the conditional, one can conclude: 'If you are terminally ill, then you should do military service'. In order to avoid such paradoxical consequences, several methods have been proposed, among them, e. g., the development of interpretative theories which constrain the premises in such a way as to permit only desirable conclusions. Another proposal has been the total replacement of standard logic by a another logic which avoids such conclusions, or the correction of classical logic using criteria of relevance. On this, cf. Moreso, José Juan, On Relevance and Justification of Legal Decisions, in: Erkenntnis 44 (1996) pp. 73-100; also id., Legal Indeterminacy and Constitutional Interpretation, Dordrecht: Kluwer 1998, esp. Chapter I, Appendix B.

[35] This notion corresponds to the so-called 'hyletic' conception of norms. Cf. Alchourrón, Carlos and Bulygin, Eugenio, The expressive conception of norms, in: R. Hilpinen (ed.), New Studies in Deontic Logic, Dordrecht: Reidel 1981, pp. 95-124. In the next chapter, I will elucidate other meanings of the term 'norm'.

been admitted. Now, if substantive reasons are to be justificatory, they must be norms. Therefore, substantive reasons too can be premise-reasons. A norm used as the foundation of an argument undoubtedly is a premise-reason which, in turn, may be – but not necessarily is – a substantive reason in favour of an action.[36] All norms are linguistic entities and, therefore, premise-reasons. But not all norms are substantive reasons in favour of an action.[37]

The situation is different when the content of the major premise-reason is not a norm, but a *normative proposition*, that is, a descriptive statement about the existence of a norm – a norm which may, in turn, be a substantive reason for action. In that case, the asymmetry between a premise-reason and a substantive reason can be seen very clearly. If the proposition (the premise-reason) is false, then the norm the existence of which is asserted does not exist and, therefore, there is also no corresponding substantive reason for action. Nevertheless, the assertion is still a premise-reason.

One aspect which may, inadvertently, lead to a confusion of these two meanings of reason is that both are linked to a justificatory function and, therefore, to norms. A justificatory nature can be predicated of premise-reasons as well as of substantive reasons for action. But the expression 'justificatory nature' means different things in the two cases. A norm is a premise-reason justifying a statement if, and only if, that statement is logically implied by that norm. In contrast, a norm is a substantive reason for action if, and only if, according to some normative theory it is an adequate standard of behaviour. An action can be regarded as substantively justified only in relation to some theory. Such a *substantive justification* may be presented in the form of a logical argument, i. e., by elaborating a *formal justification*. Therefore, the two concepts of reason (premise-reason and substantive reason for action) imply two different senses of justification.

The other entities that can be said to constitute substantive reasons for action – whether in the explanatory sense (e. g., intentional states) or in the secondary sense (e. g., so-called 'normative' or 'institutional' facts) – can never themselves be premise-reasons, because they are not the kind of entities that can form part of a formal argument; they can only be mentioned or described by a premise-reason.

Another important difference between the formal and the substantive notion of reason can be seen in the following comparison. To use or presuppose a norm of conduct as a premise-reason amounts to using it, at a particular point in time and space, in a specific empirical activity: the mental or verbal elaboration of a logical argument. But the person using a norm in an argument does not necessarily accept it as a reason for action. An anarchist can use legal norms in his arguments and still not accept them as sources of obligations, i. e., as substantive reasons for action, without committing a contradiction. The same can be said of someone who commits civil disobedience with respect to one or several specific norms. That an agent formally justifies conclusions with the help of norms does not imply that he accepts them as reasons for action. Besides, the

---

36 Note that, strictly speaking, what a general norm justifies is not an action, but a solution, i. e. the deontic qualification of an action. Cf. Alchourrón, Carlos and Bulygin, Eugenio, Normative Systems, op. cit., pp. 153 ff.

37 As explained in the previous chapter, this depends on whether or not it has been proposed and justified within some normative theory.

fact that someone accepts certain norms as reasons for action does not mean that they really are reasons for action.[38]

It may be thought that what I have characterized as the acceptance of a norm as a reason for action is the same as what Hart has called the adoption of the 'internal point of view'. But that interpretation would be misleading, above all because Hart does not distinguish between the two senses in which a norm may be 'accepted', namely, as a premise-reason or as a reason for action. At some points he asserts that those who adopt the internal point of view are those who *use* the rules, and the *use* of a rule can be understood in both senses. Thus, the expression 'adoption of the internal point of view' is ambiguous – an ambiguity the distinction I propose is intended to avoid.[39]

That one accepts a norm as a reason for action means that one is committed to, or favourably disposed towards, its content. But remember the example of the anarchist and the civil disobedient. And what about the hypocrite who pretends to accept something he actually does not accept; or the law student, the professor of law or the legal theorist who may not have that attitude, nor pretend to have it? And yet, they all elaborate practical arguments. The usual description of the situation of a person invoking a normative statement without being committed to it is based on a distinction between 'committed' and 'detached' statements.[40] The status of such statements is controversial in legal theory. According to some interpretations of Joseph Raz's proposal, detached statements must be regarded as descriptive and can therefore be true or false.[41] Most authors have accepted Raz's suggestion, albeit with minor changes. This applies even to Hart who regards it as complementary to his distinction between internal and external statements.[42]

---

[38] That means that legal norms may or may not be substantive reasons for action according to some normative theory. For example, from the standpoint of an ethical theory only legal norms with a democratic origin may be considered substantive reasons for action. From this point of view, then, agents who accept as substantive reasons norms that do not fulfil this condition can be criticized.

[39] Hart states that the adoption of the internal point of view towards primary rules is manifested most clearly in the use of these rules as a basis for the criticism of deviant behaviour or for requests of compliance. This suggests that acceptance in Hart must be understood as acceptance of a reason in the substantive (although specifically legal) sense. However, Hart says that the characterization of the internal point of view towards a developed and complex legal system is broader and more diversified. He suggests that all acts presupposing the use of secondary rules can be regarded as manifestations of the internal point of view – for instance, legislative activities, the application of norms by a court, the exercise of private and public powers, etc. Cf. Hart, H. L. A., The Concept of Law, op. cit., p. 117. This raises doubts about whether the adoption of the internal point of view necessarily implies the acceptance of the norms as substantive reasons for action. In fact, all those acts could be performed without adopting such an attitude.

[40] Cf. Raz, Joseph, The Authority of Law. Essays on Law and Morality, op. cit., ch. VIII; MacCormick makes a similar distinction when he speaks of statements made from the internal, the external and the hermeneutical point of view. Cf. MacCormick, Neil, Legal Reasoning and Legal Theory, op. cit., pp. 287 and 291; also MacCormick, Neil, H. L. A. Hart, London: Eduard Arnold 1981, ch. III.

[41] Cf. Bayón Mohino, Juan Carlos, The Normativity of Law: Legal Duty and Reasons for Action, Dordrecht: Kluwer (forthcoming), ch. 1 [Spanish original: La normatividad del Derecho: deber jurídico y razones para la acción, Madrid: Centro de Estudios Constitucionales 1991, pp. 27-34].

[42] Hart, H. L. A., Legal Duty and Obligation, in: id., Essays on Bentham, Oxford: Clarendon 1982, pp. 154 f. For a different interpretation of this kind of statements, cf. Eugenio Bulygin, Norms, normative propositions, and legal statements, in: G. Fløistad (ed.) Contemporary Philosophy. A New Survey, Vol. 3: Philosophy of

Despite its wide acceptance, I think that the classification is flawed. It projects a distinction on statements and propositions which is then justified entirely on a pragmatic level. From the point of view defended in this book, statements and their meanings do not belong to the class of objects that can be qualified as 'committed' or 'detached'. Rather than to statements, these qualities can only be applied to the agents uttering them. Committed as well as non-committed persons make use of norms in their practical arguments. A norm does not cease to be a norm only because it is not accepted as a reason for action, i. e., because an agent does not commit himself to it. The assertion that if one does not commit oneself to a statement one does not really pronounce a truly normative statement implies a change in the meaning of the word 'norm' or 'normative statement'. The assertion is true only if for a statement to be normative it must be accepted as, or believed to be, a reason for action.[43] In that case, if someone does not have one of these attitudes he obviously does not pronounce a norm. Hence, the theorist, the student, the anarquist, etc., do not make authentically normative statements whenever they utter statements they do not regard as reasons for action. All those who adopt Raz's distinction also adopt, perhaps inadvertently, a concept of norm according to which a statement is not a norm if it is not accepted as a reason for action in the substantive sense. I will come back to this in the following chapter, when I discuss the normativity of law.

In conclusion, we do not need that classification in order to show the different attitudes one can have when advancing a statement or a practical argument. From a semantic perspective, there are propositional and non-propositional meanings. From a pragmatic perspective, there is a complex spectrum of different attitudes a person can have towards such contents. For example, they can be assumed, believed, accepted, internalized, etc.[44] As something internal to an agent, the effective acceptance of a norm as a reason for action cannot be inferred merely from the fact that someone performs the speech-act of conducting an argument. The use of a premise in an argument is too weak an indicator to be regarded as corroborating evidence for an empirical statement about the existence of certain mental states in an agent. It is extremely difficult to determine a person's internal attitudes. Generally, they may be suggested by the context and the particular way in which the argument is framed, but never merely by the fact that certain words are uttered. In contrast, it is not difficult at all to determine that a norm is being assumed as a premise-reason, because that does, indeed, consist merely in its use as such, i. e., in its being invoked as part of the foundation of a logical argument.

The external manifestation of an act of formal justification may be exactly the same as that of an act of substantive justification: the verbal formulation of a sequence of statements. As has been pointed out in Chapter II, in certain contexts the external manifestation may be considered sufficient for attributing a specific intention or internal attitude to an agent. The acceptance of a norm as a reason for action is an intentional state capable of motivating action. Therefore, all that has been said about intentions (as the internal aspect of actions) also applies to acceptance. That means that in certain situ-

---

Action, The Hague: Martinus Nijhoff 1982, and id., Enunciados jurídicos y positivismo jurídico: Respuesta a Raz, in: Análisis Filosófico 1:2 (1981).

[43] As we will see later, Joseph Raz's proposal, linking norms to reasons for action, has a subjectivist and an objectivist interpretation. What I say here is compatible with the subjectivist interpretation.

[44] In Chapter V, I will present a characterization of these kinds of attitudes.

ations the mere utterance of a justificatory argument could be taken as the basis for attributing to the speaker the acceptance of the norms invoked, or the desire to promote a certain action. Examples of such situations are the legislator who cites constitutional standards to support an amendment proposal, or the judge who uses a number of norms to justify a sentence. The *attribution* of an internal attitude, however, does not necessarily mean that that attitude really exists. Under certain circumstances, one may impute the corresponding commitment and motivation of action to a person who invokes a norm; but it may, nevertheless, not be true that she really is thus commited and motivated.[45] In other cases, the attribution of the acceptance of a norm as a reason for action and, therefore, also the imputation of an act of justification in the substantive sense may be clearly discarded despite the fact that a formally justificatory argument has been formulated. Take, for example, a person who wishes to die and in seeking authorization for euthanasia wants to point out the negative consequences that would result if the request were denied. To this effect, she can argue from the norm of prohibition applied to previous cases similar to her own, where the injustice of its application is manifest. In that case, the prohibitive norm, though cited, clearly is not accepted as a reason for doing what it stipulates. It would be false to say that the person in question has substantively justified the prohibition of euthanasia in the cases she has mentioned. And yet, she obviously has formulated practical arguments, has 'used' the general norm prohibiting euthanasia, and has formally shown the particular conclusions that follow when it is adopted as a premise.

As has been said before, the adequacy of a justification in the formal sense is defined and assessed with the help of a set of inference rules. Assertions of validity, thus, are relative to such a set of logical rules.[46] And with respect to reasons for action, the correctness of a justification is judged in terms of a set of standards of rationality or morality proposed by some normative conception – political, legal, ethical, or religious. Therefore, the correctness of a substantive justification too is relative to some set of standards. Every ideological or normative conception proposes certain principles as adequate reasons for action. And it also stipulates their weight and hierarchical position. That makes it possible to resolve the conflicts that may arise when several standards are applicable to one and the same situation.[47] The possibility that there are contradictory reasons gives rise to the normative proposal of models for practical reasoning. They are intended to ground duties to act in a certain way once conflicting reasons have been considered. This kind of arguments will be analysed later.

In summary, then, what has been said in this section about the two meanings of reason (premise-reason and substantive reason for action) is a corollary of certain points I have made in the last chapter. I have underscored that justifications can always be analysed and evaluated from the point of view of their formal structure and from the substantive point of view. Formally, the justification of an action is based on norms in their condition as premise-reasons. Substantively, justification is based on norms in their condition as substantive reasons for action.

---

[45] Cf. Chapter II, sect. 5, and Chapter I, sect. 3.

[46] Klimovsky, Gregorio, El método hipotético deductivo y la lógica, op. cit., pp. 75-90.

[47] On this, cf. Richards, David A., A Theory of Reasons for Action, op. cit., pp. 214-323.

So far, I have only considered the major premise-reason of an argument. But the minor premise too is part of what permits the justification of the conclusion; only that if it were invoked as the only reason, part of the argument would be missing. The major premise is necessary, and the deduction follows only from its conjunction with the minor premise. In the substantive sense, the fact referred to in the minor premise can also be understood as a reason for action. According to Joseph Raz, this fact is part of a complete reason, and by itself can only be understood as a reason in an auxiliary sense.[48] For example, if according to some normative conception it is thought correct that parents should take care of their children, then the fact that John is Peter's son is a reason for Peter to take care of John. From the point of view adopted in the present book, this fact can be considered a reason in favour of the prescribed action only in a secondary or subsidiary sense and because it is a condition for the application of the norm.[49]

B) THE LOGIC OF SATISFACTION AND THE LOGIC OF SATISFACTORINESS

I will now very briefly turn to a kind of argument that has been proposed as a valid logical pattern but which does not fit in among the other deductive structures. It has the same form as one of the examples given of practical arguments in the non-logical sense, namely, that of a teleological structure.

The reasoning pattern according to which a given end justifies the means that make it possible to reach that end can also be attributed to Aristotle.[50] The model can be schematically presented as follows. The major premise asserts a duty, an objective or a desire to be satisfied. The minor premise states the means for reaching the end mentioned in the major premise. Finally, the conclusion asserts a decision, an intention, a duty, or a practical necessity (depending on the interpretation) to employ the corresponding means.

Generally, two criteria are proposed for assessing the validity of teleological inferences starting from a deontic statement. According to the principle of the so-called logic of satisfaction, all conditions causally necessary for the state of affairs referred to in the major premise are to be considered validly justified. On this criterion, an ought-statement prescribing the performance of an action is justified if, and only if, performance of that action is necessary for reaching a given end. Several difficulties with this principle of inference can be pointed out.[51] In the first place, from its application fol-

---

[48] Cf. Raz, Joseph, PRN, pp. 33-35.

[49] As has been pointed out before, any act whatsoever can be regarded as a (justificatory) reason only in the secondary sense. This should not be confused with the concept of reason in the auxiliary sense suggested by Raz. A fact is a reason in the secondary or subsidiary sense if it is a condition for the applicability of certain norms. And a fact is a reason in the auxiliary sense if belief in its existence does not generate a critical practical attitude in favour of an action. Incidentally, in the example given the facts that can be called reasons in the secondary sense coincide with those Raz would call auxiliary reasons. But there are cases where this is not the case. For instance, according to the point of view adopted in this investigation, the fact that a norm exists can only be a justificatory reason in the secondary sense. However, for Raz it is not an auxiliary, but an operative reason. Note that the possibility that facts can be considered reasons for action in the justificatory sense has been treated in the previous chapter.

[50] Aristotle, Nicomachean Ethics, Book III, 1112b, 1113a.

[51] Raz, Joseph, Introduction, in: id. (ed.), Practical Reasoning, op. cit., p. 9-11.

lows the duty to carry out any necessary action, even when it is known that it will not lead to the end by which it is justified. This happens, for example, when other actions, which for some reason are not possible or which depend on other agents, would also need to be carried out in order to reach the end. Second, when there are only *sufficient* ways for reaching the end, none of which is *necessary*, none of the available options can be justified with that principle.

Critics of this principle of inference have proposed another one according to which all sufficient actions for reaching a given end are to be considered justified, even if they are not necessary. This is the thesis of the so-called logic of satisfactoriness.[52] From that perspective, the duty to do what, although necessary, is known to require an impossible complement in order to bring about a sufficient condition for a given end is not justified. Following this principle, therefore, the two inconveniences of the logic of satisfaction mentioned above are, indeed, eliminated. But the plausibility of this proposal is highly controversial. Its own defenders warn that the rule, taken by itself, can lead to the justification of obvious excesses. Often, there are many different sufficient ways for satisfying an end, and all of them – even unnecessarily exaggerated or inconvenient options – would then be justified. Note, however, that this is a flaw that afflicts the logic of satisfaction as well, when there is only one way to reach the given end. As Joseph Raz remarks:

„It is important to realize that problems of overkill affect the logic of satisfaction no less than that of satisfactoriness. One has only to imagine that blowing up the house is – as it may be – the only way of getting rid of a fly or some other minor nuisance."[53]

Therefore, the teleological structure that justifies a relative duty – relative, that is, to some other, presupposed duty – is usually understood to be accompanied by another kind of practical argument which allows one to assess reasons pro and con, either concerning a given end or concerning several alternative and equally effective means for reaching that end.[54] The kind of duty justified by such an argument is based on the consideration of *all* those reasons, and not on that of one single end.

Now, according to the rules of deductive logic, from a statement asserting the desire to reach some end or the existence of some duty it does not follow that a statement asserting the desire or duty to employ the (necessary or sufficient) means leading to the satisfaction of the presupposed end or duty is true. For such a conclusion, a general premise is needed which must also presuppose the existence of the desire or duty to do whatever is necessary or sufficient to satisfy the desire or duty mentioned in the first statement. This general premise is what the logic of satisfaction and the logic of satisfactoriness add. But with this addition, the argument turns into a standard deductive structure of propositional logic.

---

52 Kenny, A. J., Practical Inference, op. cit., pp. 65 ff.

53 Raz, Joseph, Introduction, in: id. (ed.), Practical Reasoning, op. cit., p. 11.

54 According to von Wright, there are at least two completely different senses in which one can speak of a deliberation about means. One thing is deliberation about what the means to some end are, and another thing is deliberation about which of these means should be chosen for reaching the end. Cf. von Wright, G. H., Practical Inference, op. cit., pp. 7-9 and 10.

Hence, these proposals cannot be regarded as new logics. They do not suggest new formal rules of inference. Teleological structures simply are not logical arguments. And when they are complemented in order to give them logical validity, they cease to be teleological structures.

5. Practical Arguments As Models of Theoretical Reconstruction

The notion of practical argument also refers to theoretical models used to reconstruct various objects. From this perspective, two different structures receive special attention: the first is identical to the one referred to in the previous section, i. e., it is a means-end structure; the second is of a comparative nature. I will now analyse these two models and their different applications as models for the reconstruction of:

a) intentional human action,
b) the teleological or intentional explanation of action,
c) the concept of duty,
d) the process of solving conflicts between reasons.

On this view, a practical argument is a structure the function of which, as with all theoretical proposals, is to show the relevant characteristics of the respective object in order to contribute to its better understanding. It hardly needs to be said that the logical notion of validity is not applicable to practical arguments thus understood. Instead, whether or not such arguments are more or less 'correct' is assessed depending on how well they serve to represent or make comprehensible what they claim to account for.

A) A MODEL FOR THE RECONSTRUCTION OF INTENTIONAL ACTION

The use of practical arguments in the reconstruction of intentional human action has already been mentioned. The teleological structure is unanimously accepted as a model for the representation or reconstruction of human action. With its help, an action can be shown with all its constitutive elements: the cognitive and volitional aspects which make up the intention as well as the result. The volitional internal element is represented in the major premise of the argument structure, the cognitive element is shown in the minor premise, and the result is stated in the conclusion. To understand a bodily movement as an action is precisely to interpret it in the light of an intention, using this teleological model.[55] The schema of a practical argument makes it possible to show the internal structure of an action, that is, the mental states accompanying the change brought about by an agent. Here, I do not need to repeat the description of these elements, which have been treated in sufficient detail in the previous chapter: an intentional state with a world-to-mind direction of fit (e. g., a desire, or the acceptance of an end), an intentional state with a mind-to-world direction of fit (e. g., beliefs, or the acceptance of propositions), and a result to which those intentional states give rise.

---

[55] Cf. von Wright, G. H., Explanation and Understanding, op. cit., ch. III.

B) A MODEL FOR THE EXPLANATION OF INTENTIONAL ACTION

The same structure of a practical argument that is employed in understanding an event as an action can also be used for explaining an event that is already thus understood. In fact, the teleological pattern is used for explaining an action in terms of an agent's internal reasons. It is an appropriate model for showing an action in the light of the ends pursued by the agent. Although not all actions can be explained in this way, all those undertaken in order to reach further ends can. As von Wright remarks:

„The schema of the practical inference is that of a teleological explanation 'turned upside down'. The starting point of a teleological explanation (of action) is that someone sets himself to do something or, more commonly, that someone does something. We ask: 'Why?' The answer often is simply: 'In order to bring about *p*'. It is then taken for granted that the agent considers the behavior which we are trying to explain causally relevant to the bringing about of *p and* that the bringing about of *p* is what he is aiming at or intending with his behavior."[56]

Between the two applications of a practical argument mentioned above, there is a difference that should be noted. The intentional states the *premises* of the argument refer to when it is used to *understand* an action are conceptually a part of the action. They are the elements amounting to the intention or internal aspect of the action. Sometimes they are also called 'motives'.[57] In contrast. when the argument pattern is used for the intentional *explanation* of an action, the premises of the practical inference 'turned upside down' mention intentional states internal to the agent, but not internal to the action. These intentional states stand for the ends an agent may pursue, and they are also called 'motives'. However, here the expression refers to events different from those referred to in the previous situation.[58] In both cases, it is very controversial what kind of relationship these internal states have with the result of the action or with the action itself. But generally, this is understood to be a causal relation.[59]

The meanings of 'internal reason' and 'motive' denote intentional states of an agent, regardless of whether these are necessary for the action, i. e., internal to it, or whether they, contingently, explain it teleologically. Every action has a motive in the sense of an intention. But not every action has a motive that explains it teleologically. Just as there are basic actions which are not performed through any other action, there are also actions that are not a means for performing any other action. These are actions wanted for themselves, and not because they are necessary conditions for some further goal. In that case, the structure of a practical argument cannot be used for an explanation of the action, although it can serve for reconstructing its internal elements.

---

56 Ibid., pp. 96 f.

57 In the first sense of the word 'motive', that is. Cf. Chapter I, sect. 6.

58 This is what has been called the second meaning of the term 'motive'. Cf. ibid.

59 Most writers agree that it is a causal relation. In this respect, they follow Donald Davidson's proposal from his classical, already cited essay 'Actions, Reasons, and Causes' (in: id., Essays on Actions and Events, op. cit., pp. 3-19). In contrast, if one accepts von Wright's conception, then the relation between explanatory reasons and action cannot be understood as causal. For him, an action is not an event that could be explained in that way.

Finally, it should be noted that the same schema of practical inference can be used to predict an action. This is what von Wright has called the 'prospective use' of the pattern of practical inference, which is different from the retrospective use made of it in teleological explanation. In the latter case, we start from an action that has been performed and look for the intentional states which tell us why it was performed. In prediction, we start from the intentional states of an agent and try to foresee what he will do. In both cases, the applied pattern has exactly the same structure.

C) A MODEL FOR THE RECONSTRUCTION OF THE CONCEPT OF DUTY

The teleological model can also be used as a schema for the reconstruction of the notion of duty in the technical or derived sense. Von Wright, for instance, uses it to this effect when he analyses the concept of duty in terms of the practical necessity of performing some action.[60] The foundation he offers proceeds in several steps, and in order to follow them, it will be helpful to work with the example he gives:[61]

- *x* wants to make the hut habitable.
- Unless *x* heats the hut, he will not succeed in making it habitable.
- Therefore, *x* ought to heat the hut.

This reasoning pattern is called *primary practical inference*. In it, starting from an end or desire of an agent, the practical necessity to do what leads to the satisfaction of that end or desire is concluded. An action is an objective practical necessity relative to an end if it *must* be performed in order to reach that end, i. e., if its result is a necessary condition for the pursued goal to come about. An action is a subjective practical necessity relative to some end if the agent *believes* that it must be performed in order to reach the end, though he may be wrong.

Von Wright points out that duties and obligations are not, as such, practical necessities. Compliance with a duty or an obligation may, however, become a necessity of that kind. For example:

- It is *x*'s duty to make the hut habitable.
- Unless *x* heats the hut, he cannot make it habitable.
- Therefore, it is *x*'s duty to heat the hut.

This pattern is called a *secondary practical inference*. The conclusion is an obligation or duty derived from a primary duty.[62] Hence, it is a duty in the technical or instrumental

---

[60] Cf. von Wright, G. H., Practical Inference, op. cit.; Carlos Alchourrón and Eugenio Bulygin too use a teleological schema to ground what they call the Principle of Obligatoriness: „It is obligatory, according to x's commands, to perform all actions that are logically necessary in order to satisfy all obligations established by x's commands." Cf. Alchourrón, C. E. and Bulyin, E., Pragmatic Foundations for a Logic of Norms, in: Rechtstheorie 15 (1984) pp. 453-464, p. 456. This proposal can be described, I think, as the application of a teleological argument in the reconstruction of the concept of obligation.

[61] Von Wright, G. H., Practical Inference, op. cit., pp. 6-11.

[62] Cf. ibid., p. 14.

sense. A primary duty, in turn, cannot be conceived as a practical necessity for complying with another *duty*, since in that case, obviously, it would become a derived duty. In other words, the concept of primary duty cannot be reconstructed with a *secondary practical inference*.

Thus, heating the hut is a derived duty to the extent that it is a subjective or objective practical necessity relative to a given primary duty: in the case of the example, the duty to make the hut habitable. This instrumental relation is expressed in a *secondary practical inference*. According to von Wright, the primary duty to make the hut habitable could, in turn, be understood as a subjective or objective practical necessity relative to some *end* – for instance, the desire to live in the hut. The teleological structure of the reconstruction would then be that of a *primary practical inference*.

At this point, it is important to note that this teleological pattern for the foundation of a primary duty would be flatly rejected by a Kantian interpretation of that notion. For Kant, a duty is something wanted in itself and not as a means for reaching some end. Admitting the teleological structure for its reconstruction amounts to subordinating the concept of duty to the idea of the pursuit or satisfaction of further ends, and that means to deny duty the nature of an end in itself. From a Humean perspective, as von Wright's seems to be, the teleological pattern is considered adequate for showing the internal structure of the notion of primary duty.[63] On this view, a primary duty is a conclusion too, but one drawn from the recognition of certain purposes which lie 'beyond duty' and not from the acknowledgment of a duty as such, as a Kantian conception would have it.

This discrepancy is another example of the controversy between the Humean and the rationalist line of thought. From a Humean point of view, the teleological structure is well suited not only for the reconstruction of a concept of secondary duty (in the technical sense); it is also a plausible structure for the analysis of the primary, genuinely normative, concept of duty.

D) A MODEL FOR THE PROCESS OF THE RESOLUTION OF CONFLICTS BETWEEN REASONS

Finally, there is the application of the pattern of practical arguments as a schema which represents the process of the resolution of conflicts between reasons. When we think about whether a certain action ought to be performed, there may be several reasons for and against its performance.[64] An agent who wants to act rationally will compare the relevance of each one of them and act according to those with the highest weight in the case under consideration. A generally accepted proposal represents this process schematically in a model according to which the agent weighs his desires, beliefs and other motivational reasons for and against the action in the light of behavioural principles, i. e.,

63 For a similar idea, cf. Mackie, John L., Ethics. Inventing Right and Wrong, op. cit.

64 This classification of reasons as considerations for or against an action can be applied to all three kinds of reasons analysed in the last chapter (explanatory and justificatory reasons as well as reasons in the secondary or subsidiary sense). Previously, I have pointed out that a reason is always a reason with respect to an action. Every reason is a reason in favour of the action it refers to and, in turn, a reason against all actions that are incompatible with the former. Cf. Gans, Chaim, Mandatory Rules and Exclusionary Reasons, in: Philosophia 15 (1986), p. 387.

justificatory reasons.[65] In this case, the practical argument is a pattern metaphorically called a 'balance', in which reasons are assessed and compared with each other. In such an evaluation, some are discarded and others are chosen, until one has determined which of them are the 'winners'. These, then, indicate what ought to be done in a conclusive sense, that is, when all relevant questions have been considered. When a practical argument is used with this purpose, its structure is part of a psychological theory or a descriptive moral theory.

Whatever the form of a practical argument, when it is proposed as a theoretical model, it must be assessed as such. If its purpose is the reconstruction of a real mental process of reasoning, it must be judged according to how plausible it is in showing the characteristics of that process. As all theoretical proposals, it may be discarded if it becomes apparent that it is not an adequate approach to the facts or that it does not serve the formulation of fruitful hypotheses about them.

6. The Practical Argument as a Normative Model

In the last section, I have mentioned situations where there are conflicting reasons. When this is the case, the application of the teleological model of practical reasoning may lead to the justification of mutually contradictory statements. Therefore, it is an essential practical question whether we can find a rational mechanism for the foundation of a conclusive rather than a *prima facie* duty to perform a particular action. Such a duty could not be reconstructed with the help of the teleological pattern based on the consideration of one single reason. A conclusive duty can only be determined by way of an assessment of all reasons applicable to the respective case.[66] This is, then, not a technical, but a normative concept of duty.

The possibility of constructing an adequate argument for the foundation of conclusive ought-statements is a central subject of meta-ethics. A skeptical attitude would maintain that there is no possible rational argument beyond instrumental justification. The choice of ultimate ends cannot be rationally controlled.[67] The search for a non-relative answer to the question 'What ought I to do?' would itself be an irrational aspiration.[68] A non-skeptical position, in contrast, believes that it is possible to decide this question in a rational way. In this line, the notion of practical argument is not understood as an inference pattern in the logical sense nor as a theoretical model, but as a correct way of behaviour in decision making. A *practical argument* is an ideal procedure

---

65 Joseph Raz holds that besides this model of rationality there is another one in which the agent does not consider the weight of certain reasons, since they are discarded from the start because of the presence of second-order exclusionary reasons. Cf. Raz, Joseph, PRN, pp. 35-48.

66 Note that on the utilitarian conception, the teleological pattern would still be applicable. Because according to that moral theory, although all pertinent reasons must be considered, they must be assessed on their instrumental capacity to reach the end which is supposed to be good.

67 Cf., e. g., MacCormick, Neil, The Limits of Rationality in Legal Reasoning, in: id. and Weinberger, Ota, An Institutional Theory of Law, op. cit., pp. 189-206.

68 Cf. Kelsen, Hans, What is Justice?, op. cit.

designed for justifying conclusively the duty or permission to perform some action. On this hypothesis, it is qualified as 'normative' because the implementation of practical reasoning itself is considered justified as an obligatory type of conduct. It is the content of a regulatory norm and, thus, is part of a normative proposal. Here, it is useful to keep in mind what Gilbert Harman has underscored in criticizing the identification of the notions of reasoning or inference (which seem to be equivalent to what I have here called the normative model of a practical argument) with those of argument or logical implication:

„[T]he theory of reasoning is therefore not to be identified with logic. The theory of reasoning, if such a theory is possible, is a normative subject. Logic is not in the same respect a normative subject, although, as I have suggested, it is relevant in certain ways to the normative theory of reasoning."[69]

And elsewhere he asserts:

„What is required for some reasoning to be an acceptable reasoning? In order to answer this question, we might hope to state certain explicit general principles of reasoning, in the same way as we are able to state the explicit general principles of deductive logic, and so develop a rigorous normative theory of reasons. It is unlikely, however, that such a theory is really possible. There is no more evidence that there are explicit general principles of reasoning than that there are explicit general principles of esthetic appreciation."[70]

Despite Harman's skeptical conclusion, there are some theories of normative ethics which defend the obligation of conducting certain kinds of arguments in case of a conflict between reasons. According to the second distinction introduced in Section 3 above, in this case one must not confuse the argument as a mental activity or process (an empirical sequence) with the argument as a linguistic model (an abstract pattern). There is no general agreement on what the correct structure of such arguments is.[71] The teleological model is considered insufficient, since it only permits the instrumental foundation of one action relative to one end. For the kind of situations we are concerned with, a widely accepted idea requires a comparison of the conflicting considerations, and the teleological structure cannot represent that kind of assessment. An adequate pattern of practical reasoning must allow for a 'balance of reasons'. In any case, the normative proposal of a model of practical reasoning must be distinguished from the normative proposal concerning the weight or strength the reasons entering in that 'balance' are to be given. Both are part of a normative theory. Any normative theory of practical reasoning presupposes (normative) parameters attributing a value to every reason.[72]

An argument in which reasons are compared is formally identical to the one mentioned as a model for the reconstruction of the mental process that takes place in the re-

---

[69] Harman, Gilbert, The Nature of Morality. An Introduction to Ethics, op. cit., p. 128.

[70] Ibid., p.129.

[71] On this, cf. Atienza, Manuel, Las razones del Derecho. Teorías de la argumentación jurídica, op. cit. Several possible structures suggested by theories of reasoning are presented there.

[72] Raz's theory, for instance, proposes a normative conception of a practical argument. It stipulates the obligation to reason according to the weight of reasons, provided they are not affected by a valid exclusionary reason. But it does not prescribe what weight to give to each reason, nor what a valid exclusionary reason is. So far, his proposal must be considered procedural. It can be seen as becoming a substantive ethical theory, however, when it stipulates the conditions under which a legal norm constitutes a valid exclusionary reason.

solution of a conflict between reasons. Only that now it is not conceived as a reconstructive theoretical model, but as an ideal model of behaviour. In other words, through a normative ethical theory, it is justified as the appropriate model for evaluating the relevant data and grounding the duty to perform a certain action. As has been pointed out before, the conclusion based on such a 'balance' of reasons is conclusive, but not absolute.[73]

A) APPLICATION OF THE MODEL

Generally, the obligation of conducting a certain kind of practical argument is required for the foundation of all conclusive duties of a moral nature, when there are conflicting reasons. But there is no reason why it should not also apply in the case of practical conflicts where it is not a moral answer one is looking for. For example, the implementation of this kind of practical arguments may be required in the legal, the political or the religious sphere.[74] The structure of the model does not need to change in any of these cases. What does change, however, is the criterion for the selection of the reasons that will enter into the evaluation.

In this context, the characteristics specifically *legal* practical arguments should have are controversial. The main objective here is their application to the justification of judicial decisions. For example, whenever it is difficult to determine the precise premises of a judicial argument, the judge must necessarily make a choice. He must choose between different norms, or between different interpretations of one and the same provision.[75] The justification of that choice is usually called the 'external justification' of a judicial decision, and there are different positions with respect to it.[76] Some writers hold that, in the last instance, the choice of a premise cannot be guided rationally. Thus, they deny that there is any kind of 'argument' by which a correct norm could be identified.[77] Other proposals recommend the application of the teleological model of a practical argument.[78] And the most widely diffused position accepts the reason-comparing pattern

---

73 Raz, Joseph, PRN, op. cit., pp. 27 f.

74 Cf. ibid., Introduction.

75 This is one kind of what is usually called 'hard' cases, that is, cases where the difficulty is to determine the *normative* premises of an argument. Another difficulty can arise with respect to the *factual* premises. Cf. Atienza, Manuel, Para una teoría de la argumentación jurídica, in: Doxa 8 (1990) p. 52; MacCormick, Neil, Legal Reasoning and Legal Theory, op. cit., pp. 65 ff.; Aarnio, Aulis, The Rational as Reasonable. A Treatise on Legal Justification, Dordrecht: Kluwer 1987, p. 2.

76 For the time being, it will be assumed that the external justification of a judicial decision consists in the justification of a choice between premises. But that definition is questionable. The discussion of this topic, however, will be postponed to Chapter VI where it will be treated in detail.

77 In some cases, this position is a corollary to the restriction of the concept of argument to the strict sense of logical inference. Writers like Eugenio Bulygin and Carlos Alchourrón, for instance, allow only arguments in the logical sense to serve as a model for the justification of a sentence. This model permits the reconstruction of the internal justification of judicial decisions, and it can also be used for the individual justification of the premises. But if only this model of a 'practical argument' is accepted, then one must admit that it is unable to say anything about which norm is preferable to others.

78 Cf. MacCormick, Neil, The Limits of Rationality in Legal Reasoning, op. cit., pp. 189-206. MacCormick maintains that the rational control of external justification is only partial. He admits that in the last instance

as the adequate model for grounding the choice of the applicable norm. Here, the identification as well as the weight of the reasons to be compared depend on the underlying normative conception.

The normative model of an argument may be useful in solving different kinds of conflicts, for example, in determining the most adequate interpretation of a legal precept or the provision which is applicable in case of a contradiction between norms. The principles of *lex superior*, *lex posterior* and *lex specialis* can be seen as part of a normative proposal which makes it possible to justify the choice of a norm in case of conflict, i. e., they can be regarded as standards to be used in the justification of the choice of premises in legal reasoning.

Finally, it should be noted that, since we are speaking about a normative proposal, the theoretical context for the discussion of this subject is controversial. Some authors think that these matters belong to legal theory, one of the functions of which it is to propose ways of reasoning in order to resolve situations of conflict.[79] Those who subscribe to a positivist conception, in contrast, hold that this is not a subject of legal theory, but of normative ethics. Regardless of whether or not it is conceived as part of legal theory, there are different proposals concerning the identification of the reasons to be taken into account, and the criteria for the validity of that kind of argument. To these I will now turn.

B) VALIDITY

The idea of validity as applied to this kind of practical argument is not a formal one, as in the case of practical arguments in the logical sense. It is also not a matter of plausibility or adequacy, as in the case of the assessment of reconstructive theoretical models. The idea of the validity of an argument, on this interpretation, rather concerns the substantive correctness of the justified contents.

There are several conceptions of what exactly the validity of a practical argument in the normative sense amounts to. For those who adhere to the principle of the unity of practical reasoning, validity can never be relative or partial. If a practical argument is valid, it is absolutely valid. For example, it is impossible that an argument is valid from the legal, but not from the moral point of view. And even within the moral sphere, on this conception it is inadmissible that two mutually contradictory duties are both justified by equally valid arguments.[80] However, if one does not accept this principle of unity, an ought-conclusion may be validly justified within one sphere, but not within another. But that would mean that one and the same practical argument could be judged to be correct and incorrect at the same time, depending on the chosen point of view.

---

the determination of the premises is based on emotional aspects. – We can also say that Hart accepts the application of a teleological model of practical arguments when he holds, against Dworkin, that utilitarian considerations may be appropriate when it comes to the interpretation of premises. Cf. Hart, H. L. A., American Jurisprudence Through English Eyes: The Nightmare and the Noble Dream, in: id., Essays on Jurisprudence and Philosophy, Oxford: Oxford University Press 1983, pp. 123-144.

[79] Dworkin, Ronald, Taking Rights Seriously, London: Duckworth 1977, pp. 32 f.

[80] I will have to say more about this in Chapter VI, sect. 5.

As for the criteria for assessing the validity of an argument, two different methodological approaches can be distinguished. One grounds validity on the weight or substantive value of the reasons taken in to account,[81] the other on the satisfaction of a set of procedural requirements. From the latter perspective, the best option (that which ought to be regarded as conclusively justified) is the solution one arrives at by taking certain steps and respecting certain formal constraints in a process of deliberation.[82] Taken together, the different approaches to be found on this subject in practical philosophy can be collected under the name of 'theories of argumentation'. Primarily, they design models of practical arguments. Then, they justify their implementation as adequate procedures for dealing with conflicts of reasons. The theses held by different theories of argumentation exhibit great differences. For example, some of them construct an argument in a dialogical form, whereas others regard it as a monological process; some attribute a constitutive value to the conclusion, others hold that its value is epistemic. Despite all these idiosyncrasies, the element common to them all is that they offer a set of criteria for the validity of a practical argument.

Although the work of Joseph Raz, e. g., is not intended to provide a theory of argumentation, the two principles stated in *Practical Reason and Norms* constitute criteria of validity for practical arguments in the normative sense. The first criterion stipulates that in case of conflict first-order reasons must be assessed according to their weight. But if a conflict exists between a first-order reason and an exclusionary reason, the kind rather than the weight of the reasons determines which one trumps the other. The second principle requires that second-order reasons always prevail over first-order reasons. This does not mean that one must act in accordance with an exclusionary reason. They do not exclude all first-order reasons, but only those within their scope. In the last instance, Raz's principles are meant to regulate the external action based on an argument, rather than the argument itself. But what matters, in any case, is that one should act in accordance with an undefeated reason. In the present section, I will not analyse Raz's idea. What interests me here is only to point out that this is a normative proposal of a practical argument. It stipulates a model with a specific structure (i. e., a model based on certain kinds of relations: weight and kind) and determines the criteria for assessing its validity.

C) PREMISE-REASONS AND REASONS FOR ACTION

Practical arguments understood as theoretical or normative models are not arguments in the logical sense. When we say that the statements such arguments consist in are 'premises', this is only a metaphorical use of the term. Just as I have insisted that one should not confuse the different concepts of practical argument, I also insist that one should not confuse the concept and the function of the 'premises' in those different kinds of arguments.

---

[81] For example, Richards, David A., A Theory of Reasons for Action, op. cit.; Nino, Carlos S., The Ethics of Human Rights, op. cit.; Raz, Joseph, PRN; id., The Morality of Freedom, op. cit.

[82] Cf. Alexy, Robert, Theorie der juristischen Argumentation. Die Theorie des rationalen Diskurses als Theorie der juristischen Begründung, Frankfurt/M.: Suhrkamp 1978.

The distinction between reasons in the formal and reasons in the substantive sense was introduced in order clearly to bring out the difference between the elements of a logical argument (premise-reasons) and substantive reasons for action (whether justificatory or explicatory). Now, the statements that make up a practical argument in the non-logical sense are not reasons in the logical sense; rather, they describe or mention reasons in the substantive sense. The logical origin of the expressions 'argument' and 'premise', and perhaps the prestige associated with the rigour and precision of that discipline, explain the persistent tendency to transfer those meanings or to consider their metaphorical use as special versions or extensions of the logical concepts.

In conclusion it can be said that the so-called 'premises' of the last two conceptions of a practical argument (the theoretical and the normative model) can not at all claim to be a logical foundation of the statements qualified as the 'conclusions' of these arguments. The above analysis shows how one and the same expression and in some cases also structures analogous to those of logic are used with totally different meanings and purposes. The different concepts of practical argument, premise, conclusion, validity, etc. are not mutually exclusive; but, above all, none of them is an extension or development of the other. The study of models of practical arguments adequate for the reconstruction of action, intentional explanation, the concept of duty, or the process of resolving a conflict among reasons is not a chapter of logic – just as normative proposals like the different theories of argumentation are not a complement to logical investigations of arguments.

PART II

REASONS FOR ACTION IN LEGAL ANALYSIS

CHAPTER IV

NORMS AND REASONS FOR ACTION

1. Introduction

In contemporary legal theory, the concept of reason for action is thought to be relevant for the study of a broad range of questions. In general, it is considered useful for improving the approach to and the explanation of many controversial issues in the field.[1] That is why one can find writings where some conception of reason for action is adopted and applied in the respective reflection about a given subject. This is the case, for instance, with respect to the problems of normative authority,[2] the existence or validity of a rule,[3] the way how these affect the reasoning of their addressees,[4] etc. In an important aspect, the present study differs from many of these works in that it is of a meta-theoretical nature. The subjects of Part II have been chosen as examples, in order to show some of the concepts that can be analysed with the help of the notion of reason for action. Thus, in the preceding chapters, I have not tried to develop a theory of reasons; rather, I have analysed the different meanings of the term. The purpose of this second part is to test the adequacy of these concepts as tools for the analysis of other notions.

In the following three chapters, I will assess the usefulness of the different notions of reason for action for the analysis of three central ideas of legal theory:

(i) the normativity of legal provisions which regulate behaviour,

(ii) acceptance as a condition for the existence of a legal system, and

(iii) the justification of legal decisions.

---

[1] In this context, the use of the concept of reason for action forms part of an approach which can be linked to a strategy for better explanation. On this view, it is considered plausible to accept the existence of certain entities if this assumption is necessary for a better understanding of the respective object of investigation. This is the strategy pursued, for instance, by Harman and Mackie against moral realism and by M. Moore as a way of explaining our moral experience. Cf. Harman, Gilbert, The Nature of Morality. An Introduction to Ethics, op. cit., pp. 5-10; Mackie, John L., Ethics. Inventing Right and Wrong, op. cit., pp. 30-41; Moore, Michael, Moral Realism as the Best Explanation of Moral Experience, op. cit., p. 39-50.

In the present case, the thesis under discussion is that the best explanation of 'normativity' requires the presupposition of reasons for action. On this strategy in general, cf. Strawson, P. F., Skepticism and Naturalism. Some Varieties, op. cit., pp. 19 f.

[2] Cf., e. g., Raz, Joseph, The Authority of Law, op. cit.; id., The Morality of Freedom, op. cit.; Green, Leslie, Authority and Convention, in: The Philosophical Quarterly 35:141 (1985) pp. 329-346; Caracciolo, Ricardo, El concepto de autoridad normativa. El modelo de las razones para la acción, in: Doxa 10 (1991) pp. 67-90; Nino, Carlos S., The Ethics of Human Rights, op. cit., ch. 7.

[3] For example, Raz, Joseph, PRN, op. cit.; id., The Morality of Freedom, op. cit.; Nino, Carlos S., La validez del Derecho, op. cit.; id., The Ethics of Human Rights, op. cit.; Schauer, Frederick, Playing by the Rules. A Philosophical Examination of Rule-Based Decision Making in Law and in Life, Oxford: Clarendon 1991.

[4] For example, Bayón Mohino, Juan Carlos, The Normativity of Law: Legal Duty and Reasons for Action, op. cit.

In this chapter, the first of these subjects will be treated. As will be seen, the notion of reason for action plays different roles in the different theories that use it, and sometimes even in one and the same theory. Occasionally, the fact of being a reason for action is mentioned only as a potential property of legal norms (which presupposes that one has a criterion for the identification of norms other than the property of 'being a reason for action'). In other cases, it is regarded as a defining characteristic of the very concept of normativity. This is the idea that will be analysed in what follows. According to this conception, in order to account for the concept of legal norm, one must first have a concept of reason for action. For the present purpose, we must now first clarify some more what kinds of entities it is that will have to be analysed.

2. Some Concepts of Norms and the Conditions for Their Existence

Two different strands of discussion of a long philosophical tradition must be considered in this context. One is of an ontological, the other of a conceptual kind. As for the ontological discussion, a distinction widely accepted in general philosophy asserts that there are two kinds of entities: empirical and non-empirical. The former are entities that can be located in time and space. The latter are ideal universal entities without a location in time and space. Hence, there are two opposing versions concerning the specific existence of normative entities. According to one of them, norms are empirical entities; according to the other, they are abstract entities.

All ontological statements presuppose a conceptual decision. Unless one agrees about the concept of norm, the controversy about the existence of norms makes no sense. The nature of the existence of these entities obviously depends on the meaning given the term. When one goes to the root of apparent ontological disagreements, one often finds that the controversy is actually misconstrued in these terms: the disagreement turns out to be a conceptual one instead.[5]

The senses of existence presented above are exhaustive and mutually exclusive. There may be many proposals for the meaning of the word 'norm', but whichever one accepts, norms always exist either in the first or in the second sense.[6] For instance, when norms are understood as acts of promulgation or as social practices, they exist in the empirical sense. In contrast, when they are defined as a sense or meaning, they are seen as abstract or ideal entities.[7] If one chooses a concept conceiving of norms as abstract entities, there are two positions one can take from an ontological point of view. These are traditionally known by the names of *realism* and *anti-realism*. Basically, an anti-realist with respect to normative entities rejects the idea that they exist in the same way

---

[5] Cf. Hare, R. M., Ontology in Ethics, op. cit., pp. 83-98.

[6] Cf. Caracciolo, Ricardo, Sistema jurídico, in: Ernesto Garzón Valdés and Francisco J. Laporta (eds), Enciclopedia Iberoamericana de Filosofía, Vol. 11: El derecho y la justicia, Madrid: Trotta 1996, pp. 161-176.

[7] Note that what is often presented as different senses of existence refers to different meanings or concepts in which the term 'norm' can be used. On this, cf. Alchourrón, Carlos and Bulygin, Eugenio, Sobre la existencia de las normas jurídicas, op. cit.; also Bulygin, Eugenio, An Antinomy in Kelsen's Pure Theory of Law, op. cit.

as plants or rocks exist, i. e., „in nature" or as „part of the fabric of the world".[8] On the other hand, at least one current version of realism accepts that the existence of norms must not be understood in the same way as the existence of physical objects. In the present investigation, I will not analyse the plausibility of skeptical arguments about the existence of one or the other kind of entities. The metaphysical debate about kinds of existence is not the subject of this book. The main controversy between the different versions of legal theory concerns the delimitation of a concept of law or legal norm.

According to the *hyletic* notion, norms are normative meanings and, therefore, ideal entities.[9] Statements expressing norms stipulate the permission, obligation, or prohibition to perform some action.[10] Under this concept, not all provisions of a legal system are norms. For a system of statements to be a 'normative system', it is sufficient that at least one of them is a norm.[11] Let us call this conception of normativity 'normativity$_a$'. Positivist legal theory, when investigating the structure of the law, has worked mainly with this concept of normativity$_a$. It is a semantic conception according to which a norm is a non-propositional meaning that can be expressed through language.

Another notion of normativity refers to a practical capacity linked to ought-statements. In that sense, a provision is normative to the extent that it guides conduct and is a reason for action. Occasionally, normativity thus understood is regarded as a feature necessarily attached to ought-statements and, therefore, as something inherent to their condition of being norms. Here, then, the notion of norm is not used in a hyletic sense. Although it too refers to meaningful contents regulating conduct, it entails another necessary condition, namely, its practical nature. Let us call the concept of normativity connected with this practical aspect 'normativity$_b$'.[12] It should be noted that there is a difference between 'normativity$_b$', which refers only to a (possible or necessary) property of ought-statements, and the notion of 'norm$_b$' which refers to a meaningful content that is necessarily of a practical nature. This concept is radically different from the notion of 'norm$_a$' and raises a question about the kind of relationship existing between such a practical capacity (normativity$_b$) and ought-statements which, on another conception, *are* norms (in the sense of normativity$_a$). The question has been analysed extensively in ethics, since the potential practical import of moral discourse is a central subject of discussion in that field. Considering the conclusions from that controversy, two different ways of explaining the relationship can be derived.

---

[8] Cf. Strawson, P. F., Skepticism and Naturalism. Some Varieties, op. cit., p. 93, and Mackie, John L., Ethics. Inventing Right and Wrong, op. cit., p. 15.

[9] Cf. Alchourrón, Carlos E. and Eugenio Bulygin, Sobre la existencia de las normas jurídicas, op. cit., p. 47, and by the same authors, The expressive conception of norms, op. cit., p. 96.

[10] I will use the terms 'normative statement', 'ought-statement', or 'conduct-regulating statement' synonymously in order to refer to such statements.

[11] Cf. Alchourrón, Carlos and Bulygin, Eugenio, Normative Systems, op. cit.

[12] Since this notion of normativity can be analysed in terms of reasons for action, it suffers of the same ambiguity as that expression, i. e., it can be understood as referring to an empirical *capacity* of compelling to an action (that is, to a motivating capacity), or to the *duty* of compelling to that action (that is, to a moral quality). Usually, the predicate 'normative' is used without further precision. In this section, it will be used in that way too; but in the following, the different senses it may have will be duly distinguished.

So-called 'internalist' positions hold that ought-statements are internally practical, i. e., that a provision establishing a duty always is a $norm_b$ since it necessarily provides a reason for action. In contrast, 'externalist' positions deny this necessary relation. From their point of view, an ought-statement by itself does not constitute a reason for action at all. Reasons depend on facts which are only contingently linked to the existence of a duty. For internalism, motivation plays a decisive role even in the analysis of moral ought-judgments, whereas for externalism motivation is an important issue only because people must be persuaded to act in accordance with their obligations.[13] Presenting the two positions, Frankena observes:

„Again, the issue is not whether morality is to be practical. Both parties agree that it is to be practical in the sense of governing and guiding human behavior ... But one part insists that judgements of obligation must be practical in the further sense that their being efficacious in influencing behavior is somehow logically internal to them, and the other denies this. The question is whether motivation is somehow to be 'built into' judgements of moral obligation, not whether it is to be taken care of in some way or other."[14]

The controvery between internalists and externalists is a debate about the concept of *moral* duty and obligation. The arguments used in that discussion, however, are the same as those applied in legal considerations about obligations in order to underline their practical nature. One of the most hotly debated items in recent legal philosophy concerns this question, i. e., the notion of $normativity_b$. It is the meaning with which this term is used in investigations about 'the normativity of law'. Positivist conceptions do not regard $normativity_b$ (understood as a property) as a defining characteristic of legal norms, that is, they admit the notion of $normativity_b$ only as a *possible* property of legal provisions. When they regulate behaviour, they are necessarily $norms_a$, but not necessarily $norms_b$. To say that $normativity_b$ is a contingent quality of $norms_a$ implies that there are two meanings of 'normativity'. The question about the practical nature of law turns on the determination of the conditions under which what for positivism are legal norms ($norms_a$) constitute reasons for action ($norms_b$). In contrast, for adherents of natural-law theory, the question about the normativity of law presupposes that there is one single concept of norm which provides the internal link to their nature of being reasons for action. Legal provisions of obligation are not really normative, they do not stipulate a genuine duty if they do not offer reasons for action. On this interpretation, the question about the practical nature of law is formulated differently. It turns on the determination of the conditions under which legal discourse stipulates *authentic* duties or is *genuinely* normative.

3. The Practical Nature of Ought-Statements

According to what has been said so far, internalism and externalism hold opposing views about the practical nature of ought-statements. The general thesis of internalism is

---

[13] Frankena, William K., Obligation and Motivation in Recent Moral Philosophy, op. cit., p. 38.

[14] Ibid., p. 41. This idea coincides with the proposal of Falk, W. D., 'Ought' and Motivation, in: Proceedings of the Aristotelian Society 98 (1947-48).

that the nature of being a reason for action is inherent to such statements, because of the very meaning of the term 'ought'. Externalism is the negation of internalism. It does not deny the possibility that ought-statements *may* be reasons for action, but it does deny that they necessarily possess that property. That means that $norms_a$ only contingently are $norms_b$. The externalist thesis is that the existence of a $norm_b$ depends either on the respective individual's mental state or on some substantive theory of reasons for action.

An important problem is that the notion of $normativity_b$ is ambiguous. Hence, the internalist and the externalist theses about the practical nature of ought-statements can be interpreted in different senses. David Brink presents two internalist and two externalist theses. Each one of them can, in turn, be understood in two different ways, depending on how one interprets the notion of reason for action. There are, thus, eight ways of how the link between ought-statements and reasons for action can be understood.[15]

A) INTERNALISM

First, Brink distinguishes between *agent internalism* and *appraiser internalism*. Understood in the first sense, the internalist thesis holds that the very *existence* of a duty provides its addressee with a reason for action. Internalism in the second sense, in contrast, maintains that the practical nature of a duty depends on its *recognition* or on the *belief* in its existence.[16] Agent internalism is objective in the sense that it links a duty to reasons for action, regardless of whether or not they are recognized. Appraiser internalism, on the other hand, is subjective in that it links reasons for action only with duties recognized by an agent, regardless of whether they are justified or correct. And there is also another possibility which combines the two previous positions (the *hybrid* version, according to David Brink); but since it is irrelevant for our present purpose, I will not consider it here.

The expression 'reason for action' can refer to reasons in the explanatory or in the justificatory sense. Therefore, the internalist theses can be interpreted differently, depending on the underlying concept of reason for action. Brink thus distinguishes between an internalism with respect to motives and an internalism with respect to reasons for action.[17] The distinction between motives and reasons for action accepted by Brink

---

[15] Brink, David, Externalist Moral Realism, in: Southern Journal of Philosophy, Supplement, 24 (1986), pp. 23-41 (hereafter, EMR). Many ideas elaborated by this author can already be found in the classical works of Falk and Frankena. What makes his contribution interesting is the systematic distinction of the four possible readings of each one of the two rival proposals.

[16] Brink indiscriminately speaks of an agent's recognition, judgment or moral belief. In this chapter, I will treat the terms 'belief', 'recognition' or 'acceptance' as equivalent. Despite the differences between them that can be spelled out, they all have in common that they are elements of an agent's subjective motivational set, which is the only relevant property in the present context. The next chapter will be dedicated to the discussion of the concept of acceptance, and there I will introduce some refinements not considered here.

[17] In order to avoid terminological confusion, it must be noted that Brink calls 'internalism' with respect to reasons for action a thesis concerning the link between ought-statements and reasons for action, namely, the thesis that reasons for action are internal to ought-statements. But this does not say that they are internal to the agent. 'Internalism' and 'externalism' as I am using them here must not be confused with the internalist or externalist positions one can adopt with respect to the characterization of the notion of reason for action. About the latter, in Chapter II I have mentioned Bernard Williams' internalist theory, and in Chapter III I have

is comparable to that between the two meanings of the expression 'reason for action' presented earlier. What in Brink's classification is called 'motives' are reasons in the explanatory sense. Brink's notion of reason for action refers exclusively to the justificatory sense of the term.[18] Following the terminology used in the present study, we can thus distinguish two variants of the internalist position – one referring to reasons in the explanatory sense, the other one referring to reasons in the justificatory sense. The former holds that ought-statements necessarily motivate, i. e., necessarily constitute reasons in the explanatory sense of the term. The latter asserts that ought-statements are conceptually linked to reasons for action in the justificatory sense. This shows the fundamental ambiguity of the concept of normativity$_b$. And, therefore, it also shows the ambiguity of the internalist position which holds that ought-statements are, by definition. normative$_b$.

The thesis that ought-statements are intrinsically of a practical nature, if interpreted in the first sense, is untenable.[19] It maintans that every norm$_a$, as such, has the capacity to motivate the norm-subject. This requires, first of all, that one has a criterion for the identification of the existence of a duty, i. e., of a norm$_a$, that is independent of recognition. Then, the thesis asserts that even if no-one knows or accepts it, the duty in question motivates the agent whose conduct it regulates. This assumption about the practical capacity of ought-statements is obviously implausible. Therefore, internalism is usually defended in one of the other three senses.

The second interpretation implies a considerable restriction. In this case, to say that a duty is internally practical means that it constitutes a motive for whoever admits or recognizes it. The notion of motive must be taken in the weak sense of the term, i. e., as an internal disposition capable of bringing about action, but also compatible with the case that the action is not performed.[20] It may well happen that a person who accepts a duty also has other, even stronger motives which move her to behave differently from what the duty requires.

An argument in favour of this internalist conclusion says that denying it leads to a pragmatic contradiction. Whoever accepts a duty has, by definition, a motive for action. Therefore, if someone says, for instance, 'I recognize that I have the obligation to return the book I borrowed from her' or even directly 'I ought to return the book I borrowed from her' and then denies that he has a motive for action does not understand the meaning of what he is saying.

---

presented some thoughts about the sense in which the existence of external reasons can intelligibly be asserted.

[18] In the literature, the expression 'reason for action' is commonly used only in the justificatory sense. However, I will stick to the terminology proposed in the previous chapters. And this terminology requires that it is explicitly clarified when the expression is used in the explanatory sense (i. e., referring to empirical facts) and when it is used in the justificatory sense (i. e., referring to norms).

[19] Instead of 'the normativity$_b$ of ought-statements or provisions of duties' I will simply speak of 'normativity$_b$', for short. I assume that this is a property of ought-statements, i. e., of norms$_a$.

[20] This meaning of 'motive' coincides with the dispositional concept pointed out in Falk, W. D., 'Ought' and Motivation, op. cit., p. 116.

The most common objection against this version of internalism is that it makes the existence of *amoral* persons conceptually impossible.[21] An amoral agent is representative of the position that one can recognize the existence of a duty and still deny that this is accompanied by any motive to do what the duty stipulates. The amoral person requests reasons independent of the duty as such in order to comply with it. According to the present conception of the relationship between duty and reason, this request would have to be discarded as incoherent, since to recognize a duty implies having a motive for action, i. e., a reason in the explanatory sense. But, although it may seem exceptional, the position of an amoral person is conceivable. The problem is that the terms 'motive' and 'explanatory reason' are ambiguous. In some sense of these terms, it is true that the recognition of a duty does not imply a motive for the agent. Later we will see that of the three meanings of the word 'motive' mentioned before, one gives plausibility to the internalist and the other two to the externalist thesis.

According to the third reading of internalism (agent internalism with respect to reasons for action), duties are always $normative_b$, because their existence implies a justificatory reason for the addressee's action.[22]

As concepts have been defined in the first part of the book, there are two senses in which a reason can be justificatory: On the one hand, a formal logical sense according to which a generic ought-statement serves to infer (i. e., to justify formally) an individual ought-statement. From this perspective, ought-statements are justificatory premise-reasons. Certainly, those who defend the thesis that ought-statements necessarily constitute reasons for action are not referring to this formal concept of reason.

On the other hand, there is the second interpretation of the justificatory notion of reason, i. e., the substantive notion, according to which internalism must be read as follows: Moral ought-statements are, as such, correct standards of behaviour. To say that an ought-statement is necessarily $normative_b$ means to say that it is an appropriate standard of conduct. Just as the concept of motive was interpreted in a weak sense (such that it could be overridden by another one), this notion of justificatory reason for action too must be interpreted in a defeasible instead of a conclusive sense. In conclusion, then, on

---

[21] Brink, David, EMR, p. 30. Most of those who have written on this topic have endorsed this objection. It puts into doubt that the fact that there is some duty decides the question of whether there are reasons for acting in conformity with it. This is also what the classical question 'Why should I be moral?' alludes to.

[22] This third interpretation of internalism is possible only if one admits two independent concepts of reason for action: reason as motive and reason as justified duty for performing an action. Cf. Brink, David, EMR, p. 28. From this perspective, the assertion that an ought-statement implies the existence of a reason for action is not a thesis relating an agent's considerations of duty to his motives. It does not say that considerations of duty imply the existence of a good or justified motive, that is, of that internal attitude which supposedly ought to guide the agent. A justified or good motive is still a motive that explains, and not a reason for action that justifies something. Juan Carlos Bayón offers the opposite interpretation when he says about the distinction between explanatory reasons ('reasons why') and justificatory reasons ('reasons for'): „In the first case, we try to identify the factors that *motivate* an actor, while in the second we are talking about what *ought* to motivate him, regardless of whether they actually do". What is not clear is whether the factors that ought to motivate an agent are motives he has and which ought to make him act, or whether they are motives he doesn't have, but ought to have. In any case, the notion of justificatory reason is not independent of the notion of explanatory reason. Both are characterized as factors which are internal to an agent. The difference is that the latter actually motivate while the former ought to motivate. Cf. Bayón Mohino, Juan Carlos, The Normativity of Law: Legal Duty and Reasons for Action, op. cit., Introduction to ch. 2.

this internalist thesis every duty is a substantive *prima facie* reason, but not a conclusive reason for some action.

Finally, the internalist conception can be interpreted as a thesis referring only to those who accept a duty. In this case, the intrinsically practical character of ought-statements means that, if they are recognized by an agent, they constitute a justificatory reason for action. Here too, we can distinguish between the two senses of a justificatory reason – the formal and the material sense. And this enables us also to distinguish two senses of the word 'acceptance'. An ought-statement can be accepted as a justificatory reason in the formal sense, that is, as a premise of an argument, without being accepted as a substantive reason for action, that is, as an adequate standard requiring the performance of that action.[23]

The thesis which claims to show the internal link between acceptance of a duty and justificatory reasons for action either does not distinguish between these two senses of acceptance[24] or holds that acceptance in the formal sense entails acceptance of the norm as a substantive reason.[25] In view of these two kinds of acceptance, when one asserts that someone accepts a duty it must be determined which of the two senses of acceptance is meant. In one case, one will acknowledge only a reason in the formal sense; in the other, a substantive reason. Acceptance of a duty as a reason in the formal sense is something that is manifested merely by uttering a sentence. When a person says that she ought to, or that she acknowledges that she ought to, do a certain thing, she necessarily accepts this ought-statement as a justificatory reason in the formal sense. Acceptance of a duty as a substantive reason for action, in contrast, is not ensured merely by the utterance of some sentence.[26] Acceptance in this additional sense presupposes a commitment to some standard of conduct.

B) EXTERNALISM

So far, four interpretations of the internalist position have been presented. Each one of them can be opposed with an externalist conception consisting in adherence to the thesis

---

[23] Some authors take this difference into account and express it through the terminological distinction between 'assuming' a statement (which corresponds to what I have called formal acceptance) and 'accepting' it (which corresponds to what I have called substantive acceptance). In the next chapter, this distinction will be treated in more detail.

[24] This is the case, for example, of Hart in *The Concept of Law*. Some authors who analyse his proposal hold that acceptance on the part of the officials entails a commitment of a moral nature. In later works, Hart has reacted to this and criticized the idea that the mere acceptance of a norm as a foundation for justification implies its acceptance as a morally correct consideration in favour of the action in question, i. e., as a reason in the substantive sense. Cf. Hart, H. L. A., Commands and Authoritative Legal Reasons, in: id. (ed.), Essays on Bentham. Jurisprudence and Political Theory, Oxford: Clarendon 1982, pp. 243-268.

[25] Carlos Nino, for instance, identifies the two senses of acceptance when he says that all judicial justification necessarily presupposes the acceptance of moral norms. Cf. Nino, Carlos S., El constructivismo ético, Madrid: Centro de Estudios Constitucionales 1989, p. 30. This conception of justification will be discussed in Chapters V and VI.

[26] As explained in Chapter I, the imputation of an intentional attitude to an agent on the basis of (verbal or non-verbal) conduct depends on the rules for the use of language in certain situations. Thus, the presumption that a person accepts a duty as a substantive reason also underlies those rules. Cf. Chapter I, sect. 3.

contradicting that kind of internalism. In all cases, externalism denies the *necessary nature* of the relationship between a duty and a kind of reason (i. e., an explanatory or a justificatory reason). On this view, ought-statements are only contingently normative$_b$.

Interpreted in terms of *motives*, externalism holds that the existence of a duty does not imply the existence of *explanatory* reasons – neither for addressees nor for acceptants. Thus, whether we can say that ought-statements are of a practical nature depends on people's psychological make-up, and that varies from one person to another.

Understood in terms of justificatory reasons, externalism claims that the existence of a duty does not imply the existence of justificatory reasons – neither for addressees nor for acceptants. Whether or not a duty is a justificatory reason depends on its content. What the substantive content of a justificatory reason may be depends, in turn, on a substantive theory of reasons for action. As an example, Brink mentions the conception of rational egoism according to which the duty to do *p* is a justificatory reason for action to the extent that doing *p* satisfies the agent's interests. He also refers to rational altruism. From this point of view, the duty to do *p* is a reason for action just in case doing *p* satisfies somebody's interest. For more examples, we could use the proposal of whatever normative ethical theory we could think of. The standards an ethical theory holds to be correct or justified are substantive reasons for action from the perspective of that theory. Hence, from an externalist point of view an ought-statement does not necessarily provide a substantive reason. In order to do so, it must first satisfy the criteria of some moral theory.

Summing up, then, in the preceding paragraphs I have shown the two possible foundations for the practical nature of ought-statements, i. e., that they are explanatory reasons, or that they are justificatory reasons. We thus get two different senses in which a norm$_a$ can be qualified as being normative$_b$. According to the proposals mentioned, these properties can be attributed either to ought-statements in general (with respect to all their addressees) or only to accepted duties (with respect to those who have recognized them). In any case, it should be noted that the practical nature is conceived as a quality of ought-statements. Either they are said necessarily to have that property, from which four internalist positions arise; or it is denied that this is part of their defining characteristics, which leads to four externalist positions. In condensed form, this can be presented as follows:

NORM ↗	1. NORM$_a$:	meaningful content which makes a conduct obligatory, permitted or prohibited
CONCEPTS ↘	2. NORM$_b$:	normative content which makes a conduct obligatory, permitted or prohibited *and* has a practical nature, i. e., constitutes a reason for action

NORMATIVITY AS A PROPERTY →	PRACTICAL NATURE ↗	1. constitutes an explanatory reason for action
	↘	2. constitutes a justificatory reason for action

INTERNALIST THESIS: Because of the concept of duty, ought-statements necessarily are of a practical nature, i. e., constitute reasons for action. Every duty is a $norm_b$.

1ST INTERPRETATION: *Agent-internalism with respect to reasons in the explanatory sense*: All duties are $normative_b$. The existence of a duty necessarily constitutes a motive for an addressee.

2ND INTERPRETATION: *Acceptant-internalism with respect to reasons in the explanatory sense*: A duty is $normative_b$ if, and only if, it is recognized. A recognized duty necessarily constitutes a motive for an acceptant.

3RD INTERPRETATION: *Agent-internalism with respect to reasons in the justificatory sense*: All duties are $normative_b$. The existence of a duty necessarily constitutes a justificatory reason for an addressee.

4TH INTERPRETATION: *Acceptant-internalism with respect to reasons in the justificatory sense*: A duty is $normative_b$ if, and only if, it is recognized. A recognized duty necessarily constitutes a justificatory reason for an acceptant.

EXTERNALIST THESIS: It is not the case that ought-statements necessarily constitute reasons for action. Ought-statements only contingently have the property of being $normative_b$.

1ST INTERPRETATION: *Agent-externalism with respect to reasons in the explanatory sense*: It is not true that the existence of a duty necessarily constitutes a motive for an addressee. That depends on the agent's mental states.

2ND INTERPRETATION: *Acceptant-externalism with respect to reasons in the explanatory sense*: It is not true that every recognized duty necessarily constitutes a motive for an acceptant. That depends on the agent's mental states.

3RD INTERPRETATION: *Agent-externalism with respect to reasons in the justificatory sense*: It is not true that the existence of a duty necessarily constitutes a justificatory reason for an addressee. That depends on the content of the duty.

4TH INTERPRETATION: *Acceptant-externalism with respect to reasons in the justificatory sense*: It is not true that the existence of a duty necessarily constitutes a justificatory reason for an acceptant. That depends on the content of the recognized duty.

C) EVALUATION

Keeping in mind the different internalist and externalist interpretations, it will be useful to make explicit the consequences that arise if one applies the concepts adopted in the first section.

(i) If the practical nature of a duty is defined in terms of explanatory reasons for action, then a $norm_a$ can never be of such a nature. As the concepts of explanatory reason and $norm_a$ are defined, such norms cannot be explanatory reasons – neither for a norm-subject nor for an acceptant. A $norm_a$ is not a mental event, but an ideal entity. Therefore, if 'practical nature' is understood as a causal ability to give rise to action, the internalist as well as the externalist thesis are untenable.

The following should, however, be taken into consideration: When that causal ability is linked to accepted or recognized ought-statements, that *recognition or acceptance* may be understood to be the source of a motive capable of triggering action. That a duty is accepted implies that there is a motive for the acceptant. If the internalist and externalist theses are understood in these terms, one must admit that internalism is true with respect to the third meaning of the word 'motive'. *Acceptance*, that is, of a legal provision is an element of the subjective motivational set of the acceptant and can give rise to action. Externalism, in turn, is then true in the remaining two senses of 'motive'. That is, *acceptance* of a duty is only contingently an intentional state which in fact gives rise to, or explains, an individual act. That is so because, although the acceptant has the disposition to act, he may not come to perform a certain act that would be caused or explained by that disposition.[27]

An important clarification about the preceding observations is in order. In both cases, it is not the ought-statements themselves which are of a practical nature. What constitutes an explanatory reason for action cannot be a norm_a but only the *recognition* or *acceptance* of such a norm_a. On this interpretation, then, to assert that provisions of duty are of a practical nature is not false, but nonsense.

(ii) If the notion of 'practical nature' is interpreted in terms of justificatory reasons in the substantive sense, the adopted concepts imply an externalist position. As for the addressee, an ought-statement is not by itself a substantive reason for action. Rather, that depends on whether the conditions stipulated by some conception of normative ethics are satisfied.

For an acceptant too, the externalist thesis is true. An ought-statement is not a justificatory reason for an acceptant just because it has been accepted or recognized. It is perfectly possible that standards are recognized or accepted as justificatory reasons which, from an objective point of view, are no such thing. If one adopts the internalist conception with respect to acceptants then one must also adopt a subjective concept of justificatory reason. If someone believes in, or accepts, a standard as a justificatory reason, then it *is* such a reason for him. From the point of view adopted in the present work, that position must be rejected, since an accepting agent may well be wrong. To accept, or believe in, a principle as a justificatory reason for action does not imply that one actually *has* a justificatory reason for action.[28]

In conclusion: *(i)* That ought-statements or norms_a are of a practical nature can only be said in terms of justificatory reasons. Ought-statements or norms_a can never be reasons in the explanatory sense. *(ii)* If one is unwilling to hold that any ought-statement is a justificatory reason (in the substantive sense), or that its mere acceptance by an agent is sufficient to make it such, then one must accept the externalist thesis about their practical nature.

---

[27] These distinctions are based on the different meanings of the term 'motive' elaborated in Chapter I, sect. 6.

[28] Cf. Chapter II, sect. 5.

4. The Normativity of Duty-Imposing Laws

The same question as that about moral ought-statements can also be raised with respect to legal provisions regulating conduct. Are legal provisions normative? And if so, then in what sense? In the previous chapters I have used the notion of normativity$_a$, i. e., the hyletic conception of norms. Norms$_a$ (or meaning-norms) are abstract entities which can, even though they may not need to, be expressed through language. They prohibit, command, permit or authorize the performance of some action, and they cannot be true or false. In that sense, they are clearly different from propositions.

The notion of norm$_a$ is widely used in legal theory. Evidently, not all meaning-norms are conceived to be legal norms. In order to be regarded as such, generally, several conditions must be satisfied. One usual prerequisite is that norms$_a$ are legal if they belong to at least one legal system.[29] Hence, the question about the legal nature of a meaning-norm can be translated into a question about the conditions such a norm must satisfy in order to belong to a system of that kind. In studying the criteria of membership, positivist legal theory has paid particular attention to legality and deductibility in the procedure of admission or elimination.[30] This approach has been criticized for its lack of attention to other elements which also function as membership criteria in most actual legal systems. Among such elements are, e. g., a habitual practice of behaviour in conformity with some norm$_a$, or the moral correctness of such a behaviour. As a criterion for the identification of legal norms, the first of these is often explicitly excluded in positivist studies; and if it is not, this creates serious problems for them.[31] That the second aspect is not considered is justified with the strict line positivism draws between law as it is and law as it should be. From the positivist point of view, a theory describes and explains its object of investigation. In order to do that, one of its purposes is to identify that object; but never does it aim at judging how it should be. The problem of the identification of the law must be distinguished from the question of its substantive correctness.[32] Critique and moral assessment belong to the realm of normative ethics which does not claim to be descriptive.

---

[29] The most typical advocate of this proposal is, of course, Hans Kelsen. Note that this is not to say that he subscribed to a hyletic conception of norms, but only to the condition of belonging as a criterion of existence. It must also be emphasized that this is not the only criterion considered by Kelsen. On this, cf. Kelsen, Hans, General Theroy of Law and State, Cambridge, Mass.: Harvard University Press 1945; also id., Reine Rechtslehre, 2nd ed. Vienna: Deuticke 1960.

[30] Concern for the analysis of this problem is shown, for example, in: Alchourrón, Carlos and Eugenio Bulygin, Normative Systems, op. cit.; Caracciolo, Ricardo, Sistema jurídico. Problemas actuales, op. cit.; Moreso, Juan José and Pablo E. Navarro, Orden jurídico y sistema jurídico, Madrid: Centro de Estudios Constitucionales 1993.

[31] Cf. Guibourg, Ricardo, Derecho, sistema y realidad, Buenos Aires: Astrea 1986, where, the difficulties the admission of customary rules presents for Kelsen's theory of law are spelled out.

[32] This kind of independence between law and morality is denied by legal naturalists who argue that the very identification of the law presupposes a moral evaluation. This is what Carlos Nino has called the interpretative connection between law and morality. Cf. Nino, Carlos, Derecho, moral y política. Una revisión de la teoría general del Derecho, Barcelona: Ariel 1994. It should be noted that in the positivist ranks, there are authors who admit that there is a justificatory connection between law and morality. Cf. Raz, Joseph, Author-

Generally, critics of the positivist criteria for the identification of legal norms do not question the concept of normativity$_a$, that is, they agree that legal ought-provisions are norms (in the hyletic sense). Thus, when legal norms are regarded as *standards* which are expressed in enacted provisions, or deduced from other standards, or accepted as a social practice, or which correspond to a set of correct moral norms, one and the same concept of norm is involved, namely, the hyletic concept. For the purposes of the present study, we do not need to discuss which of the criteria mentioned is the best for the identification of legal norms. I have mentioned them only in order to underline a distinction of fundamental theoretical importance: One thing is the concept of norm$_a$ or of normativity$_a$, and quite another the empirical or moral conditions required for a norm$_a$ to be incorporated into (be valid in, or belong to) a legal system.

According to the concept of norm$_a$, not all meaning-norms are necessarily legal norms. That is, not all standards of conduct satisfy the membership criteria of a legal system. On the other hand, not all legal provisions are necessarily meaning-norms, since there may well be provisions which satisfy the conditions for belonging to the system, but which do not regulate behaviour. For instance, legal provisions which introduce definitions do not prohibit, command or permit any conduct. Therefore, they are not norms$_a$.

The notion of norm$_b$ is more comprehensive than the former, because the property of being a reason for action is included in its defining characteristics. In order to avoid linguistic confusion, it is important to note that the notion of norm$_b$ implies the notion of norm$_a$. Now, when the notion of normativity$_b$ is interpreted as a property, it is also inevitably linked to the notion of norm$_a$. This has an important consequence. As we have seen, since normativity$_b$ is perceived as a quality of legal ought-statements, it is wrong to define it in terms of motives or explanatory reasons. Ought-provisions are not the kind of entities that can be regarded as motives or explanatory reasons. Therefore, the attribution of normativity$_b$ or of a practical nature must be interpreted in the sense of a justificatory reason. In other words, to say that a legal provision is normative$_b$ is to say that it constitutes a binding standard conforming to which it is correct to act.[33]

Remember that according to the two versions of internalism, if something is a duty (agent-internalism) or a recognized duty (appraiser-internalism), then it is necessarily normative$_b$, i. e., it is a reason for action. The polemic between internalism and externalism is, among other things, of a conceptual nature. For an internalist, the notions of duty and reason for action are conceptually linked. An internalist is not committed to the thesis *that* legal provisions impose duties and are reasons for action, but he is committed to the thesis that *if* such provisions establish duties, then they are reasons for action. In contrast, because externalism does not necessarily link the notions of duty and reason, it can conceptually admit that there are legal provisions which are only norms$_a$, that is, which establish duties without constituting reasons for action.

ity, Law, and Morality, in: id., Ethics in the Public Domain. Essays in the Morality of Law and Politics, Oxford: Clarendon 1994, 210-237.

33 As with 'duty' in general, the discussion about whether or not legal ought-provisions are reasons for action is not about whether or not they are premise-reasons, i. e., reasons in the logical sense. For simplicity's sake, in the remainder of this section, whenever reasons are mentioned without further attributes it should be understood that I am referring to justificatory reasons in the substantive sense.

Next, I will show two different conceptions of the 'normativity' of law. Each one of them can be linked to an internalist position about the connection between duties and reasons for action.

5. Two Examples in Legal Theory

As it is not the purpose of this study to review how different theories of law conceive of the relationship between legal provisions and reasons for action.[34] Only two such positions will be presented as examples. They explain in different ways what the 'normativity$_b$' of the law consists in. However, they share the idea that this characteristic can be analysed with the help of the concept of justificatory reason for action.

(i) Legal provisions are not always normative. They are normative only when they constitute justificatory reasons for action.

In this section, I will discuss an argument advanced by Carlos S. Nino in some of his works. As Nino points out, the positivist concept of law requires that legal provisions are always identified on the basis of empirical sources.[35] Hence, what from a positivist perspective is called legal 'norms' must be understood as empirical entities – for example, commands backed by threats, or social practices.[36]

---

[34] Such an analysis, albeit not including all theories of law, can be found in Shiner, Roger A., Norm and Nature. The Movements of Legal Thought, Oxford: Clarendon 1992. In this book, Shiner classifies positivism as simple or sophisticated, among other things, by how the definition of legal norm is connected to reasons for action. He considers several meanings of 'reason for action', but he does not distinguish between the position according to which the notion of reason is part of the definition of legal norms and that other one in which the notion of reason refers to a contingent property of such norms. That is what enables him to put Austin and Hart (as opposed to Raz) into one and the same category, as regards their respective conceptions of norms as reasons for action. Cf. Shiner, op. cit., p. 45.

If one uses the distinctions proposed here, it becomes clear that the conceptions of these two authors of the relationship between law and reasons for action are very different. In Austin's theory, the notion of legal norm does not presuppose that of a reason for action. For Austin, a certain kind of explanatory reasons, as, e. g., a fear of sanctions, become relevant when it comes to explaining why norms are complied with. But such reasons are far from being an integral element of legal provisions. Cf. Soper, Philip, A Theory of Law, op. cit., pp. 18-22. In contrast, in Hart there is a central kind of legal norm, namely, the rule of recognition, which is a social norm. The explanation of this kind of rule presupposes a concept of reason for action. However, in Hart's conception the notion of reason for action is not always necessary for analyzing the concept of norm. Hart uses different concepts of norms, and not all of these norms are social rules.

[35] It is unanimously acknowledged that the social-source thesis is one of positivism's central dogmas. Cf. Raz, Joseph, The Authority of Law, op. cit., or Bobbio, Norberto, El problema del positivismo jurídico, transl. by E. Garzón Valdés, Mexico-City: Fontamara 1991. Nino also includes the concept of norm as prescription among the empirical notions. Whether presciptions must be understood as empirical entities is, however, controversial. For an expressivist conception, a prescription is a speech-act, i. e., an empirical fact; but for a hyletic conception, a prescription is a semantic category, i. e., an ideal entity. Cf. Bayón Mohino, Juan Carlos, The Normativity of Law: Legal Duty and Reasons for Action, op. cit., ch. 6.1.

[36] Cf. Nino, Carlos S., La validez del Derecho, op. cit., pp. 134 f.; also id., Derecho, moral y política, op. cit., pp. 23 and 24. Nino regards Kelsen's proposal as an exception from this characterization of legal norms. Cf.

Following the so-called Humean principle, Nino holds that an ought-conclusion can be reached only from an argument in which at least one of the premises is of that nature too. From this, he infers that so-called legal 'norms', which are empirical entities in the positivists' conception, are unable to found such a conclusion. For Nino, any attempt to justify an ought-conclusion with a legal norm, as identified according to a positivist criterion, contains a logical mistake. To claim such a thing means to commit the naturalistic fallacy.

According to this argument, then, for logical reasons, in order to be able to justify ought-conclusions, the law must rely on morality, since only morality provides genuinely normative provisions.[37] The plausibility of that thesis rests on two ideas which allegedly can be attributed to positivism. One of them is the inadmissibility of the step from 'is' to 'ought'; the other one is the empirical conception of norms. Indeed, if norms are facts, they cannot serve as a basis for justifying a normative conclusion – nor can they serve to justify a descriptive conclusion. From facts, no conclusion whatsoever can be drawn. In order to be able to speak of norms as entities which justify or permit to conclude something, they must be conceived as linguistic or semantic entities. A conception of legal norms as empirical entities is not the right one to account for what is unanimously said to be one of their functions, namely, the possibility to justify sentences and, indirectly, actions.[38]

According to Nino, if a legal provision is a fact, then the only way how it can form part of a practical argument is by way of a descriptive sentence which mentions it as a relevant fact for the application of a genuine norm. In order to come to an ought-conclusion, an authentically normative premise stipulating that one ought to do what the legal provision says is absolutely necessary. Carlos Nino proposes the following reconstruction of a justificatory argument:

„1) One ought to obey those who have been democratically elected to legislate. 2) Legislator L has been democratically elected. 3) L has dictated a legal norm providing 'Those who kill another person shall be punished'. 4) Those who kill another person shall be punished. 5) John has killed someone. 6) John shall be punished."[39]

In Nino's view, premise 1) expresses a moral norm since it has the characteristics of autonomy, generality, universality, supervenience and integration, which are the necessary conditions for a moral norm. Legal provisions cannot justify a duty, i. e., they are not justificatory reasons, unless they rely on a moral norm or they are themselves directly considered a moral norm – which means to give up the positivist criterion of identification and to regard as legal norms only those having all the characteristics just men-

---

Nino, Carlos S., La validez del Derecho, op. cit., pp. 7-27; also id., Introducción al análisis del Derecho, Buenos Aires: Astrea 1984, pp. 78-81.

[37] Cf. Nino, Carlos S., El constructivismo ético, op. cit., p. 115. In a paper I published together with Pablo Navarro and José Juan Moreso, we have called this proposition the 'inseparability thesis'. Cf. Moreso, José Juan, Pablo E. Navarro and Cristina Redondo, Argumentación jurídica, lógica y decisión judicial, in: Doxa (Alicante) 11 (1992) p. 248.

[38] A position similar to Nino's on this point can be found in Bayón Mohino, Juan Carlos, The Normativity of Law: Legal Duty and Reasons for Action, op. cit., ch. 1.

[39] Nino, Carlos S., Normas jurídicas y razones para la acción, in: id., La validez del Derecho, op. cit., p. 139.

tioned. On this basis, Nino concludes that it is reasonable to hold, against the thesis of authors like Joseph Raz, that legal provisions do not express operative reasons for justifying decisions, except when they are identified as moral judgments.[40]

So far, the thesis that legal provisions cannot be justificatory reasons was based on the contention that they are not norms. In order to justify an ought-conclusion, it is logically necessary to go all the way back to morality. The appeal to moral norms is not the result of a search for moral correctness, but the result of a search for something that constitutes a duty, i. e., a reason for action. This alone can justify action. If we thus complete Nino's argument, it turns out that only moral norms are genuine norms (norms$_b$). The only concept of normativity that is admitted is coextensive with the notion of moral precept.

This argument of Nino's is different from the one which claims a connection between law and morality, not because one should avoid the naturalistic fallacy, but because only substantively correct premises justify anything. The appeal to morality based on the necessity to ensure the material correctness of the justificatory argument can be held jointly with the thesis of the necessary connection for logical reasons. But it can also be defended independently. Its foundation does not rest on Hume's principle, but on the adoption of a concept of justification which requires the material correctness of the argument. That is the strategy followed by theories of argumentation. These theories admit that legal statements can express norms (in the sense of normativity$_a$) and that they can formally justify ought-conclusions. But since the justification they are interested in is the one ensuring the adequacy of the justified content, the legal argument must possibly be complemented or corrected with a consideration of moral norms.[41]

---

40 Nino, Carlos S., La validez del Derecho, op. cit., p. 143. Here, we have a concept that has not appeared so far, namely, that of an 'operative reason'. This notion is defined as distinct from so-called 'auxiliary reasons'. The difference between operative and auxiliary reasons is based on Joseph Raz's idea that, in the last instance, there is only one concept of reason for action. All reasons are facts. Operative reasons, Raz says, are facts which, if an agent believes in their existence, provoke a practical critical attitude in favour of an action. This mental attitude *explains* the action, and the fact that brings it about, i. e., the reason, *justifies* it. From the point of view of the present study, that conception is inadmissible. According to what has been explained above, a fact can never be said to be of a justificatory nature (neither in the formal nor in the substantive sense). The categories of operative and auxiliary reason reflect a unification of mental (empirical) and justificatory (logical or moral) aspects, which in all the preceding analysis I have always tried to keep apart.

Besides, Raz – and with him, Nino – admits that this classification is projected also onto language when reasons are mentioned in a formal practical argument. In this sense, the premises of an argument are operative or not, depending on the kind of reasons they represent. If what is represented is a fact belief in which generates a practical critical attitude, that premise is an operative reason; if not, it is an auxiliary reason. This idea too is incompatible with the thesis held in the present study about norms as premises of arguments. According to Raz and Nino, within a practical argument a norm functions as an operative premise which justifies decisions to the extent that it expresses or represents an operative reason. In the present work, norms themselves are thought to be justificatory reasons in the formal sense and, under certain conditions, also in the substantive sense; but not because they represent, reflect or express a fact. The language which represents or reflects facts is a descriptive, not a normative language.

41 Carlos Nino sometimes also appeals to this way of connecting the law to morality. See, for example, Nino, Carlos, Respuesta a J. J. Moreso, P. E. Navarro y M. C. Redondo, in: Doxa 13 (1993) pp. 261-264. The mixture of the two strategies leads him to hold that the material correctness of an argument is necessary for logical reasons. The expression 'logical reasons' is, however, ambiguous. Sometimes, it presupposes Hume's principle and is at the root of the requirement that all justificatory arguments must be supported by norms.

Nino is right when he says that if legal provisions are characterized as empirical entities they cannot constitute the foundation of a justification. That is what would be the case, for instance, were one to adopt the expressive conception, or an extreme positivist position. It is, however, a mistake to think that the positivist thesis of the social or empirical sources of the law identifies norms with empirical entities. The thesis of the empirical sources requires that nothing be regarded as a valid legal precept, or as belonging to a legal system, if it has not been enacted or accepted through human acts. This idea, which is strongly defended by positivism, is totally independent of the concept of norm in general. Among positivists, the hyletic conception of norms is a viable and common option. Thus, the fact that enactment, acceptance or some other empirical event is proposed as a condition for the admission of a norm to a legal system does not convert such norms into empirical entities.[42] Nino correctly points out that, according to positivism, legal provisions must be identified through empirical sources. His mistake is to believe that, therefore, norms are no longer abstract entities which can justify something in accordance with Hume's principle. As Roberto Vernengo has observed:

„That such a norm has its source in an order given by a politician, and that this politician held the belief that the norm had to be enacted through a decision by him, are things concerning the effective existence of the norm in a social system. These facts, however, do not form part of the deductive argument, and therefore do not lead to the logical mistake of wanting to infer a normative conclusion from purely factual premises. After all, any premise of a normative nature originates in some act of intention; but the fact from which the norm arises does not affect the normative nature of the proposition."[43]

There is no logical reason why legal provisions, in order to be 'normative', must be connected to morality. The problem of Nino's argument is that he combines two notions of normativity and of justification. Hume's principle requires a norm in order to justify something. Nino does not see that the hyletic notion of normativity (what has been called $normativity_a$) is necessary *and* sufficient for a formal justification of an ought-statement. A proposition logically justifies an ought-conclusion only if it is $normative_a$. That is what Hume's principle stipulates. A very different concept of justification is that which associates it with $normativity_b$, understood in terms of substantive reasons for action. In that case, in order to justify, it is not only necessary to invoke a $norm_a$; that norm must also constitute a substantive reason in favour of the action. According to Nino, only such standards are genuinely normative; from his standpoint, therefore, Hume's principle makes it necessary to take recourse to norms which are reasons for action. Fol-

---

And sometimes it presupposes a specific concept of justification which requires the truth or correctness of justificatory premises. If, by definition, an argument justifies only if it is sound or correct, then for conceptual or 'logical' reasons the premises must be true or correct. If they are not, there is a mistake. That mistake then is not the illicit step from 'is' to 'ought', but the incoherence with respect to the adopted concept of justification. Once these two different logical or conceptual reasons are elucidated, we can understand the requirement that the premises of a justificatory argument must be, first of all, norms (this is required by Hume's principle) and, secondly, also materially correct (this is required by the concept of justification which presupposes the material correctness of the argument). In Chapter VI, I will discuss different concepts of justification. Although the thesis defended in the present work admits the existence of a substantive concept of justification, it does not coincide with Nino's thesis.

[42] Cf. Caracciolo, Ricardo A., Sistema jurídico, op. cit.

[43] Vernengo, Roberto J., Relativismo ético y justificaciones morales, in: Doxa 4 (1987) p. 248.

lowing Nino's theory, then, only moral norms constitute that kind of reason. And, therefore, only moral norms can justify.

In summary, Nino's argument is committed to the following ideas:

(1) An internalist conception of duty with respect to justificatory reasons: If something is a duty, then it is a justificatory reason for action, i. e., it is normative. This is the only genuine sense of normativity, and it is exemplified by moral norms.

(2) Legal dispositions are not justificatory reasons. Therefore, they are not normative (they satisfy that condition only when they are indistinguishable from moral norms).

(3) Conclusion: If a normative decision is to be justified, for logical reasons it is necessary to invoke normative entities, that is, the kind of entities mentioned in *(1)*: moral norms.

Nino's thesis of the justificatory connection between law and morality is based on these ideas. Only if the law is connected with moral norms, it can justify ought-conclusions. In Nino's conception, the notion of reason for action is necessary for analyzing the concept of genuine norms, but not for analyzing legal provisions, because these are not always genuine norms.

The perspective offered in this book coincides with Nino's on thesis *(2)*. That is, in my view legal provisions do not necessarily constitute reasons for action. It also coincides with it concerning the acceptance of Hume's principle, i. e., that a norm is needed to justify an ought-statement. However, it is clearly opposed to the conclusion drawn in *(3)*; and that is because I do not accept premise *(1)*. This means that I do not agree that there exists merely one single concept of normativity linked to the constitution of substantive reasons for action. Unless this conceptual restriction, according to which only moral norms are genuine norms, is adopted one cannot reach the conclusion of *(3)*. The adoption of premise *(1)* entails a confusion of two aspects the difference between which was emphasized in the first part of this investigation. It blurs the distinction between formal and substantive justification and, therefore, confuses the notion of premise-reason (justificatory reason in the formal sense) with that of a reason for action (a justificatory reason in the substantive sense). If that confusion is to be avoided, one must reject Nino's proposal.

(ii) Legal provisions are normative because even when they are not reasons for action agents believe that they are.

It is a widely held thesis that the law is intrinsically practical and, in that sense, normative. Within contemporary legal theory, this idea is rooted in Hart's conception according to which in an effectively existing legal system legal norms are considered justificatory reasons for action.

A further development of this Hartian thesis can be found in the work of Joseph Raz. In Raz's view, in order to understand the normativity of the provisions created by an authority Hart's proposal must be strengthened and different kinds of reasons must be taken into account.[44] According to Raz's proposal, mandatory legal norms must be analysed in terms of protected reasons. These are a special kind of reasons which combine a first-order reason with an exclusionary reason.

First-order reasons are reasons directly affecting, or referring to, actions. They are considerations claiming that one should act in conformity with them.[45] Conflicts between this kind of reasons are resolved by their force or weight. In contrast, second-order reasons are reasons for acting, or not acting, *for* certain (first-order) reasons. In the first case, they are positive second-order reasons; in the second case, they are exclusionary reasons. Raz is primarily interested in exclusionary reasons since they have a characteristic that is typical for commands issued by a norm-authority. An exclusionary reason is not a reason for not acting *in conformity with* first-order reasons, but for not acting *for* them. An exclusionary reason affects a set of first-order reasons which are within its scope. They must, therefore, not be taken into account in the motivation for an action. In the conflict between the affected reasons and the exclusionary reason, if the exclusionary reason is valid it always prevails.

Ever since Raz's proposal, the notion of exclusionary reason has been extensively discussed, first of all because of the difficulties encountered in giving a precise account of the very concept and, secondly, because of the consequences it may have if one admits this idea as a defining element of legal norms. Concerning these difficulties, Raz's own reasoning follows a twofold purpose. One is to try generally to justify the admission of reasons of that kind, i. e., reasons which exclude reasons; and the other is to try to justify the recourse to that notion for an adequate characterization of legal norms. If one thinks that he fails with respect to the first purpose, obviously one must also reject the second part of his argument.[46] But, inversely, one can accept the existence of that special kind of reasons and still deny that the definition of legal norms presupposes that concept.

The notion of reason used by Raz has been interpreted in different ways.[47] According to the replies the author has given to his critics, reasons are, in the last instance,

---

[44] Joseph Raz specifies that his objection to Hart's proposal is conceptual, not moral. He thinks that the precisions he has introduced give a more adequate account of the elements necessarily involved in the notion of authoritative rule. Cf. Raz, Joseph, PRN, pp. 192 ff. For his critique of Hart's conception, cf. ibid., pp. 49-58.

[45] Raz asks himself whether reasons, in general, are reasons for behaving in conformity with them (reasons for conformity) or for behaviour to be guided by them (reasons for compliance). In the former case, it is sufficient that the behaviour conforms to what the reason requires, regardless of the motives guiding the action. In the latter case, the reason also requires that behaviour is motivated by its consideration. That means that although externally one may do what the reason stipulates, one can act wrongly if one does not act in order to comply with the reason. In Raz's view, except for special circumstances, reasons for action are only reasons for conformity. Cf. ibid., pp. 178-182.

[46] Some authors hold that the notion of exclusionary reason does not really differ from that of first-order reason, and show that their way of operation can be explained without creating a special category. Cf., for example, Perry, Stephen, Judicial Obligation, Precedent and the Common Law, in: Oxford Journal of Legal Studies 7 (1987); Schauer, Frederick, Playing by the Rules. A Philosophical Examination of Rule-Based Decision Making in Law and in Life, op. cit., pp. 81-93.

[47] Michael Moore, for instance, observes that Raz's proposal can be interpreted in terms of explanatory as well as in terms of justificatory reasons. Cf. Moore, Michael, Authority and Razian Reasons, in: Southern California Law Review 62 (1989) pp. 854 ff.

objective facts which justify action.[48] Since my purpose here is not an exhaustive presentation of Raz's conception, I will simply accept this last option. Considering the distinctions I proposed earlier, that means that the notion of reason must be understood in the justificatory and substantive sense.

Raz suggests a certain reasoning pattern for the case of conflicting reasons. His proposal has the characteristics of what I have earlier qualified as a normative model of practical reasoning.[49] The model suggested by Raz is basically defined by two principles. The first does not need much arguing since it corresponds to a notion of rationality widely accepted in practical philosophy. Raz asserts:

„According to our intuitive conception of practical conflicts such conflicts are to be resolved by assessing the relative strength or weight of the conflicting reasons and determining what ought to be done on the balance of reasons. To put it another way, one ought always to do whatever one has a conclusive reason for doing.“[50]

In Raz's view, this principle must not be applied when there is an exclusionary reason. In that case, a different reasoning pattern is appropriate. In such a situation, one should not act in accordance with a balance of reasons if the reasons that would tip the balance in favour of one side are excluded by an undefeated exclusionary reason.[51] Many writers have discussed the justification of that principle. Raz himself has presented several arguments intended to show not only that the principle generally works, but also that it is legitimate.[52] The two principles of reasoning presuppose and refer to a substantive theo-

---

[48] Cf. Raz, Joseph, Postscript to the Second Edition, in: PRN, p. 198. It should be remembered that Raz's approach does not analyse norms as justificatory reasons in the formal or logical sense.

[49] Cf. Chapter III, sect. 5.

[50] Raz, Joseph, PRN, p. 36. Note that from the standpoint adopted in this investigation, such a 'practical argument' is not an agrument in the logical sense. But there are different interpretations which attempt to reconstruct this kind of argument in logical form. Cf. Alchourrón, Carlos, Para una lógica de las razones prima facie, unpublished manuscript, 1994.

[51] Raz, Joseph, PRN, p. 40.

[52] Raz invokes two kinds of arguments, one phenomenological, the other one functional. Phenomenological arguments point towards the particular features of a concept (in this case, that of an exclusionary reason), based on how it functions in an individual's speaking and thinking. There are three features supporting the existence of exclusionary reasons phenomenologically. First, the experience of conflicting assessments of what one ought to do (for example, a desire that contradicts the content of a given promise). Second, the impression that one is dealing with a case that should not be resolved by the agent on the basis of ordinary reasons, but which should be decided by someone who has been given the competence to do so (for instance, when one is dealing with a situation that is regulated through the directives of an authority). And finally, the feeling that one's capacity for action is restricted, that one's hands are tied by a commitment (this characteristic is different from the others, but it is also present in the examples given).

Through the functional argument, Raz shows how exclusionary reasons play an important role in practical reasoning when a decision must be made. They provide a middle level of reasons enabling one to avoid having recourse to a deeper level of considerations, and at the same time they function as a strategy for an indirect approximation to such considerations. On the one hand, we cannot resolve each case according to its specific characteristics (among other things, time and mental capacities are limited). On the other, it they had to be resolved in accordance with rights, virtues and moral last ends, severe disagreements would surely arise. Rules constitute an intermediary level between particular characteristics and final principles, which makes it possible to reach agreements in the resolution of conflicts even when there is disagreement about the basic values supporting those agreements. Rules could not fulfil this important social function if they would not

ry of reasons for action. For the first, such a theory is necessary in order to identify the reasons applicable in a particular situation, and their respective force or weight. For the second, it is necessary in order to determine which are the *valid* exclusionary reasons, i. e., the circumstances in view of which it is thought to be correct to disregard the balance of first-order reasons. Raz's purpose is not to provide a substantive theory of reasons. Hence, he mentions possible valid reasons only by way of example – first-order as well as (positive and exclusionary) second-order reasons. With those examples he shows how in certain situations the need to save time, work or worries leads to justified exclusionary reasons, i. e., to cases in which the second principle of reasoning should be applied. Raz does not provide a complete list of the kind of circumstances in which the balancing of reasons should be suspended. His aim is to show that there are at least some valid exclusionary reasons.

Here, I will not question the different concepts of reason proposed by Raz. I will take as given that, in general, reasons require conformity, i. e., that they are satisfied when there is merely the external manifestation of the action in question. The principles of reasoning mentioned above are, in the last instance, strategies for maximizing that conformity. Through them, Raz stipulates the criteria according to which some reasons prevail over others in case of conflict. Generally, a balance of first-order reasons should be performed (principle I). Under certain circumstances, however, the requirement of rationality (the necessity to conform to existing reasons) is that certain first-order reasons are excluded from the balance (principle II). The overall principle guiding all reasoning imposes that, all things considered, one should always act for an undefeated reason.

Legal norms are among the cases that can constitute valid reasons for action. From the point of view of their content, such norms are first-order reasons; and because of their (content-independent) authoritative nature they are exclusionary reasons. That is the kind of reasons legal norms are when they are valid. But even when they are not, their existence as norms must be analysed in terms of reasons for action. On this, Raz observes:

„In discussing authoritative directives and other rules and commitments, there is no need to distinguish between justified and unjustified directives and rules. The basic structure of reasoning involved in relying on either is the same. Since those who rely on them believe that they are justified, their basic structure is determined by that of justified, or valid, rules.“[53]

That means that even when the authorities are wrong and a legal provision is, therefore, unjustified, it is still regarded as a justificatory reason from the point of view of the subjects who believe in it. Rules, even when invalid, „by their nature“ always function as reasons.[54] Thus, if one wants to understand what a directive issued by an authority consists in, this characteristic must be taken into account.

---

function as exclusionary reasons. Cf. Raz, Joseph, Facing Up: a Reply, in: Southern California Law Review 62 (1989) pp. 1164-1168; also id., The Morality of Freedom, op. cit., p. 58; and the Introduction to Raz, Joseph (ed.), Authority, Oxford: Basil Blackwell 1990, pp. 1-19.

[53] Raz, Joseph, PRN, p. 191.

[54] It must be pointed out that Raz's characterization is ambivalent. First, being a (first-order or exclusionary) reason is presented as a defining characteristic of norms issued by an authority, even though not all of them are valid or ought to be obeyed. Cf. Raz, Joseph, PRN, pp. 62 ff. In other works, however, he says that not all

This conception of legal provisions has some noteworthy consequences. First of all, norms are ordinary reasons for action, but they are also exclusionary reasons, i. e., reasons for deliberating in a certain way. Either the existence of a legal norm is a reason for two different actions: an external action, in view of a first-order reason, and an internal action (the action of deliberating or reasoning), in view of an exclusionary reason. Or the existence of a legal norm is a reason which regulates the external aspect of the addressees' actions as well as their internal aspect.[55] Second, according to that conception of normativity, directives issued by an authority always have a positive rationality value since they maximize the possibility of conforming with existing reasons.[56]

Raz's characterization of authoritative provisions can be analysed using the categories proposed throughout this book:

(i) Legal norms are exclusionary, content-independent reasons: If this assertion were based on the hyletic conception of norms, it would make no sense, because according to that conception, norms are nothing but meaningful contents.

In Raz's conception, the exclusionary reason is not constituted by the norm (in the hyletic sense), but by the fact that it has been issued by an authority. It is their authoritative origin which gives legal norms their exclusionary character. In this sense, Raz's theory is not only a conceptual reconstruction, but also implies a normative proposal. It asserts that if there is a directive issued by a legitimate authority the second principle of reasoning *ought to be* applied, i. e., the respective reasons *ought to be* excluded. This standard of conduct is what enables us to say that the *fact* that a legitimate authority issues a norm is a valid reason for excluding the corresponding first-order reasons.[57] On this hypothesis, it becomes comprehensible why, in Raz's theory, the duty of exclusion is based on the authoritative nature of legal norms rather than on their content.

(ii) Legal norms are first-order reasons, with respect to their content: Norms in the hyletic sense are meaningful contents which deontically qualify behaviour. From the point of view adopted in this book, that a norm is a justificatory reason can mean two different things. On the one hand, every norm in the hyletic conception is a justificatory reason in the formal sense. On the other hand, if some moral theory qualifies the conduct conforming to a norm as correct, then from the point of view of that theory the norm is a justificatory reason in the substantive sense. In that case, to say that legal norms are (first-order) reasons for action is a substantive thesis of a moral kind.[58]

---

authoritative directives are reasons for action. This is only the case when they are issued by a legitimate authority. Cf. Raz, Joseph, Authority and Justification, in id. (ed.), Authority, op. cit., pp. 124 f.

55 Cf. Redondo, Cristina, Las normas jurídicas como razones protegidas, in: ARSP 79 (1993) pp. 321-332.

56 That value derives from the fact that normative authorities are experts, a property which justifies the belief that they are probably right. It therefore also justifies that norms coming from authorities are regarded as strategies which maximize conformity with the right reasons. Note that this value is lost when the authorities are wrong. If it is admitted that an authority has erred, the probability of correctness cannot be invoked as a foundation of the duty of compliance. Cf. ibid., pp. 328 f.; also Caracciolo, Ricardo, Autoridad sin normas y normas sin autoridad, op. cit.

57 Note that not only norms issued by legitimate authorities can be exclusionary reasons. Raz's conceptual proposal introduces this property in the definition of legal norms, not all of which are valid.

58 It could be objected that the kind of justificatory reason constituted by law must not necessarily be moral; it could also be prudential or strategic. That is true. But a widely accepted argument emphasizes that pruden-

However, in Raz's characterization, that legal directives are (exclusionary or first-order) reasons does not mean that they possess a moral quality. For Raz, there are two ways of explaining the normativity of legal provisions: either because they *are* valid reasons, or because those who accept them *believe* that they are valid reasons.[59] In view of this alternative, first of all, Raz's approach differs from Nino's, since Nino adopts the first and Raz the second option. In Nino's view, the fact that legal provisions are not valid reasons prevents them from being normative. In Raz's opinion, this is not so. Second, although Raz's explanation of normativity rests on the participants' beliefs, his approach has nothing to do with legal realism. He does not want to explain (as realists do) why citizens *believe* that the law is normative; rather, he wants to explain why it *is* normative. Because according to Raz, the law does have that quality.

Taking into account the classification proposed by David Brink, this conception of the normativity of ought-statements presupposes the position of appraiser-internalism concerning reasons in the explanatory sense. The practical nature of ought-provisions is guaranteed by the agents' recognition or beliefs. There are two ways of expressing this idea of normativity applied to the law. The individuals' recognition or beliefs are reasons in the explanatory sense, capable of motivating action. Therefore, all legal provisions recognized as duties imply the existence of a motive for action. If normativity is understood in this way, that is, as a motivating capacity, there is a problem. As we have seen, an ought-statement cannot constitute a 'motive' in any one of the senses of the term. One would thus have to admit that normativity, or being of a practical nature, is not a characteristic of legal provisions, but a property of the agents' attitude, i. e., of recognition, beliefs or acceptance. This difficulty can be avoided when the situation is interpreted in a different way. Because we can also interpret that for Raz the acceptants' belief transforms legal provisions into justificatory reasons. In other words, they are justificatory reasons from the participants' point of view, even if not from an objective point of view. This conception implies a subjective notion of justificatory reasons which are constituted when the acceptants *believe* that directives are valid reasons. In that case, in contrast to the previous interpretation, normativity is a property of the respective ought-provisions. Although he does not say so explicitly, Raz must adopt a subjective concept of reason according to which a reason is constituted by the mere fact that an agent believes in its existence. This notion of reason enables him to say that normativity is an internal quality of existing law, even when it does not come from legitimate authorities and must not be obeyed.

---

tial reasons are applicable only to situations where one imposes a duty on oneself, and that is not the case with legal norms: they impose a (generic or individual) duty on persons other than those who accept them. Therefore, the kind of justificatory reason they constitute cannot be of a prudential nature. Cf. Nino, Carlos S., El concepto de Derecho de Hart, in: Agustín Squella (ed.), H. L. A. Hart y el concepto de Derecho, special issue of the Revista de Ciencias Sociales, Universidad de Valparaíso, Valparaíso 1986, p. 51.

One could argue that the justificatory reasons constituted by law are not moral, but specifically legal. That thesis (which is Hart's), however, must be rejected by those who adopt the principle of the unity of practical reasoning. From that point of view, there is one single authentic sense of a justificatory reason, and that is of a moral kind.

[59] Cf. Raz, Joseph, PRN, p. 170.

From the point of view adopted here, two observations about Raz's proposal on this point are in order. First, from the fact that legal provisions are accepted or that they are believed to be valid reasons, it only follows that the agents have a reason in the explanatory sense, but not that the norms are justificatory reasons. I have stressed the usefulness of distinguishing between the existence of a reason and the belief in its existence. The existence of a reason is objective, i. e., independent of individuals' beliefs. When a subjective concept of justificatory reasons is adopted, this distinction disappears: Whoever believes to have a reason then has a reason.

Second, if the key to normativity is to be found in the beliefs of those who participate in a legal system, then it cannot be regarded as a defining characteristic of law or of legal provisions in general, but only of those which are in effect accepted or recognized.

6. Reasons as Tools for the Conceptual Analysis of Legal Norms

Concerning the relation between norm and reason as it is established in current legal philosophy, it is suggested that the concept of reason for action is the primary one, and absolutely necessary in order to understand what norms are. Hence, the notion of reason for action is regarded as an indispensable tool of analysis.

As a methodological suggestion, this idea is independent of whether one adopts the internalist or the externalist position about the practical nature of legal provisions, i. e., their normativity$_b$. One can say that the notion of reason is useful as an analytical tool for certain concepts of norm, without entering into the debate about whether or not legal provisions necessarily are reasons for action. Take the notion of social norm as an example. This concept alludes to a practice of behaving in conformity with some standard, but also to an internal attitude of those participants who consider that standard a justificatory reason for their actions. Therefore, the concept of social rule presupposes

(i) the concept of meaning-norm (since the participants act conforming to a *standard* of behaviour),[60]

(ii) the concept of reason for action in the explanatory sense (since the acceptance of that standard is a *motive* for acting),

(iii) the concept of reason in the justificatory sense (since the acceptants believe that standard to be such a reason).

The fact that participants believe or accept that a standard is a justificatory reason does not imply that it actually is. An assertion of the existence of a social rule says nothing about the existence of a justificatory reason for action, although the analysis of that notion presupposes the concept of justificatory reason.[61] In summary, then, the defini-

---

[60] Cf. Hund, John, Wittgenstein versus Hart. Two Models of Rules for Social and Legal Theory, in: Philosophy of the Social Sciences 21:1 (1991) pp. 72-85.

[61] This interpretation of social rules does not coincide with that proposed by H. L. A. Hart. For Hart, rules are reasons for action, i. e., one ought to act in conformity with them. But it is important to note that for Hart such reasons and duties are strictly legal. They are different and independent from moral reasons and duties.

tion of a social rule presupposes the different concepts of reason and also, necessarily, the concept of meaning-norm. From this point of view, the hyletic conception of norms and the concepts of reason are primitives with respect to the notion of social rule.

However, a topic which requires taking a stand with respect to the internalist or externalist position is the controversy about the relation between the notion of duty and that of reason for action. For an externalist position like the one adopted here, the two notions can be defined independently of each other, and that is what enables us to identify the two concepts of norm presented above: $norm_a$ and $norm_b$. Only the analysis of $norms_b$ presupposes the notion of reason. With respect to $norms_a$, the notion of reason for action is irrelevant as an analytical tool. An ought-provision is a norm in the hyletic sense, independently of its practical nature (understood as the property of being a reason for action). The practical nature predicated of norms in the hyletic sense can mean only that they prohibit, command or permit conducts, not that they constitute reasons for action. For an internalist position, the notions of duty and reason are necessarily related. Analysing the notion of duty (and therefore the notion of duty-imposing norm) presupposes the notion of reason for action. From this perspective, the concept of norm includes the property of being a reason for action. The thesis that the concept of reason is primary with respect to the concept of norms is linked to this internalist conception.

An important problem is that the very notion of normativity, understood in terms of reasons for action, is ambiguous. For example, the two positions analysed in the previous section sustain two different conceptions of normativity. For Nino, authentic duties are necessarily normative, i. e., constitute justificatory reasons for action. Since legal provisions not always constitute reasons of that kind, they are not always normative. For Raz, in contrast, all recognized duties are normative because that recognition makes them part of an individual's practical reasoning. That means that all duties are normative in the sense that they play a role in the motivation of actions. All existing law presupposes that recognition, and therefore all existing law is normative.[62]

Raz and Nino hold diverging theses about the normativity of legal provisions because they use different concepts of normativity. In any case, the notion of justificatory reason is necessary in order to analyse the concept of normativity in the sense of a practical nature. The notion of norm in the hyletic sense, in turn, is prior to and indispensable for explaining the nature of a justificatory reason. A justificatory reason is a meaning-norm in conformity with which one ought to act.

---

[62] Note that not all provisions of the legal system are recognized as reasons for action. Hence, one must admit that either not all law is normative or that it is normative only because some of its provisions are recognized as such.

CHAPTER V

THE ACCEPTANCE OF NORMS AND REASONS FOR ACTION

1. Introduction

In contemporary legal theory, a common starting point for the analysis of the existence of a legal system is that proposed by H. L. A. Hart who asserts:

„There are therefore two minimum conditions necessary and sufficient for the existence of a legal system. On the one hand, those rules of behaviour which are valid according to the system's ultimate criteria of validity must be generally obeyed, and, on the other hand, its rules of recognition specifying the criteria of legal validity and its rules of change and adjudication must be effectively accepted as common public standards of official behaviour by its officials. The first condition is the only one which private citizens *need* satisfy: they may obey each 'for his part only' and from any motive whatever ..."[1]

From this perspective, the 'acceptance' of certain norms is an indispensable prerequisite for the existence of a legal system. The present chapter will be dedicated to an analysis of this notion which, as presented by Hart, seems to be inseparably linked to the concept of reason for action.

Hart's proposal has given rise to several controversies, above all about the concept of acceptance, about who must have such an attitude, and with respect to which norms of the system. Hart thinks that in a developed legal system the attitude of acceptance must be adopted above all by the officials, and not with respect to all norms of the system, but at least with respect to its rule of recognition. Acceptance is an essential ingredient in order to be able to predicate the existence of that rule itself – a rule which, as conceived by Hart, consists in a complex practice for the identification of valid norms by reference to certain criteria. That complex practice has all the characteristics of a social rule.[2] On the one hand, most members of the group identify the valid rules by reference to the same criteria. On the other, some of them not only regularly behave that way, but also adopt what Hart calls the 'internal point of view', i. e., an attitude consisting in the acceptance of a common standard of behaviour which supports the justifi-

---

[1] Hart, H. L. A., The Concept of Law, op. cit., p. 116.

[2] The rule of recognition can be understood in different ways, depending on the point of view one adopts. On this, cf., for example, the controversy between Juan Ruiz Manero and Eugenio Bulygin, published in Doxa 9 (1991). This is not the place for going into the different interpretations of that rule. From the perspective taken in the present study, the interesting concept is that of a social rule as a practice which presupposes the acceptance of a standard of behaviour. According to Hart, all existing legal systems are based on such acceptance. When Hart speaks of the 'existence' of a legal system, he does so in the same sense as when he speaks of the existence of a social rule. That means that to assert that a system exists is to assert a fact that can be apprehended from an external point of view. Cf. Hart, H. L. A., The Concept of Law, op. cit., p. 110. In this context, the analysis presented in the previous chapter should be kept in mind. The development of a practice conforming to some standard is a *contingent* property of the concept of norm in the hyletic sense, but it is a *defining* property of social rules.

cation of social pressure in favour of the practice as well as criticism of deviating behaviour. It also implies the development of a normative language in which criticism and justification are expressed.

There are other theses about acceptance as a condition for the existence of a social rule. While Hart says that it is indispensable, others deny that it is necessary for the constitution of a rule, or for its maintenance once the rule has been established.[3] The controversy has its origin in the different ways how the concept of acceptance can be reconstructed in legal theory. The characterization proposed by Hart in *The Concept of Law* is so vague that it gives rise to different opinions. Before we take a look at different analyses of Hart's idea, it may be useful to say a few words about the notions of 'acceptance' in general, and 'acceptance of norms' in particular. By comparing these attitudes with other, similar ones, we will be able to bring out their distinctive features. To begin with, the notion of *acceptance* will be contrasted with the concepts of *belief* and *assumption*. Then, I will analyse the difference between the *acceptance* of norms and their *internalization*. Finally, applying these notions to the analysis of the existence of a legal system, it will be possible to distinguish the *acceptance of norms* from the *strategic attitude* one can adopt with respect to norms.

2. The General Idea of Acceptance

Acceptance can be directed towards any kind of meaningful content. That means that one can accept propositional as well as non-propositional contents. In this and in the following section, I will analyse acceptance in general, regardless of the contents to which it may be directed. Because of its peculiarities, the acceptance of norms deserves a separate section.

A) ACCEPTANCE AND BELIEF

In epistemology, there is consensus about the necessity to distinguish carefully between the notions of belief and acceptance. In legal analysis, however, the distinction is usually ignored. There are several ways of how to reconstruct these concepts, among them the one proposed by Jonathan Cohen.[4] According to Cohen, to believe some content *p* is „a disposition to feel it true that *p*".[5] In contrast, to accept a content *p* is to have, or adopt, a policy of taking *p* as a premise, that is, to agree with *p*, in some or in all contexts, on the basis of evidence and arguments. The notion of acceptance refers to an intentional mental act (or its result) which is compatible with not affirming or feeling that *p* is true. For professional reasons, for instance, a lawyer may accept that his client is innocent although he does not believe it. This shows a significant difference between the mental

[3] Cf. Bayón Mohino, Juan Carlos, The Normativity of Law: Legal Duty and Reasons for Action, op. cit., ch. 7.1 (ch. 8.1, pp. 458 f. of the Spanish original).

[4] Cohen, L. Jonathan, Acceptance and Belief, op. cit. (hereafter, 'AB'). According to Cohen, the notion of acceptance does not entail that of belief. Against this interpretation, cf. Klarke, D. S., Does Acceptance Entail Belief?, in: American Philosophical Quarterly 31:2 (1994).

[5] Cohen, op. cit., p. 368.

state of believing and the mental state resulting from acceptance. In addition, it brings to light that the reasons for an act of acceptance must not be epistemic reasons, i. e., that it is not necessary that the foundation of the acceptance of *p* is belief in the truth of *p*.[6]

Acceptance involves an internal act of decision, which means that it is always voluntary. *Accepting* is something an agent does and for which he is responsible. Beliefs, in contrast, are involuntary. One cannot decide to believe something. Cohen refers to this peculiarity as the passive nature of beliefs. Passivity here is not to be understood in the Humean sense according to which beliefs cannot motivate action, but in the sense that they cannot be adopted or discarded voluntarily.[7] The answer to the question of whether or not one accepts *p* is an information about a decision one has taken. In contrast, in order to answer the question of whether or not one believes *p* one must perform an introspection, trying to find out something one may never have had consciously to think about before.[8] This feature is a consequence of regarding acceptance as a mental act and beliefs as involuntary dispositions.[9]

Concerning the involuntary nature of beliefs, Bernard Williams has presented a clear argument.[10] If we could acquire beliefs voluntarily, then we would have to be able to acquire them regardless of their truth or falsehood. If we really had the capacity to decide, then even if an agent always *chose* to believe what he holds to be true, he would have to be able to acquire or keep a belief even when he knows that it is false. Besides, if it were true that an agent can control his beliefs, then he would have to know that, i. e., he would have to be aware of the fact that he can choose true or false beliefs. Bernard Williams's question is: Is it possible to say that a person can decide to believe something she knows to be false? According to the concept of 'belief', such an event could not be called an acquisition of a belief, since beliefs are defined as states of mind which are thought to represent reality, that is, to be true. That beliefs are involuntary is implied by one of the defining characteristics of a belief, namely, the claim of truth. In summary, Williams's argument is the following: If we could decide what beliefs to have, then we could also decide to have false beliefs. But one cannot decide to have a false belief. Therefore, one cannot acquire beliefs at will. According to Williams, it is impossible consciously to regard something as one's own belief (and that means: to think that it is

---

6 Ibid., p. 369.

7 In that sense, they are just as passive as spontaneous desires. Both are states that are 'suffered' and which one cannot voluntarily bring about.

8 Cohen, L. Jonathan, AB, p. 367. Note that Cohen's presentation is not an analysis of the different uses of the term 'believing that'. He does not deny that there is a way of speaking in which the expression 'believing that' is used as a synonym for what in his contribution he calls 'accepting that'. But that is not a counterexample to his thesis. On the different uses of the expression 'believing that', cf. Mosterín, Jesús, Racionalidad y acción humana, Madrid: Alianza Universidad 1978, pp. 108-115. Mosterín distinguishes several linguistic usages and, based on them, different kinds of beliefs. In his terminology, conscious and assertive beliefs imply acceptance.

9 On this point, see the dissenting opinion of Michael Bratman for whom belief as well as acceptance are internal states both of which can be the subject of mental acts. Cohen and Bratman agree, however, on that the passive nature of beliefs is a fact that distinguishes them from acceptance. Cf. Bratman, Michael, Practical Reasoning and Acceptance in a Context, op. cit., p. 11 (hereafter, 'PRAC').

10 Williams, Bernard, Deciding to Believe, op. cit., pp. 136-151 (hereafter, DtB).

true) and at the same time to know that it was brought about by a voluntary decision.[11] In contrast to the inability, for example, to blush at will, this human inability is not a contingent one. Rather, it is conceptually impossible to believe something voluntarily. Williams calls attention to the strong link between beliefs and acts of assertion: beliefs are expressed through acts of assertion. But he also insists that this should not lead to confusion. One can very well decide to say or not to say what one believes, but one cannot decide to believe.[12]

According to this approach, there is one last important difference. Beliefs are states that can come in degrees, whereas acceptance is all-or-nothing. We can say that someone believes more strongly in *p* than in *q*. But with respect to acceptance, although we can say that someone has a stronger or weaker disposition to accept *p* (depending, perhaps, on the quantity or quality of judgmental elements in favour of that attitude), acceptance itself is not a matter of degree. It is a policy that is either adopted or not.[13]

Unlike other attitudes, beliefs cannot be valued pragmatically.[14] Only things that can be voluntarily intended can be valued that way. The fact that *z* is brought about by an attitude *x* can be a reason for adopting that attitude only if the agent can do this intentionally. In the case of beliefs, that is impossible. For instance, for a sick person it may be true that if she believed to have been cured that would in fact make things easier (for herself as well as for the people around her). But even if the patient knows this and wishes to make things easier, she cannot intentionally decide to believe that she is cured, simply because that would satisfy this, or some other, end. That is why beliefs can be explained causally, but not teleologically. Perhaps the strong desire to be cured works as a *cause* for the patient to come to believe that she is cured; but it cannot be the *reason why* she comes to believe it.[15] That beliefs cannot be valued pragmatically does not mean

---

[11] Ibid., p. 148.

[12] This topic has already been touched upon in Chapter I. There, I underlined that internal intentional states, unlike illocutionary acts, must necessarily be sincere.

[13] Cohen, L. Jonathan, AB, p. 374.

[14] A valuation is pragmatic only if what is valued is appreciated because it is a means or an adequate way for doing some other thing. For instance, by being or doing something that falls under a description *x* (as, for example, being a hard-working man, or working hard) someone (say, John) can do something that falls under another description *z* (e. g., help his family). A valuation of the fact that John is or does *x* (is a hard-working man, or works hard) is pragmatic to the extent that this fact is valued because by this means John does *z* (helps his family). Working hard is something one can do in order to reach some end. In contrast, one cannot believe something in order to reach some end, just as, for example, one cannot feel warmly dressed in order to bring about a certain result – for instance, to feel comfortable. Cf. Edgley, Roy, Reason in Theory and Practice, op. cit., p. 63.

[15] Although Edgley acknowledges that believing is not a voluntary act, in a very broad sense, he includes it among the things an agent can do – though, of course, not for pragmatic reasons.

On this point, it is interesting to consider Bernard Williams's ideas when he analyses the possibility that one may wish to believe or have motives for believing. He distinguishes between „truth-centered motives" and „non-truth-centered motives". One of the defining characteristics of beliefs is their claim of truth. Therefore, it seems incoherent to say that one wishes to believe or has a motive for believing something one knows to be false. Assertions apparently expressing the wish to believe something that is false, as, for instance, 'I wish I could believe that my child is not dead', actually do not express the wish for a certain belief, but the wish that reality were not as it is.

that they cannot be evaluated at all. For example, they could be evaluated by reference to the truth or falsehood of the propositions they contain.

Since beliefs cannot be voluntarily manipulated, a person who does not believe some proposition after having seen that there is sufficient evidence for it can be punished or admired, but cannot be *required to believe* it.[16] Something that cannot be done at will cannot be obligatory. In contrast, according to certain rules of rationality, in such a situation one can and must require that the proposition in question is *accepted.*[17]

The fact that one believes something may be a reason that explains why one accepts a certain meaningful content; but that must not necessarily be the case. For example, belief in the moral adequacy of a standard of behaviour normally is one of the reasons why it is accepted. But there might be other reasons which conflict with that belief and may lead the agent to decide not to accept that standard. Belief in truth or correctness is neither necessary nor sufficient for acceptance. The fact that the two usually

---

Since beliefs cannot be acquired by decision, the only thing a person can do is put herself under the causal conditions that may bring about a certain belief or make her forget another one. If one could say that beliefs can have „non-truth-centered motives", there would be no problem in saying that a person may take drugs, let herself be hynotized, or use any other means that will lead her to believe what she thinks is convenient (though false), or to forget what she doesn't like (although it is true). But here Williams indicates an asymmetry between implementing the means for believing something one knows to be false and forgetting something one knows to be true. In his view, beliefs carry a claim of truth, but not of completeness. That means that the elimination of true beliefs does not have the same relevance as the incorporation of false beliefs. Considering the number of beliefs one would have to change in order to believe something that is false, succeeding in such an undertaking would amount to paranoia. Cf. Williams, Bernard, DtB, pp. 149-151.

16 Bernard Williams thinks that empirical beliefs can be based on evidence: If one receives new information (evidence for or against something) that will causally provoke the corresponding beliefs. Thus, one can expect that a person with sufficient evidence for the truth of some content will come to believe it, although she cannot *decide* to do so. The assertion that someone believes that *p* because he believes that *q* – or, directly, because *q* – can only be understood in this causal (not in the teleological or intentional) sense; i. e., 'because' must be understood as causal here. Cf. Williams, Bernard, DtB, pp. 141-144.

17 According to the concepts adopted here, beliefs cannot be rational in the sense that they cannot be the products of actions carried out for some reason. This marks an important difference between the meaning of 'rationality' when applied to beliefs and when applied to intentional action, as for example, to acceptance. An action is commonly judged to be rational on the condition of being an appropriate means for reaching some given end. Such ends are said to be the reasons that explain why the agent acted as he did. In contrast, by definition, the rationality of beliefs cannot consist in their being appropriate means for some given end. What is usually called a reason in favour of a belief is not an end of the agent, but a fact regarded as evidence of the truth of the believed proposition. Although one cannot directly require someone to believe or not to believe something, one can require that all available evidence for and against a proposition is taken into account and assessed. And just as there is a theory of knowledge stipulating under what conditions it is rational to accept a proposition, one can propose an ethical theory stipulating under what conditions it is rational to accept a norm. If the content of his beliefs does not fit to what an agent has sufficient evidence of, the beliefs can be said to be irrational. But even then, one could not require the agent to abandon or modify his mental state concerning these beliefs. In short, one should not confuse the fact that beliefs are excluded from the realm of internal attitudes that are voluntary – and, therefore, rational, in a teleological sense – with the fact that the content of beliefs can be qualified as rational or irrational, depending on the evidence for their truth.

Against this interpretation, see the critique of Cohen's position presented by Colin Radford. According to Radford, beliefs are not beyond the reach of a rationality requirement, since they can be causally produced, but they can also be justified by good reasons. Cf. Radford, Colin, Belief, Acceptance and Knowledge, in: Mind 99 (October 1990), p. 610.

coincide makes it difficult to separate them, but conceptually there is a clear distinction.[18]

B) ACCEPTANCE, SIMULATION AND ASSUMPTION

When the attitude of acceptance is characterized, there is generally a reference to external behaviours of the acceptant. Such conduct is regarded as a manifestation necessarily connected with the attitude to be characterized. In the case of norms, for instance, acceptance is associated with the use of normative language when criticism or requests of conformity are formulated.[19] If that were the only basis of the characterization, however, it would not be possible to „distinguish very clearly the ideas of 'accepting a rule', 'behaving (towards others) like someone who accepts a rule', and 'obeying a rule'".[20] The same external behaviour may be shown by someone who does and by someone who does not accept a corresponding norm. What distinguishes acceptants from non-acceptants is a typical internal attitude. In order to underline the defining characteristics of acceptance, it seems useful not only to compare it with believing, but also with other attitudes an individual may have, such as assuming or simulating.

The acceptance of *p* implies that the agent in question admits *p* and actually uses it when reasoning about action.[21] *Acceptance* is the result of an intentional act by an agent in which he commits himself to some meaningful content even though he may not believe it. Accepting implies the incorporation of the accepted content into the foundations of the agent's internal reasoning. Because this incorporation is voluntary, it has an important consequence: it is subject to a consistency requirement with respect to all other contents accepted in the same context.[22] This is what distinguishes an acceptant

---

[18] I will not go into the question of the hierarchy of a person's reasons here. In any case, an agent would be subjectively irrational if he would not respect his own hierarchy of reasons.

[19] Cf. Hart, H. L. A., The Concept of Law, op. cit.; also Gibbard, Allan, Moral Judgement and the Acceptance of Norms, op. cit., p. 18.

[20] Bayón Mohino, Juan Carlos, The Normativity of Law: Legal Duty and Reasons for Action, op. cit., ch. 7.1 (ch. 8.1, pp. 459 of the Spanish original).

[21] On this, Michael Bratman offers a characterization which basically coincides with that of Cohen, except for the following two points. In the first place, although this is not entirely clear in Cohen's text, Cohen apparently does not concede the contextual relativity of acceptance. It should be recalled that Cohen says that accepting *p* implies adopting a policy. The idea of adopting a policy in some sense is at odds with the contextual nature indicated by Bratman. Secondly, for Bratman beliefs as well as acceptance are internal states which must be distinguished from the mental acts of positing or bracketing a meaningful content. According to Bratman, that is what an agent does in each context in order to adjust the „cognitive background" on which he carries out his deliberations and plans. Thus, in certain contexts one can posit *p* although one does not believe it, i. e., although *p* does not belong to one's cognitive background. In other contexts, one may bracket *p* although one believes it, that is, although *p* does belong to one's cognitive background. Such adjustments give rise to a „context-relative adjusted background". This background, together with our plans, shapes our practical deliberation. Cf. Bratman, Michael, PRAC, pp. 10 f.

[22] Cohen, L. Jonathan, AB, pp. 371 f. Cohen explains that acceptance, in contrast to belief, indirectly commits an agent also to accept all logical and mathematical consequences of any conjunction of propositions directly accepted by him. That is why it is so important that accepted propositions be mutually consistent. It may be the case, for instance, that a person inadvertently accepts two logically inconsistent propositions.

from someone who merely acts toward others *as if* he were an acceptant, i. e., it distinguishes him from someone who is *simulating* acceptance. An agent who simulates does not sincerely incorporate the meaningful content in question into his internal practical reasoning.

On the other hand, one can also assume *p*. Assuming consists in proposing some premise merely as a conjecture which does not commit one to any action. For instance: 'Suppose I have a million dollars. What should I do with it?'[23] Unlike assumption, the acceptance of a content creates an expectation for a behaviour conforming to the accepted content. With respect to standards of conduct, we must therefore distinguish the assumption of a norm (which only implies that it is used as a premise-reason of an argument) from its acceptance as a substantive reason for action. Acceptance, unlike assumption, is necessarily associated with action. Although it does not guarantee its performance, it is a motive capable of bringing it about.

These ideas require a few comments concerning distinctions presented earlier. In previous chapters, I sustained that if *p* is a standard of behaviour it may be the subject of two kinds of acceptance: either as a premise of an argument in the logical sense, or as a reason for action. This distinction is perfectly compatible with that presented by Cohen and Bratman. The only difference is that they reserve the name 'acceptance' exclusively for the second case. In the terminology of these authors, the uncommitted positing of a proposition, as a premise of a logical argument, is merely an assumption.[24] According to the terminology used in the present study, an assumption must be regarded as a kind of acceptance, i. e., as acceptance in the formal sense.[25] Once the concept is clear, it does not matter which word is used. What is important is to underline that we are dealing with two different mental acts and that because of their characteristics only the attitude of non-formal acceptance can be identified with an (explanatory or motivational) reason for action. In the terminology of Bernard Williams, the formal acceptance or the assumption of a meaningful content is not an element of an agent's subjective motivational set, that is, not even in the weakest sense of the term is it a motive.

In conclusion, comparing the concept of acceptance with those of simulation, belief and assumption brings to light three points. First, unlike simulation, acceptance implies positing a content in internal deliberation. Unlike belief, acceptance is a voluntary attitude which can be consciously intended. Finally, unlike assumption, acceptance is linked to a pragmatic requirement with respect to the agent's external conduct.

Now, when non-formal acceptance specifically refers to norms, it not only constitutes an explanatory or motivational reason, but it can also be associated with the notion of justificatory, substantive reason. Before I analyse that double link, it will be useful to review, just as was done with respect to acceptance in general, some proposals about the acceptance of norms.

Since (according to the principles of standard formal logic) a contradiction implies any other proposition, that person, without being aware of it, is then committed to any other proposition.

[23] The example is taken from Bratman, Michael, PRAC, p. 9. The distinction between acceptance and assumption is also made by Cohen.

[24] In fact, that is the name given to the logical rule which permits one to introduce a content as a premise of an argument: 'rule of assumption'. Cf. Lemmon, E. J., Beginning Logic, op. cit., pp. 8 f.

[25] Bratman observes that Stalnaker too regards it as a kind of acceptance; cf. Bratman, Michael, PRAC, p. 9.

3. Accepting a Norm

Following a similar strategy as that developed in the previous section, in order to give precision to the concept of accepting a norm it will be useful to compare it with the concept of internalizing standards of behaviour. This comparison is of particular interest because it brings to light two very different ways of understanding what it means to 'accept a norm'.

A) ACCEPTANCE AND INTERNALIZATION

According to Allan Gibbard, there are different kinds of practical conflicts, depending on which sources of an individual's motivation are opposed to each other.[26] One very common example of this is the conflict between the disposition to act in conformity with *our best judgment* and the pressure exerted by certain powerful socially generated motivations. In Gibbard's view, in this kind of conflict we can see the difference between the psychological act of accepting a norm and the internalization of standards of behaviour. The acceptance of a norm is necessarily linked to the notion of rationality. To act rationally is to act on the basis of the norms one accepts. What is called 'rational' is what is permitted by the accepted norms. In contrast, when an agent acts because of a standard he has internalized, he is subject to a causal pressure of a social kind which he, individually, cannot control. Suppose, for instance, a group of people accepts the norm not to inflict harm on others as a standard that has greater weight than the social rules of politeness which requires them to be friendly and to cooperate with those around them. That means that even when, in order to avoid a harm, it is necessary to violate certain rules of courtesy they think that the rational thing to do is to avoid the harm. Suppose also that the same group, nevertheless, has internalized the rules of politeness. In case of conflict, these people, according to their best judgment, recognize that the rule prohibiting harm is more important than the rules of courtesy. And yet, they will probably try to do what the internalized rules require, contrary to what they themselves believe they should do. That is, it is possible that agents violate standards they accept as being more important and do what they consider to be irrational. This class of conflicts is typically accompanied by certain manifestations (some agents protest, others are very agitated) which show that this is not a conflict between different accepted standards. The agents do not think that they are confronted with two equally rational courses of action. In the conflict between respecting the norm which requires not to harm or the rules of courtesy, the agents think that there is only one rational action: to respect the norm requiring not to do harm. If even under this hypothesis they act in conformity with the rules of courtesy, we can say that they do so under the compulsion of certain standards which, in their own opinions, are not the ones that should determine their conduct. That does not mean that they act because they accept these norms, but that they are 'in the grip' of them.[27]

---

[26] For example, weakness of will involves a conflict between the norms a person accepts and her spontaneous appetites or desires. In Gibbard's view, the latter belong to the motivational system human beings share with animals. Cf. Gibbard, Allan, Moral Judgement and the Acceptance of Norms, op. cit. (hereafter, MJAN).

[27] As an example, Gibbard invokes Milgram's experiments about compliance. The individuals taking part in these experiments were asked to give electric shocks to other people. The shocks were explained to be increa-

What is typical of agents in such a situation is precisely that they do not act in conformity with the norms they accept. They think that to abstain from harming is much more valuable than to be polite, and yet they find themselves inflicting harm on someone else in order not to be impolite.

In Gibbard's view, situations like those just mentioned show the contraposition of two kinds of attitudes toward norms. *Acceptance* is the attitude one arrives at by conscious deliberation (generally, not individual but joint deliberation), in the course of which agents identify a norm, discuss its foundation, anticipate situations of application, commit themselves to it, and prepare themselves to act accordingly when the situation arises. This attitude is acquired through participation in shared evaluations and debates which are a central characteristic of all complex forms of social life.[28] To accept a norm means to be willing to defend it openly in normative discussion, keeping in mind those requirements of consistency. The difference between acceptance and internalization of a standard of behaviour is precisely the internal attitude underlying actions of conformity with that norm. The comparison can be formulated in terms of reasons for action. Both the acceptance and the internalization of norms can motivate action, and in that sense both can be explanatory reasons. The difference is that the mental state which constitutes acceptance results from a deliberate act of decision which can be explained and justified with reasons. Internalization, in contrast, is not the product of an intentional act, it is not a kind of attitude that could be explained or justified with reasons. If we compare the ideas presented in the previous section, we can say that internalization is a disposition one acquires basically by social conditioning; it is passive in the same sense as beliefs are. It can be explained in causal, but not in teleological terms. Internalizing a norm is not something one can do voluntarily.

It is important to note that for some authors this difference does not justify the distinction of the two concepts. They speak of acceptance in both situations, although they admit that this attitude is sometimes rationally adopted and sometimes acquired without reflection. With respect to the acceptance of a legal system, for example, William McBride suggests that 'acceptance' can designate *(a)* a long-term dispositional attitude toward the system, which may be highly irreflective, or *(b)* a choice taken at a specific point in time, which may, however, be repeated in any other instance, or *(c)* a set of short-term dispositions or a prolonged series of acts of decision which can be regarded as somewhere in between *(a)* and *(b)*.[29] This conception, obviously, is broader than Gibbard's: under certain circumstances, acceptance is an act of choice, and in other cases it is an irreflective disposition. From this perspective, although a voluntary and a non-voluntary attitude are distinguished, both are considered to be forms of *acceptance* of a system. In other words: a narrow concept defines 'acceptance' as the intentional act of adopting the policy of following a norm; a broader concept also includes those cases in which a norm is followed because it has been internalized, i. e., in which an agent irreflectively comes to be 'in the grip' of a social standard. For the purposes of the present investigation, the broader concept of acceptance will be left aside, since if we admit-

---

singly more painful, and on the highest level, lethal. Despite their protests and visible uneasiness, about two thirds of the candidates did whatever they were ordered to do. Cf. Gibbard, Allan, MJAN, pp. 15 f.

28 Ibid., p. 19.

29 McBride, William L., The Acceptance of a Legal System, in: The Monist 49 (1965) pp. 382 f.

ted it we would lose one of the features enabling us to distinguish between those who accept a norm and those who merely conform to it.[30] Of course, those who have acquired the disposition of following a norm conform to it too, but that disposition does not give us any relevant information about whether or not an agent has the critical practical attitude typical of those who consciously commit themselves to a standard of behaviour.

A precise concept of acceptance is needed especially when it comes to answering the empirical question about the kind of attitude towards norms characterizing the participants of an existing legal system. Following Cohen, the acceptance of a norm by an agent will be understood to mean that the agent has decided to adopt the policy of assuming that standard of conduct as a basis for his actions. Such an internal decision is necessarily associated with two pragmatic commitments: consistency with all other accepted contents, and the adaptation of one's external conduct.

B) MORAL AND STRATEGIC REASONS FOR ACCEPTANCE

There is still another, even more restricted way of understanding the notion of 'acceptance' of norms. Here, not only all situations not involving an intentional act of choice are excluded from the concept, but also all those where the decision is not based on a specific kind of reason. From this point of view, the decision to follow a norm is not a case of acceptance when it is based on strategic or prudential reasons. An acceptant, on this view, is someone who adopts a directive because he believes that it is a correct standard of behaviour. An example for such a conception can be found in the writings of Ernesto Garzón Valdés:

> „Those who adhere to the system, that is, who adopt the internal point of view, do so because they accept its norms as standards of behavior. Since this acceptability, by definition, cannot be due to prudential reasons (e. g., the fear of possibly being punished, or the hope of gaining some sort of reward), it seems to follow that it must be grounded on the belief that these norms coincide with the supreme principles and rules for the justification and guidance of conduct held by the persons in question."[31]

This is one of the most common interpretations in legal theory. It is endorsed, among others, by authors such as Joseph Raz, Carlos Nino, Juan Ruiz Manero, Manuel Atienza, Philip Soper, and Robert Alexy. On this conception, acceptance is necessarily linked to the belief of moral correctness. It is that belief which allegedly distinguishes someone who accepts a norm from someone who merely adopts it for strategic reasons. But note that the strategic attitude that is distinguished from acceptance is, likewise, an attitude *toward norms*. As such, it presupposes the decision to follow the rule, only that here the decision is based on prudential reasons. This must not be confused with adopting a stra-

---

30 Cf. Bayón Mohino, Juan Carlos, The Normativity of Law: Legal Duty and Reasons for Action, op. cit., ch. 7.1 (ch. 8.1, p. 482 of the Spanish original).

31 Garzón Valdés, Ernesto, Algo más acerca de la relación entre Derecho y moral, in: Doxa (Alicante) 8 (1990) p. 114. Cf. also the slightly different wording in the English version: More on the Relation Between Law and Morality, in: A. Aarnio, K. Pietilä, J. Uusitalo (eds.), Interests, Morality and the Law, University of Tampere, Research Institute for Social Sciences 1996). For Garzón Valdés, those supreme principles are of a moral nature.

tegic attitude *toward actions*. The latter is the position of those who are unwilling to follow a rule and in each particular case evaluate all the relevant reasons in order to determine the most appropriate course of action. The strategic perspective Garzón Valdés opposes to acceptance is not that of an individual who in each case newly decides what to do. The distinction he emphasizes is that between two attitudes both involving the adoption of a policy of rule-following, and it is based on the different kinds of reasons for which an agent may adopt such a policy. From this point of view, an agent cannot be said to be an acceptant if the reason is not his belief in the moral correctness of the standard. This interpretation thus necessarily unites the two concepts Cohen and Bratman wished to keep apart. The main thrust of Cohen's work is to show that the rational attitude of acceptance, first, should not be identified with a belief and, second, also does not need to be founded on a belief. Likewise, Bratman's interest is to bring out the necessarily contextual nature of acceptance, which presupposes that it is distinguished from beliefs.

4. Acceptance and Reasons for Action

Acceptance implies an internal act of decision which can motivate an agent's behaviour and, therefore, explain his action. In addition, when acceptance refers to normative contents, it implies that those contents are regarded as justificatory reasons for one's actions. Therefore, when we characterize the acceptance of norms, both kinds of reasons for action are involved: explanatory reasons and justificatory reasons. Let us now take a look at this double link.

A) NORM-ACCEPTANCE AND EXPLANATORY REASONS

The term 'acceptance' designates a mental act as well as the result of such an act. The result of an act of acceptance, as identified above, can be regarded as an element of the agent's subjective motivational set.[32] That result may be described in terms of an explanatory reason for action. It is a mental state which can determine the agent's behaviour, that is, it can be regarded as a motive in the third sense of the term.[33] As the result of an intentional act, besides itself being a reason capable of explaining an action, it is a fact which can, in turn, be explained in terms of reasons (just like the result of any other action). From this point of view, everything that has been said about actions in general also applies to acceptance. The difference is that, in this case, we are dealing with an internal act which can take place without any external physical or verbal evidence. A person may accept a norm even though she has not had the opportunity to manifest her acceptance explicitly.

On the basis of the arguments presented, it does not seem plausible to restrict the kind of reasons for which a normative content may be accepted. When Bratman shows the varieties of acceptance, he also reveals certain kinds of reasons which may explain

---

[32] Williams, Bernard, Internal and External Reasons, op. cit., pp. 101-113.

[33] Cf. Chapter I, sect. 6.

the adoption of that attitude. They are, among others, the wish to simplify an argument in order to avoid undesirable costs, the need for social cooperation, the existence of special relationships with other persons, etc.[34] Belief in correctness may be, but not necessarily is, a reason which determines the acceptance of a norm, just as the belief in the truth of a proposition may be, but not necessarily is the reason why one decides to accept that proposition.[35]

In conclusion, then, acceptance is an explanatory reason for behaviour as well as a behaviour which is performed because of reasons which explain it. Both the attitude of acceptance and the reasons motivating it must not be confused with the content, the object, of that attitude. The properties characterizing the act of acceptance and its reasons cannot simply be identified with the properties of the accepted content, and *vice versa*. This is an important point. For instance, an accepted norm, but not the fact that it is accepted, may be a justificatory reason. Likewise, the fact that the explanatory reasons for an act of acceptance are of a moral, an esthetic or a prudential nature does not make the accepted content a moral, aesthetic, or prudential content. One may decide to accept the rules of a game for moral reasons; but that does not transform the rules of the accepted game into moral rules.[36]

B) NORM-ACCEPTANCE AND JUSTIFICATORY REASONS

Two ways of linking the attitude of acceptance and justificatory reasons for action can be presented. The first is based on the fact that acceptance itself is a conscious act which is something that can be justified. The second takes into account that acceptance may regard meaningful contents which constitute justificatory reasons for action.

(i) The attitude of acceptance as an object of justification[37]

As defined above, the justification of an action is an act in which substantive reasons are invoked as a foundation for a statement saying that the action ought to be performed. Acts of justification always involve the application of a normative conception or theory since only on the basis of such a theory can certain norms be identified as reasons for action. As already mentioned, acceptance as an intentional act can be explained in terms of reasons for action and, at the same time, it can be justified from the perspective of a specific normative conception. The two possibilities are systematically confused in discussions of this topic.

In legal theory, most interpreters of Hart discuss the acceptance of the rule of recognition on the part of the judges. Generally, their method leads them to consider the reasons why a judge may or may not accept the rule of recognition. In most cases the conclusion is that acceptance is necessarily reached for moral reasons. The argument

---

34 Bratman, Michael, PRAC, pp. 4-7.

35 Cohen, L. Jonathan, AB, p. 369.

36 This asymmetry between the act of acceptance and the accepted contents has been overlooked by Carlos Nino who maintains that the nature of accepted contents depends on the reasons why they are accepted. Thus, the premises invoked by a judge, when accepted for moral reasons, could not be distinguished from moral judgments. Cf. Nino, Carlos S., El constructivismo ético, op. cit., p. 30.

37 In this context, justification must be understood not in the formal, but in the material sense.

given for this conclusion is typically that another kind of reasons would not yield the kind of justificatory reasons needed for grounding a judicial decision.

For instance, in his book *Jurisdicción y Normas*, Juan Ruiz Manero points out that concerning the issue of the acceptance of the rule of recognition what matters are justificatory reasons.[38] He distinguishes between explanatory and justificatory reasons and asserts that facts cannot be justificatory reasons. In other words, he accepts the so-called Humean principle. He discards the possibility that a judge's acceptance could be justified by legal or prudential reasons. Following Raz, he holds that in order to be justified the attitude must be adopted for moral reasons. In Ruiz Manero's view, Hart fails in his attempt to indicate non-moral kinds of reasons for which an agent could accept the law.[39] Hart's alleged mistake is said to be evident in the examples he gives, since, according to Ruiz Manero, none of them mentions justificatory reasons:

„[T]he reasons presented by Hart as possible alternatives to the acceptance of the rule of recognition for moral reasons either are no justificatory reasons at all, but mere facts, or they are *prima facie* justificatory reasons of a moral kind.“[40]

A judge accepts a rule for moral reasons when his acceptance is based on the „*belief* in the moral legitimacy of the sources indicated in the rule of recognition".[41] And he also does it when he accepts

„not because he *believes* in the moral legitimacy of those sources but because he *believes* that if the judiciary acted otherwise that would lead, for instance, to an anarchical situation which would be a greater moral evil than the persistence of illegitimate legislation".[42]

Finally, Ruiz Manero, quoting Nino, also mentions the possibility that a judge may believe to have moral reasons which justify the acceptance of legal provisions without the need to take recourse to the rule of recognition:

„when a judge *believes* to have the moral obligation to apply a certain legal provision [...] because he regards that provision, whether or not it satisfies the criteria of the rule of recognition, as morally obligatory for him, in view of its content".[43]

Because of Hume's principle, justifications must always be based on normative judgments. What is incomprehensible is why for Ruiz Manero the *belief* that a standard is morally correct has a justificatory (normative) nature which other – for example, egoistic or prudential – *beliefs* lack. All this criticism of Hart seems to be based on a confusion between *justificatory reasons* and a *belief in justificatory reasons*. The latter are the

[38] Ruiz Manero, Juan, Jurisdicción y normas, op. cit., pp. 177 f. A similar approach can be found in the works of authors like Joseph Raz or Carlos Nino.

[39] Hart indicates various kinds of non-moral reasons on which acceptance may be based, among others a traditional or an inherited irreflective attitude.

[40] Ruiz Manero, Juan, Jurisdicción y normas, op. cit., p. 178.

[41] Ibid., p. 179.

[42] Ibid.

[43] Ibid.

reasons why an agent accepts something, i. e., they do not justify, but only explain his attitude. What Ruiz Manero's considerations overlook is that all elements of judgment mentioned by Hart as reasons for acceptance are explanatory reasons. None of the alternatives given by Hart is a justificatory reason, not even the *belief* in moral correctness.

Throughout this investigation, I have maintained a strict distinction between the concepts of the explanation and the justification of an action. This is paralleled by the recognition of two independent concepts of reason: explanatory reasons and justificatory reasons. Many authors explicitly reject this separation and defend the priority of the idea of justification over that of explanation. This relation of dependency is possible if one adopts a subjective concept of justification, that is, if we call 'justification' the set of considerations which, from the point of view of the respective agent, were the reasons that made him act. Thus, for example, one says that an agent *justified* his action with his fear of punishment, or with his acceptance or rejection of a certain norm. Therefore, an adequate explanation depends on the justification given by the agent, since to explain an action means to report what for the agent is his justification.

Those who do not recognize the independence between the two kinds of reasons are committed to admit that the attitude of acceptance is an explanatory reason which, in turn, constitutes a justificatory reason. It is an explanatory reason from the point of view of an observer, and it is a justificatory reason from the point of view of the agent. This conception must admit the existence of two kinds of justification: a subjective one, which refers to what the agent regards as justifying his action (for instance, his belief in the moral correctness of some normative content); and an objective one, based on norms which apply to the agent even though he may not accept them. The latter notion of justification is the one used in the present investigation, and it is the only one admissible for those who agree with Hume's principle. On that view, a 'subjective justification' is nothing but another explanation, and cannot be considered a justification in the strict sense, because it is based on an agent's beliefs, which are not the kind of entities that can possibly be justificatory reasons, i. e., norms.[44]

The concept of subjective justification is interesting because it is where explanatory and justificatory reasons overlap. Of course, if one assumes a single concept of reason and therefore rejects Hume's principle, this does not involve a confusion. That is the case, e. g., of Joseph Raz for whom, in the last instance, all reasons are facts, and such facts can justify. In contrast to this view, if one concedes that in order to justify one needs reasons of a different quality than explantory reasons, then it is wrong to identify the reasons *why* someone does (for instance, accepts) something with the reasons which justify that action. When we speak of acceptance, or of the reasons why an agent adopts that attitude, we refer to psychological states. A psychological fact does not become a norm, i. e., does not acquire a justificatory nature for the mere fact that its object is a normative content. The fact of accepting a norm, or of believing in the correctness of a norm, does not give a justificatory nature neither to the acceptance nor to the belief. Hence, the requirement that acceptance be based on the belief in moral correctness cannot be supported with the argument that that kind of reasons, as distinct from the others invoked by Hart, constitutes justificatory reasons. The belief in moral correctness has

---

[44] The different notions of justification have been analysed in Chapter II, sects. 2 and 3.

the same ontological status as the desire to continue with an established practice: as psychological facts about the agent, none of the two is a justificatory reason.

The idea that a necessary condition for the existence of a legal system is that acceptance is based on the belief in moral reasons can be founded on a number of different arguments.[45] An empirical argument, for example, regards that belief as a necessary element of the social cohesion required for a system to come into, or stay in, force. A conceptual argument suggests that it is a distinctive feature of the meaning of 'legal system' or 'law', as opposed to coercive systems based only on the exercise of force. In that case, an adequate reconstruction of the notion of law must show that such a moral belief is a necessary defining characteristic.[46] According to these arguments, acceptance for moral reasons is a conceptually necessary condition for the existence of a legal system. But from this it does not follow that there really are moral reasons for the acceptance of that system, nor that it actually is accepted for reasons of that kind. The question about the existence of moral reasons for acceptance can be answered neither with an empirical nor with a conceptual argument. The answer can only derive from a normative conception. In fact, when Raz says „Therefore it seems to follow that I cannot accept rules imposing duties on other people except, if I am sincere, for moral reasons"[47] he is referring to a normative rather than a factual impossibility. He grounds his conception in a normative principle which is also adopted by Nino and Ruiz Manero: When an accepted content imposes obligations on people other than the acceptant, acceptance *must* be based on moral reasons. In other words, when one accepts a standard which provides an obligation for others, it is morally wrong to do so for prudential reasons. But, as all principles, this one too can be violated. Therefore, it is empirically possible that judges or other relevant participants do not accept the rule of recognition for moral reasons.

Undoubtedly, Hart did not mean to elaborate a normative theory about the reasons for which officials *ought* to accept a system. His purpose, rather, was to underline that officials regard the accepted standards as justificatory reasons for action.[48] Such an attitude is necessary for the existence of a legal system. Like all intentional attitudes, it can be explained and justified with different reasons. The *wish* to uphold a practice, the *disposition* to imitate certain conducts, the *belief* in moral correctness, or the presence of strategic *interests* are all reasons which explain the adoption of that attitude.

---

[45] Cf. Caracciolo, Ricardo, L'argomento della credenza morale, in: Paolo Comanducci and Riccardo Guastini (eds.), Analisi e Diritto 1994. Ricerche di Giurisprudenza Analitica, Torino: Giappichelli 1994, pp. 97-110.

[46] That is Soper's argument, among others. His approach identifies the idea of acceptance with that of the belief in, or claim of, justice, and clearly adopts the idea of subjective justification. What matters is not only the fact that certain norms are accepted, but also that they are defended as being worthy of acceptance, i. e., that they are believed to be just. Cf. Soper, Philip, A Theory of Law, op. cit., p. 56.

[47] Raz, Joseph, Hart on Moral Rights and Legal Duties, in: Oxford Journal of Legal Studies 4:1 (1984) p. 130.

[48] The fact that officials accept that certain standards are reasons for action does not imply that these standards actually are justificatory reasons from a moral point of view. Neither the acceptance nor the belief of the judges converts the accepted contents into justificatory reasons for action.

(ii) The object of acceptance and justificatory reasons

The contributions of Bratman and Cohen concentrate on the acceptance of propositional contents and its importance for the problem of knowledge. In the present study, in contrast, I am interested basically in the acceptance of normative contents and its relevance for the problem of the existence of legal systems. This does not mean that the acceptance of certain propositional contents is not relevant to my topic. For example, the fact that participants accept certain propositions about the existence of their own or others' explanatory reasons (dispositions, wishes, beliefs, etc.) or about the occurrence of facts leading to the application of the norms they accept may well be decisive. Nevertheless, the object of acceptance Hart specifically refers to is a *standard of conduct* adopted as a justificatory reason for the pressure exerted in favour of a practice and for the critique of deviating behaviour. Hart's proposal is compatible with the interpretation that only norms can be justificatory reasons for action.[49]

From the point of view adopted here, not all norms are reasons for action in a substantive sense. Whether they are or not can only be established within a normative theory and does not depend on their being accepted by some group or individual. The mere fact that a norm is accepted does not convert it into a justificatory reason for action, just as the fact that one identifies a norm as a justificatory reason for action (according to some theory) does not yet mean that one accepts it. When we say that an agent acts for a justificatory reason, what we say is that the agent internalizes, accepts, or believes in, a normative standard as a justificatory reason. Such an attitude explains his action, but it does not imply that what has been internalized or accepted or is believed actually is a justificatory reason for action.

If whether or not a norm is a substantive justificatory reason depended on whether or not it is accepted or on the motives for which it is accepted, there would be no place for rational controversy about justificatory reasons. For this to be possible, there must be an objective parameter. Otherwise, disagreement about whether or not one ought to do a certain thing, i. e., about whether or not there are justificatory reasons for an action would not be a cognitive disagreement.[50]

Every normative theory proposes a set of standards as justificatory reasons, regardless of their individual acceptance. The thesis that something is a reason only relative to some theory does not preclude that from the point of view of each one of them the respective reasons are regarded as universally valid and as the only admissible reasons. An altogether different question is which theory is the correct or the most adequate one. Concerning normative theories, one can make the same distinctions as with respect to individually considered normative standards. A particular theory may be assumed, accepted, or believed to be true. The *identification* of a substantive reason for action

---

[49] According to Hart, the norms of a legal system are *legal* justificatory reasons. That does not imply that they are also justificatory reasons from a *moral* point of view. Therefore, we can say that in his philosophical conception the fragmentation of justificatory discourse and of the notion of obligation is admitted. In Hart's proposal for the identification of the norms belonging to an existing system (the legal reasons of a social group) the criteria of validity accepted by a qualified set of agents must be known. That means that acceptance of a common standard of recognition (not of every single norm) is necessary for the identification of the reasons which are valid within a system.

[50] Cf. MacIntyre, Alasdair, The Claims of *After Virtue*, in: Analyse & Kritik 6 (1984), pp. 3-7.

presupposes the *assumption* of a normative theory, and the *acceptance* of a substantive reason for action presupposes the *acceptance* of a normative theory. What is not necessary is the belief in the theory's truth. This distinction between assumption, belief and acceptance is enormously important for a typical controversy in practical philosophy. It shows that one can rationally accept a set of standards, with all the implications of the notion of acceptance – as, for instance, a pragmatic commitment to an action and the commitment to internal consistency with respect to the accepted contents –, even if one is a skeptic as regards the truth or falsehood of moral discourse.

5. Acceptance as a Condition for the Existence of a Legal System

In the first part of this chapter I have presented an idea formulated by Hart and widely accepted, namely, that there are two necessary conditions for the existence of a legal system. They are, on the one hand, that its valid rules are obeyed and, on the other, that at least its rule of recognition is accepted. Depending on the different meanings given to 'acceptance' there are three ways how the difference in attitude between those who accept and those who merely obey can be understood. First, in a broad sense, an acceptant of a norm is someone who simply has the disposition to act in conformity with it. Here, it makes no difference whether that disposition has been acquired irreflectively or is the result of an act following deliberate decisions. In this version, whoever has the disposition to do what legal norms stipulate is an acceptant, even those who follow them 'like sheep', provided they have the clear tendency to do what the standards say. In this case, then, there is no difference between an acceptant and someone who merely obeys. The only distinction one could perhaps make is between someone who accepts a rule and someone who does what the rule says only because that is what his balance of reasons tells him to do on some particular occasion.[51]

On the other extreme, those who advocate a narrow concept of acceptance say that acceptants are only those who have the disposition to follow the norms because they believe in their moral correctness. Hart's proposal, interpreted from this point of view, not only requires that the officials adopt certain standards as justificatory reasons for action. It is also necessary that they do so because of a moral belief. In this version, those who are committed to following the rule of recognition for prudential reasons have exactly the same effect on the existence of a legal system as those who do not respect the rule of recognition at all. None of them is a genuine acceptant.

Finally, from the perspective adopted in this book, someone is an acceptant of a norm if he *has decided* to adopt it as a justificatory reason for action. Those who accept the rule of recognition as a justificatory reason for action not only adopt the policy of using it as a premise in their practical arguments, but are also committed to the duty of acting in conformity with it. Acceptance is a mental state resulting from an internal act, where the object, in this case, is a standard guiding the recognition of valid norms. This

---

[51] Both attitudes can be distinguished from that of someone whose conduct conforms to the norm, but who neither accepts it nor regards it as a reason that should enter the balance. This may be the case when an agent does not know that the norm exists or when, knowing that it exists, he does not admit it as a reason for action. Cf. Navarro, Pablo E. and Redondo, Cristina, Aceptación y funcionamiento del Derecho, in: Doxa 9 (1991).

presupposes, on the one hand, that the acceptant admits the standard, from a subjective point of view, as a justificatory reason for action, and on the other, that this admission is the result of a decision. These two prerequisites are indispensable. For example, a judge who acts as the rule of recognition provides, either because of a circumstantial interest in avoiding reproof or because it coincides with his interests in a particular case, neither obeys nor accepts that rule. Such a judge does not regard the rule of recognition as a reason for action. And someone who has internalized the rule of recognition has a motive for action, but that attitude is not the product of a deliberate decision.[52] The involuntary nature of internalization prevents it from being regarded as a case of acceptance. Finally, this characterization does not include the belief in moral correctness, neither as a part of the concept of acceptance nor as its necessary foundation. Hence, it is compatible with Hart's idea that agents accept norms for different kinds of reasons.[53] The presence or absence of a belief in correctness neither subtracts nor adds anything regarding the conditions which, according to Hart, are necessary for the existence of a legal system. First, an accepted standard of recognition does not acquire nor lose the nature of a justificatory reason for the fact of being or not being accepted for moral reasons. Secondly, if the commitment of respecting it and making others respect it has been deliberately assumed, the quality of this commitment does not change for the fact that its adoption is explained by prudential reasons.

Concerning the acceptance of the norms of a legal system, two different reasoning strategies can be found. One consists in taking as a starting point some concept of acceptance and then looking at whether or not the conduct of the members of the system manifests that attitude. In that case, semantic agreement is assumed and what is debated is an empirical question about whether the members of the system actually accept it. This line of argument opens up the possibility of reaching the conclusion that accept-

---

[52] It is not even clear whether the internalization of a standard implies its recognition as a reason for action. The internalization of a guideline of behaviour seems compatible with the possibility that the agent in question does not clearly know which standard he is following, for example, because he has never thought about it. In that case, despite having internalized a standard, the agent could not invoke it as a justificatory reason for an action of his. This is the idea Hart seems to adopt when he characterizes those who obey habitually, as distinct from those who see in a norm a reason for action.

[53] Thus, when Hart juxtaposes those who really accept to those who obey 'like sheep', he seems to be committed to a concept of acceptance which excludes mere internalization. This is how Shiner, who criticizes the restrictiveness of Hart's use of the concept, interprets it; cf. Shiner, Roger, Norm and Nature. The Movements of Legal Thought, op. cit., pp. 161-183. On the other hand, when Hart admits that acceptance may be an attitude merely based on imitation or tradition, he seems to admit within the scope of the concept what Gibbard has qualified as the internalization of a norm. This is the interpretation, for instance, of Nino and Bayón who criticize Hart precisely for the broadness in which he uses the concept when he says that acceptance may rest on a traditional, inherited or irreflective attitude. Cf. Nino, Carlos S., El concepto de Derecho en Hart, op. cit., p. 51; Bayón Mohino, Juan Carlos, The Normativity of Law: Legal Duty and Reasons for Action, op. cit., ch. 7.1 (ch. 8.1, pp. 482 of the Spanish original).

Remember also the criticism presented by Soper against Hart's characterization of acceptance. Soper observes that in Austin's model the sovereign as well as his subjects accept his position for reasons which do not essentially depend on the fear of sanctions. If this is the kind of acceptance regarded as sufficient to explain the normativity of the law, then Hart's model does not add anything that had not already been implicit in Austin's model. Cf. Soper, Philip, A Theory of Law, op. cit., pp. 18-20.

ance is not necessary for the existence of a legal system.[54] The alternative is to assume that all existing law implies the acceptance by some of the respective society's members. In this case, what remains open is the meaning of 'acceptance'. Hence, what is needed is not an empirical investigation, but the reconstruction of a concept which will help elucidate the presupposed thesis. This second way of approaching the subject is the more common one among legal philosophers. Generally, they adopt Hart's idea that for a legal system to exist certain norms must be accepted. For example, this is the strategy of authors such as Philip Soper or Roger Shiner who think that acceptance is the essential characteristic for the distinction between law and merely coercive regimes.[55]

Shiner observes that in the discussion of this topic two kinds of attitudes must be distinguished. Both come in degrees, between opposing extremes. *(a)* The first range of attitudes goes from blind, irreflective obedience to the adoption of a fully conscious and rational commitment to norms. *(b)* The second goes from a disposition to obey because of a fear of sanctions to the disposition to do so because of a commitment to the moral value of the norms. Acceptance is a disposition acquired somewhere along the second continuum.[56]

For Shiner, what has been defined earlier as the 'acceptance of norms', i. e., the adoption of a policy of using some standard as a premise, accompanied by the deliberate commitment to act in conformity with it, is an attitude that is compatible with the external point of view. In his view, acceptance has nothing to do with the first range of attitudes. The value measured on this scale is that of the rationality of an agent's attitude. According to Shiner, all the attitudes on this first continuum can be adopted from the external point of view. That means that the internal point of view is not directly linked to the rationality of the agent's attitude. In characterizing acceptance, Shiner uses a comparison with virtue in the Aristotelian sense. A virtuous person is someone who has developed the capacity to do what is right, even without thinking about it. Hence, there is no reason to think that those who have developed a habit of obedience because of the internalization of certain standards of conduct obey 'like sheep'. Such an apparently irreflective conformity is not incompatible with the internal point of view; on the contrary, it presupposes it.[57]

The two ranges of attitudes pointed out by Shiner reveal the basis of the different meanings of 'acceptance' previously discussed. That is, they show the two values or properties the respective concepts depend on. On the one hand, the value in question is

---

[54] An approach of this kind is proposed by McBride when he underlines that two aspects involved in this issue must be distinguished. One refers to the meaning of 'rule-governed behaviour' and the other one to the empirical investigation of the attitudes individuals actually have toward the rules of a legal system. Cf. McBride, W. C., The Acceptance of a Legal System, op. cit., p. 378.

[55] Philip Soper expressly acknowledges this approach. First, he shows a weak and a strong conception of the attitude of acceptance. If Hart's ideas are to be sustained and the theory is to be consistent, the weak interpretation must be chosen. In contrast, if the theses defended in Soper's theory are assumed, then the strong interpretation is needed. Cf. Soper, Philip, A Theory of Law, op. cit., p. 38.

[56] One of Shiner's criticisms is based on the argument that Austin and Hart place the point corresponding to acceptance very close to the first pole of this continuum of attitudes, that is, very close to a strategic disposition.

[57] Shiner, Roger, Norm and Nature. The Movements of Legal Thought, op. cit., pp. 174-180.

rationality; on the other, it is morality. When the property taken to be relevant is rationality, what is controversial is whether acceptance comprises only the reasoned adoption of a policy or also includes the irreflective following of internalized standards. When acceptance is defined with morality as the relevant property, the discussion focuses on whether this attitude can be attributed only to someone who believes in the correctness of the standard or whether it also applies to someone who respects it merely for strategic reasons. I have tried to show that this second option (which proposes to identify the acceptance of a norm with the belief in its moral correctness) is questionable. It does not take into account the difference between voluntary and involuntary attitudes – in this case, between acceptance and belief. This position either reduces acceptance to belief in correctness, or it restricts the concept of acceptance to a commitment based on involuntary attitudes, i. e., on beliefs.

According to Hart, the idea of the acceptance of a rule of recognition shows, on the one hand, a relevant characteristic of all legal systems and, on the other, the typical position of some of a society's members. Specifically, it enables one to show the position the officials of the system, in contrast to ordinary citizens, must necessarily assume.

(i) The attitude of the citizens: Most legal theorists adopt Hart's thesis that for the existence of a legal system it is not necessary that all the norm-addressees accept the rule of recognition. Otherwise, Hart says, one would have to assume that they all know about a number of complex constitutional questions, which in fact they don't. Thus, the attitude of ordinary citizens differs from that of the officals of a system, and that difference is captured by the concepts of obedience and acceptance. The notion of acceptance presupposes epistemic and volitional elements which can hardly be attributed to the citizens as such.[58]

Shiner agrees that the attitude of ordinary citizens is different from that of the officials. But he criticizes Hart for adopting an excessively restricted meaning of 'acceptance' which prevents us from showing that in all legal systems the citizens too have that attitude toward the norms. His opinion is not based on empirical evidence different from that taken into account by Hart, but on the introduction of a new concept of acceptance: judges 'accept' in one sense, and ordinary citizens in another. It thus becomes possible to say that acceptance is much more widespread among the subjects of a legal system than what Hart assumes. Citizens express their acceptance through all acts in which they present legal claims and exercise the faculties given to them by the law. For example, „I manifest, i. e., give evidence of, my acceptance of criminal statutes every time I do *not* murder, do *not* steal, do *not* commit contempt of court, and so forth ..."[59]

---

[58] The cognitive and volitional elements involved in the internal aspect of a social rule are spelled out in MacCormick, Neil, H. L. A. Hart, op. cit., pp. 33 f.

[59] Shiner, Roger, Norm and Nature. The Movements of Legal Thought, op. cit., p. 178. Shiner distinguishes the manifestation of the acceptance of legal obligations from that of legal prohibitions. In the latter case, an agent shows his acceptance through an omission. In Shiner's view, only a prejudice in favour of the commission of actions can lead one to underestimate the value of 'passive' attitudes as evidence for acceptance. Cf. ibid., pp. 178 f.

(ii) The attitude of the officials: In principle, most legal theorists agree with Hart that for the existence of a legal system at least acceptance by the officials is necessary. However, this is not really an agreement, since there are different views about what Hart means with his thesis. According to many of his critics, Hart does not see that officials, and especially judges, accept the rule of recognition in the strictest sense of the term, i. e., on the basis of a moral belief. As we have seen before, the assertion that such a belief is a necessary condition for the existence of a legal system is not based on an empirical investigation of the attitudes of judges, but on a specific normative conception. It is founded on the idea that the norms accepted by the officials in applying the law impose obligations on other people, and that standards imposing obligations on third parties *ought* to be accepted for moral reasons. Since this attitude is thought to be necessary, an official who does not have it would have to *pretend* to have it. Hart has openly expressed his disagreement with this thesis.[60] On his conception, there is no need to simulate this attitude which itself is not necessary. Again, this is not based on different empirical data, but on a different concept of acceptance.

Whether a concept is more or less plausible depends on the theoretical or practical purpose it is intended to serve. If the existence of a legal system is understood to depend on acceptance of a moral kind, then the concept of law only refers to orders the officials of which believe that they have moral legitimacy. All other orders would not be legal orders, but mere coercive regimes not deserving that name. The advocates of such a conception, who are currently in the majority, do not share Hart's theoretical purposes. In conformity with Hart's positivist position, the purpose of his theory is descriptive. Its function is not to determine what the acceptance of the judges must be like in order to be justifiable as a morally correct attitude or in order to detect moral differences between different kinds of institutionalized systems and genuinely legal systems.

Summing up, according to Shiner's proposal acceptance is not *one* of the several attitudes members of a legal system may adopt with respect to its norms. Given his definitions, acceptance is *the* attitude which applies to the entire group. The typical feature of legal systems is that the citizens as well as the officials accept it. Acceptance is not distinguished from other possible attitudes toward the law, but serves to distinguish between what can rightly be called 'law' and something that is only a system of coercion. In Shiner's own words:

„We need a way of understanding how citizens accept the law which none the less preserves the real difference between the role of citizen and the role of official. We need a conception of how the ordinary citizen interacts with the law that manifests acceptance, while acknowledging that this acceptance is not manifested in the way that the officials' daily and continuous intentional operation of the system in accord with its secondary rules manifests their acceptance of those rules."[61]

Shiner clearly wants to present a concept which makes it possible to say that ordinary citizens too accept the law, even if they show a passive attitude toward its norms. From his point of view, the citizens' attitude must be qualified as a case of acceptance. Other-

---

[60] Cf. Hart, H. L. A., Commands and Authoritative Legal Reasons, op. cit., pp. 243-268.

[61] Shiner, Roger, Norm and Nature. The Movements of Legal Thought, op. cit., p. 176.

wise, the law would only be a coercive order for them, and any set of norms could then be identified as law simply because it is accepted by the officials.[62]

6. Conclusions

The idea of acceptance is crucial in the controversy beteween legal positivists and their critics. Seeing acceptance as a necessary attitude for the existence of a legal system and defining it in a way that links it internally to the belief in moral correctness, Hart's critics claim to have proved the central thesis of legal naturalism: that the existence of a legal system presupposes a necessary connection between law and morality. One of the questionable premises of that argument is the meaning of the notion of acceptance. To identify it with the belief in moral correctness, as one must do in order to reach the desired conclusion, means to ignore certain relevant aspects. It is a much less subtle characterization than the one offered by those who emphasize the independence of the concepts in question. And this greater subtlety is important because it clearly brings out certain consequences.

Linking acceptance to beliefs either means to reduce it to an involuntary attitude (when it is identified with the belief in correctness) or to found it exclusively on such a kind of attitude (when it is restricted to an attitude based on moral beliefs). But if the acceptance of norms is an attitude that can be required or criticized, it cannot be made to depend necessarily on the belief in moral correctness, just as the acceptance of a proposition, when it is understood as an attitude that can be required, cannot be conceived as depending necessarily on the belief in its truth. If one defines acceptance as an attitude supported by a belief, one renounces the possibility to require that it be adopted or given up, with respect to some content or to all those contents logically related with previously accepted ones. It makes no sense to require of someone to do something which he cannot do intentionally, and believing is of that kind. What one can decide are the ends and policies one accepts, but not one's beliefs. To reduce the notion of the acceptance of norms to something that can only be predicated of those who believe in the moral correctness of certain standards is to put this issue beyond the reach of rational discussion and convert it into a matter of faith. Jonathan Cohen shows that the distinction between belief and acceptance is one of the parameters for distinguishing a religious from a rational attitude. Beliefs are similar to religious faith. They are mental states one may wish to reach or lament to have lost. But, in any case, they cannot be acquired, regained or maintained by decision. Acceptance, in contrast, as the product of an intentional act, can be decided on the basis of reasons. For instance, a rational approach, as the scientific approach claims to be, requires that the acceptance of a proposition must be able to be decided by deliberation, depending on available evidence. In Cohen's opinion, the ideal of a scientific attitude toward a proposition is to forget the beliefs one may have about it and to decide whether it should be accepted or not according to the evidence. As the history of science shows, beliefs, whether favourable or negative, may

[62] Ibid., p. 182. According to Shiner, if one adopts Hart's concept of acceptance the notion of legal system could be satisfied even by a cruel dictatorship. Although this is no problem at all for Hart, it is a problem (commonly called 'Payne's problem') for those who want to distinguish between legal and coercive orders.

even come to turn into a prejudice which hinders the progress of investigation. What kinds of evidence must be regarded as adequate for the justification of the act of acceptance that *p* is, of course, a normative question. We need rules which establish under what conditions an agent *ought* to accept *p*, though he is still free to do so or not.[63] These rules are then the reasons which justify the acceptance of *p*.

The theoretical purpose of Hart's proposal in introducing the concept of acceptance is to show that mere conformity with the norms is not sufficient to explain the existence of a legal system. Commitment with certain rules is necessary. From the point of view of this theoretical purpose, the characterization of acceptance as a belief in the moral correctness of the accepted contents is superfluous. For the ideas of commitment, responsibility, and coherence which are supposed to be captured with the notion of acceptance we do not need to presuppose a moral belief. In other words, epistemic reasons, i. e., beliefs, are not the only reasons on which the adoption of an attitude with these characteristics can be founded. In addition, the separation of the attitudes of acceptance and belief shows how those who do not believe in the moral truth or falsehood of some norm are in a better position to evaluate it than those affected by such beliefs. The rational way of judging whether or not a normative content should be accepted is in conformity with a normative theory.[64] If the reasons one takes into account in the decision are those stipulated by a normative theory, then it may well be that an agent has reasons to reject certain norms, and indeed comes to reject them, despite the fact that he finds himself unable to shed his belief in them. Or, *vice versa*, he may find reasons to accept a norm and indeed come to accept it, although he is unable to convince himself, i. e., to acquire the belief that that norm is a moral truth. Understood in this sense, the acceptance of a norm always ensures a rational attitude not based on prejudices or unjustified beliefs of the agent in question.

The concept of acceptance, when disconnected from moral beliefs, in no way affects the factual and ideal connections that may exist between law and morality. But it does not allow one to stipulate a *conceptual* relationship between them.[65] In contrast, the narrow concept of acceptance leads to the conclusion that there is a necessary relationship between these two normative orders. In fact, the introduction of a meaning of acceptance necessarily linked to moral beliefs transforms this conclusion about the nexus between law and morality into a *petitio principii*.[66]

---

[63] Cohen, L. Jonathan, AB, pp. 386 ff.

[64] The acceptance of a theory cannot be justified in the same sense as the acceptance of certain rules of conduct, namely, in conformity with such a theory. The very notion of justification presupposes the prior choice of a theory which provides the axioms from which the justification proceeds. For instance, the standards stipulated by a moral theory are the criteria of validity for a moral evaluation, and therefore they are not themselves justifiable value-judgments, at least not in the same sense as the judgments justified in reference to the former. Cf. Pap, Arthur, The Verifiability of Value Judgments, op. cit., p. 183.

[65] On these different kinds of relations, cf., e. g., Alexy, Robert, On Necessary Relations Between Law and Morality, op. cit. In this and in other works, Alexy holds that the connection between law and morality is neither empirical nor normative, but conceptual.

[66] Note that even if one admits that the foundation of acceptance is a moral belief this still leaves open the question of whether this fact proves that there is a necessary connection between law and *ideal* morality, or only between law and *positive* morality. The legal naturalist must claim that it is a connection between law and ideal or critical morality. Whether this thesis can be upheld merely on the argument that acceptants do

Finally, it should be noted that the moral definition of acceptance excludes an important variable for the comparison between different legal systems, between successive instances of one and the same system, and between different attitudes towards it. In contrast, if one admits that acceptance is an attitude that can be adopted for various reasons, it becomes possible to compare the kinds of acceptance different sets of norms receive, or the same set of norms in different points in time, or the acceptance a set of norms receives from different sectors of society. Such comparisons are not possible if acceptance by definition presupposes the belief in moral correctness.

The notion of acceptance sketched in this chapter shows how the distinction indicated by Hart, between those who merely obey and those who are committed to a system, can be maintained without the need to appeal to moral beliefs. The acceptance of a norm is an attitude which constitutes a possible explanatory reason for actions performed in conformity with it. This distinguishes acceptance from belief, assumption, and internalization. Because of the voluntary nature of acceptance, it is possible to construct a normative theory about what should be regarded as reasons which justify adopting it. That is, it opens up the possibility of establishing a basis from which acceptance may be required or criticized. The notions of a duty of, or a justificatory reason for (or against), acceptance are meaningless if that attitude cannot be deliberately adopted, i. e., if it is not independent of beliefs. This is the most important feature the distinctions introduced above reveal: a normative theory about the conditions in which a norm may or ought to be accepted makes absolutely no sense if acceptance is characterized as necessarily based on a moral belief.

have some moral belief is questionable. On this point, cf. Caracciolo's critique of Garzón Valdés's opinion in Caracciolo, Ricardo, L'argomento della credenza morale, op. cit., pp. 97-110.

CHAPTER VI

LEGAL JUSTIFICATION AND REASONS FOR ACTION

1. Introduction

The task of justification accompanies judicial decision-making at the point of the creation of general norms as well as at the moment of their application in particular decisions. In this chapter I will treat only questions concerning the latter, i. e., the justification of judicial decisions.

Most contemporary studies about the justification of the individual decisions of judges rely primarily on the notions of 'practical argument' and 'reason for action'. Generally, it is the meaning given to these terms which enables one to present the justificatory activity of legal officials as a cogent proof of the necessary connection between law and morality.[1] Concerning this topic, the following discussion will begin with a consideration of the distinction between internal and external justification, the difficulties this classification entails, and the models of practical arguments applicable in the different cases. I will then analyse in some detail one of the central assumptions of the argument of the necessary connection between law and morality, namely, the postulate of the unity of practical reasoning. Here, I will mainly refer to Carlos Nino's contribution to the controversy. The application of the concepts spelled out in the first section will, finally, allow me to indicate some difficulties for the possibility of reaching the conclusion Nino claims to have proved.

2. The General Idea of Justification

The notion of justification was discussed in Chapter II of this book. Reviewing briefly what I have said there, it should be recalled that a common feature of the different concepts of justification is that they all allude to a relation between a n element that is to be justified and an element on which the justification is based (thus, the set of the latter elements can be seen as constituting a 'dominium' to which the set of the former is the 'condominium')[2] Another feature apparently shared by the different concepts is that the dominium of a justification always refers to *reasons*. As has been pointed out before, however, there are different kinds of justification each of which is linked to a different meaning of the word 'reason'.

---

[1] The thesis that in the justification of judicial decisions, especially concerning the application of the law, the necessary connection between law and morality clearly reveals itself is defended by many authors, with a variety of arguments. In Chapter IV I have presented some of those arguments in the context of an analysis of the normativity of law.

[2] Caracciolo, Ricardo, El sistema jurídico. Problemas actuales, op. cit., pp. 75-77.

From a pragmatic as well as from a semantic point of view, two meanings of justification – a formal and a substantive one – have been distinguished. As acts, they differ in their internal aspects as well as in their results, although they have the same external appearance. Acts of justification are performed by presenting arguments. Formal justification requires only the *assumption* of a normative statement as a premise-reason of the argument. Substantive justification requires *acceptance* of a normative statement as a substantive reason for action. Both notions of reason are justificatory, although in different senses. And from the perspective adopted here, both are independent of the explanatory notion of reason.

In this context, two considerations are fundamental. The first regards the process-product ambiguity of justification, that is, the distinction between justification as an act and justification as a set of statements resulting from that act.[3] The second concerns the distinction between justification in the subjective sense, i. e. the act of justification (including its result), and justification in the objective sense, i. e. the relationship existing between the connected contents. This last distinction with respect to the notion of justification runs parallel to another one applying to the notion of reason. From a subjective point of view, in order to justify something formally one invokes as a foundation what one considers to be a premise-reason, i. e., a norm. In contrast, in order to justify something in the substantive sense, one invokes as a foundation what one holds to be a substantive reason for action, i. e., that there is a duty to perform a certain action. In both cases, the agent could be wrong. That is, he may not have invoked a norm at all, although he believes to have done so; or the norm he invoked may not be a substantive reason for action, in accordance with some normative theory, even though the agent accepts it as such. The fact that the term 'justification' refers either to an action (in speaking or writing), or to a resulting set of statements, or to a (formal or substantive) relationship between meaning contents suggests a need of special caution in its use. A theoretical study, in any case, should not use the term with all the ambiguity it has in ordinary usage. Within legal theory, the confusion of those meanings has been shown to be one of the main causes for the mistake made by legal realism in its thesis about the justification of judicial decisions. Later I will show that a similar confusion also affects the thesis of current approaches to the same problem.

3. Justifying a Judicial Decision

Judges normally solve individual cases by dictating a sentence. A sentence includes a set of decisions which can be classified in different groups: for instance, decisions about factual or decisions about normative questions, and among the latter, decisions regarding general or individual duties, personal duties of the judge or third-party duties, etc. Each one of these decisions may or may not be justified. The following discussion will be concerned only with the justification of individual norms which terminate a judicial controversy. As a prototypical example, I will take the justification of a duty, imposed on a third party, to perform a certain action. Note that, strictly speaking, judges do not

---

[3] Cf. Caracciolo, Ricardo, Justificación y pertenencia, op. cit.; cf. also Chapter II, sects. 3.a and 3.b.

justify actions, but meaningful – propositional or normative – contents.[4] In the present case, what is justified is a normative statement qualifying a certain behaviour as obligatory.

In the literature on judicial justification a difference between internal and external justification is usually made.[5] Unfortunately, the concepts are vague, and it is not clear what distinction they are actually thought to capture. Generally, it is understood that the final individual decision is grounded in an *internal* justification, whereas the premises of that internal justification are grounded in an *external* justification. But this is not always the criterion used for the classification. It is a rather common idea that one and the same individual norm issued by a judge must, at the same time, be internally and externally justified.

(i) The criterion of the externality of the premises: The terms 'internal justification' and 'external justification' suggest that the distinction is based on the internal or external nature of the dominium of the relationship. But the criterion for qualifying those reasons as internal or external is not clear. If, for instance, the judicial sentence is taken as the relevant parameter, then an internal justification would be a justification based on the premises recognized by the judge, and an external justification would be a justification based on reasons which are external to the sentence, but which may nevertheless belong to the legal system.[6] If, in contrast, one takes as the parameter the set of norms and principles of the legal system, then an external justification necessarily is one based on extra-legal reasons. The distinction between internal and external justifications would, in that case, lead to a classification which takes into account the substantive content of the argument. Internal justification would then be specifically legal justification; whereas an external justification would be a justification based on extra-legal standards such as political or moral directives. Usually, this last idea is the one underlying the distinction between those two kinds of justification.

The requirement that judicial decisions be externally justified is connected with the idea that the legal system is an open system with limited autonomy. Through this kind of justification it is shown that the legal argument is adequate with regard to a more encompassing normative system into which, it is assumed, the law ought to be integra-

---

[4] Cf. Alchourrón, Carlos and Eugenio Bulygin, Normative Systems, op. cit., pp. 169 f.

[5] Cf. Wróblewski, Jerzy, Legal decision and Its Justification, in: H. Hubien (ed.), Le raisonnement juridique, Proceedings of the World Congress on Legal and Social Philosophy, Brussels 1971, pp. 409-419; id., Legal Syllogism and Rationality of Judicial Decision, in: Rechtstheorie 5 (1974) pp. 33 f.

[6] Although it is an interesting matter, the internal-external distinction derived from this parameter has not received much attention from the authors who have treated this topic. After all, on this view, to identify the premises of an external justification amounts to identifying the norms which belong to the legal system. In order to do that, a criterion is needed, and, notably, that criterion cannot be the judge's own criterion of recognition. If the norms belonging to the system were simply the norms recognized by judges in their sentences, then the distinction between internal and external justification would entirely lose its sense. The norms which justify a decision internally would be precisely the same as the norms serving as premises for an external justification. In order to have a (legal) parameter for the justification of the premises of a judicial decision, one must have a criterion of identification for the norms of the system which does not refer to those norms directly recognized by the judges. Cf. Caracciolo, Ricardo, El sistema jurídico. Problemas actuales, op. cit., p. 82.

ted.[7] It is a widely shared opinion that the encompassing normative system must be the moral system. On this view, internal justification is justification relative to legal premises. External justification, in turn, shows that the legal premises satisfy moral norms. Since the moral system involved here is that of critical or ideal morality, this kind of justification ensures that the strictly legal internal justification is substantively correct.[8]

(ii) The criterion of the difficulty of the case: Usually, internal and external justification are linked to so-called easy cases and hard cases. The criteria for distinguishing an easy case from a hard case are controversial.[9] According to Manuel Atienza's proposal, hard cases are those in which there are discrepancies in the formulation of the premises. This may happen because of different evaluations of factual evidence, because of different interpretations of applicable norms, or because of disagreement about which norms are applicable to the case in question.[10] According to Atienza, they are „cases in which the task of establishing the factual and/or the normative premise requires new reasoning which may or may nor be deductive".[11] Starting from this distinction, Atienza asserts that the judge's task of justification is different in simple, routine cases and in hard cases. He calls justifications of the first kind *internal justification*, and those of the second kind *external justification*. On this view, although the classification seems to be the same, what matters is not the nature of the premises. The difference now lies in the concept of justification itself and in the kind of argument used for it:

> „Internal justification is only a matter of deductive logic, but in external justification we must go beyond logic in the strict sense. This second kind of justification is what [...] theories of legal reasoning are basically concerned with."[12]

---

[7] The limited-autonomy thesis according to which under certain circumstances judges should resort to moral premises is defended by most of the authors who have analysed the problem of judicial justification as, for example, Robert Alexy, Manuel Atienza, Neil MacCormick, and many others. A different opinion is maintained by Ronald Dworkin.

[8] This conception presupposes a distinction between the principles of positive morality and those of an ideal morality. Generally, the latter are thought to be *valid*, while the former are those *de facto accepted* by some social group. Carlos Nino compares this distinction with the one we could make between positive or actual science and ideal science. The propositions of actual science are *believed* to be true, although they not necessarily *are* true; those of ideal science are true even if no-one believes them. Cf. Nino, Carlos S., The Ethics of Human Rights, op. cit., p. 64.

[9] The literature on this question is abundant. Different ways of drawing the line between the two kinds of cases are proposed, and there is no consensus on the matter. Despite the on-going disagreement about its meaning, the terms proposed by Dworkin are widely used. Cf. Dworkin, Ronald, Hard Cases, in: Harvard Law Review (1975), reprinted in: id., Taking Rights Seriously, op. cit., pp. 81-130.

[10] Cf. Atienza, Manuel, Tras la justicia. Una introducción al Derecho y al razonamiento jurídico, Barcelona: Ariel 1993, p. 24.

[11] Atienza, Manuel, Las razones del Derecho. Teorías de la argumentación jurídica, op. cit., pp. 45 f. Note that according to this criterion, the difficulty apparently cannot be attributed to generic or individual cases, but only to 'cases' in the sense of a lawsuit or trial. On the concept of 'case', cf. Alchourrón, Carlos and Eugenio Bulygin, Normative Systems, op. cit., pp. 21-34; Carrió, Genaro, Cómo estudiar y cómo argumentar un caso, Buenos Aires: Abeledo-Perrot 1987, pp. 22-42; Navarro, Pablo, Sistema jurídico, casos difíciles y conocimiento del Derecho, in: Doxa 14 (1993).

[12] Atienza, Manuel, Las razones del Derecho. Teoría de la argumentación jurídica, op. cit., p. 46.

Although this is a controversial topic, there is generally agreement that for the internal justification of a judicial decision the model of deductive reasoning applies.[13] This is not the case with respect to the model of reasoning applicable to external justification, on which there is an on-going controversy.[14]

There are, thus, several different questions involved in the distinction between internal and external justification which must not be confused. Under this label, we find discussions about *(i)* whether the reasons of judicial justification are internal or external to the system, *(ii)* whether or not it is a duty of the judge to ensure the moral correctness of the argument, and *(iii)* the kinds of (logical or non-logical) arguments adequate for each kind of justification.

In order to avoid this ambiguity, I will discard the distinction between internal and external justification and consider, separately, some problems concerning the justification of the individual norms issued by a judge and of the premises of judicial arguments. In both cases, the discussion will be connected to the different notions of reason for action.

4. Justifying the Conclusion of a Judicial Decision

What kind of justification is required of a judge? What concept of justification applies in the reconstruction of a judicial sentence as a justified decision? These are the questions I will attempt to answer in this chapter.

Earlier, I distinguished two kinds of justification: formal and substantive. I also emphasized that they can be seen from two perspectives: the subjective and the objective one. Based on these distinctions, the justification of a judicial sentence can be understood in four different senses. In legal theory, however, only two of these have received major attention. Some conceptions hold that an objective formal justification is necessary and sufficient; it must be possible, that is, to reconstruct the content of a sentence by way of an argument in the logical sense. Others think that, in addition, a substantive justification, at least in the subjective sense, is indispensable, which means that in their formal justifications the judges also accept the norms, that they are committed to them as reasons for action and therefore perform an act of justification in the substantive sense. Later, I will consider all four alternatives; but I will mainly review those answers arising from the two most often discussed options.

If one adopts a concept of justification in the formal and objective sense, then for a sentence to be justified the final part which states the legal consequence must follow

[13] This question is discussed under several aspects as, for example, whether the premises may be norms or must be normative propositions, what kind of logic is applicable, whether the deductive model has descriptive or reconstructive relevance, etc. As an example of such a discussion, cf. Alchourrón, Carlos and Bulygin, Eugenio, Limits of logic and legal reasoning, op. cit.

[14] Among the models thought to be applicable to this kind of justification, we find, e. g., the reason-comparing practical argument mentioned by Joseph Raz, the ideological model chosen by Vincent Wellman, the coherentist model suggested by Aulis Aarnio and Nilo Jääskinen, etc. Manuel Atienza reviews several models proposed by different theories of argumentation. Cf. Atienza, Manuel, Las razones del Derecho. Teorías de la argumentación jurídica, op. cit.

logically from the premises invoked by the judge. This idea is one of the theses of positivist legal theory; but it is also accepted by advocates of other approaches.[15] As Eugenio Bulygin observes:

„[I]n a well-grounded sentence the solution is a logical consequence of (can be deduced from) the premises, that is, the general norm applied to the case and the description of the facts (plus the definitions), all taken together."[16]

For this conception, the justification of an individual norm issued by a judge is linked to the performance of a practical argument in the logical sense. In this kind of argument, the applicable legal provisions are normative premises which are sufficient for the justification of the final decision. This proposal has given rise to two severe objections against positivism. They aim to show

(i) that the logical model of a practical argument cannot be applied to judicial justification, and
(ii) that for such a justification to be valid, one must refer to moral norms.

(i) Legal realism denies that it is possible for a judicial sentence to be a decision that is justified according to a pattern of subsumption. On this view, the process by which judges arrive at a solution cannot be reconstructed as a deductive argument. It does not start from the general norms of the legal system (as premises) and then proceed to an individual norm (as conclusion). The decisions taken by judges are determined by irrational attitudes which for the purpose of being presented in a sentence are merely rationalized. According to the realistic thesis, rather than following rules, judges always decide as they see fit. According to legal realism, this proves that the logical model of practical reasoning is inapplicable in the justification of judicial decisions.

It has been repeatedly noted that this conclusion is based on a wrong interpretation. Bulygin observes that realism here commits the mistake of

„confusing the logical with the psychological level. One thing is the logical relationship between the norms (mentioned in the premises) and the final legal consequence established in the sentence, and quite another the psychological (causal) motivation of the judge".[17]

---

[15] Some authors, however, reject this possibility. Vincent Wellman, for instance, points out several problems with the application of the deductive model to the justification of a judicial sentence. One of them is the fact that a deductive argument can be formulated from propositions which may be true or false. Norms, he says, do not have the proper logical form for being part of such a kind of argument. If a judicial justification must refer to norms, its reconstruction therefore cannot be deductive. Cf. Wellman, Vincent, Practical Reasoning and Judicial Justification: Toward an Adequate Theory, op. cit. (hereafter, 'PRJJ').

[16] Bulygin, Eugenio, Sentencia judicial y creación de Derecho, in: Alchourrón, Carlos E. and Eugenio Bulygin, Análisis Lógico y Derecho, op. cit., p. 360.

[17] Bulygin, Eugenio, El concepto de vigencia en Alf Ross, in: Revista del Colegio de Abogados de La Plata, pp. 1-16, reprinted in: Alchourrón, C. E. and E. Bulygin, Análisis Lógico y Derecho, op. cit., pp. 339-353, here pp. 349 f.

Referring to a similar model, Atienza points out that the mistake of realism is that it confuses the context of discovery and the context of justification:

„Thus, one thing is the procedure by which a premise or conclusion is established, and another the procedure by which that premise or conclusion is justified.“[18]

In other words, what is at issue is the difference between the explanation of the act of decision performed by a judge and the justification of the content of that decision.[19]

According to what has been said in Chapter III, the explanation as well as the justification of an action have the structure of so-called 'practical arguments', and both are related to psychological processes with the same name. In a non-logical sense, generally, what is called 'practical arguments' are patterns representing different kinds of relationships with theoretical or normative ends. As has been observed, the model of a practical argument used in the reconstruction of the psychological process explaining action is a theoretical schema which mentions an empirical relationship between means and ends. It is a teleological model which shows the instrumental relationship existing between the internal and the external aspect of an action, or between the action and the elements which explain it. In contrast, the model of a practical argument applied in the justification of judicial decisions refers to a logical relation of entailment between statements. The implementation of such a 'practical argument' (logical schema) by a judge is performed through a psychological process which can be reconstructed in the form of a 'practical argument' in another sense (theoretical scheme).

Realists confuse the practical argument in the sense of a valid pattern of inference with the practical argument in the sense of a theoretical schema reconstructing action. At least they don't see that when positivism refers to the application of a deductive practical argument, it does not mean to reconstruct the psychological process going on inside the judge, but the relationship the content of his final decision must have to the premises he uses.

Realism attempts to show to the legal positivist that judicial decisions are not deductively justified and that logic and rationality are of little relevance in the practical reasoning of judges. If we pay attention to the different concepts of practical arguments we can disentangle the problems realism confounds. The application of a *teleological* practical argument may enable one to show that judicial decisions cannot be explained

[18] Atienza, Manuel, Tras la justicia. Una introducción al Derecho y al razonamiento jurídico, op. cit., p. 125.

[19] Note that the realist thesis can also be understood differently. As Caracciolo has suggested, realism has drawn attention to the circularity of the criterion for the recognition of norms: The norms of a system S are those which are recognized in judicial sentences which, in turn, are recognized as belonging to the system only if they apply the norms of S. Thus, a sentence is always adequately justified in the norms of S, whatever the interpretation of those norms. Cf. Caracciolo, Ricardo, El sistema jurídico. Problemas actuales, op. cit., p. 82. From this point of view, one can say that realism does not confuse the logical and the psychological level, but instead the problem of formal justification with that of the substantive correctness of the argument. In fact, if recognition by the judges is the only criterion for the identification of the norms of a legal system, it is impossible to criticize the premises recognized by the judges as incorrect or as a bad interpretation of the norms of the system in question. From a legal point of view, a judicial argument would always have to be considered substantively correct. This problem leads to a critique of the criterion of judicial recognition, but it is completely independent of the thesis of formal justification defended by legal positivism.

on the basis of the acceptance of rules. That is, it may be possible to show, by reconstructing the action of a judge, that his decisions are arbitrary and have been adopted in disregard of established norms. But that has nothing at all to do with an application of the *logical* model of practical reasoning. Logic can still be applied in the justification of the content of a judge's decisions.[20]

(ii) Another critique of positivism's deductive conception of judicial justification is not intended to prove that judges actually do not follow norms or that logic is irrelevant for judicial justification. On the contrary, positivism is reproached for failing to grasp all the implications of the application of an argument in the logical sense. More specifically, on this view positivism does not see that the elaboration of an argument of that kind implicitly presupposes an appeal to moral norms. According to Carlos Nino, such norms are necessarily present in the practical arguments of judges, and this can be seen by making explicit the reasons for which a judge accepts the premises of his argument:[21]

„Elsewhere, however, I have rejected the idea that legal norms, understood as deontic judgments, can be autonomous reasons for justifying decisions. The arguments I offered there can be summarized as follows: if the judgments in question are *accepted* as premises of the practical argument because of their content, then they are indistinguishable from moral judgments ... In contrast, if legal judgments are *accepted* because of their origin, then – since this origin is a fact which as such does not determine the *acceptance* of a norm – there must be an underlying normative principle making that origin relevant for that acceptance."[22]

Based on this idea, Nino concludes that strictly legal justification is impossible. Justification, in his view, is always necessarily moral. And he reaches this conclusion by different ways.[23] In the present case, two different meanings of the term 'practical argument' are confounded in the argument given. In contrast to the realists, Nino does not confuse the logical and the teleological patterns, but the logical argument and the psychological process of its implementation. The *acceptance* Nino mentions is the psychological attitude of a judge who is committed to certain premises – specifically, to the norms he applies. This is an attitude adopted voluntarily and, therefore, adopted always for some reason which explains it. Nino's formulation refers to the 'practical argument' understood as the empirical course that runs from the *acceptance* of the norms which operate as the premises of a logical argument (and the explanatory reasons which determine that acceptance) to the *acceptance* of an individual norm constituting its conclu-

---

[20] Note that this kind of argument against realism is different and independent from the one presented by Hart in his reply to legal realism. Hart defends a thesis which, in his view, can be proved empirically. He holds that in most cases judicial decisions „are reached ... by genuine effort to conform to rules consciously taken as guiding standards of decision"; cf. Hart, H. L. A., The Concept of Law, op. cit., p. 141. On this point, Hart, just like realism, advocates a psychological thesis about the reasons of judges.

[21] Cf. on this proposal the discussion in Moreso, José Juan, Pablo E. Navarro and Cristina Redondo, Argumentación jurídica, lógica y decisión judicial, op. cit., and Nino, Carlos S., Respuesta a J. J. Moreso, P. E. Navarro y M. C. Redondo, op. cit.

[22] Nino, Carlos S., El constructivismo ético, op. cit., p. 30.

[23] As we have seen in Chapter IV, Nino also says that this position is logically necessary if one wants to be able to draw genuine deontic conclusions.

sion. His thesis says that if we study the arguments through which judges come to *accept* legal norms, we will find that they necessarily presuppose moral norms.

The thesis of positivism asserts that in order to justify a judicial decision, besides the respective definitions and the description of the facts, only legal norms are needed. This idea is the result of an analysis of the notion of justification, not an empirical proposition about the reasons which explain why judges *accept* certain norms. Nor is it a moral thesis about the substantive reasons which should justify that act of *acceptance*. The positivist thesis simply does not refer to the reasons (whether explanatory or justificatory) for *acceptance*. And, therefore, it cannot be criticized for not accounting for them. Even if Nino's suggestion were true, i. e., if in fact judges necessarily would presuppose moral reasons in their *acceptance*, it would not follow that legal norms are not sufficient for the deductive justification of final decisions. Besides, the fact that the reason which explains the *acceptance* of legal norms is, in turn, the *acceptance* of moral norms does not convert the legal norms in moral norms, nor does it require that the argument refer to such norms – just as, for example, if someone *accepts* the axioms of a mathematical system for religious reasons (norms) this does not make it plausible to infer that the mathematical arguments based on those axioms must include religious norms, or that the mathematical axioms are indistinguishable from such norms.

In conclusion, then, if one admits, as Nino does, that the model of deductive reasoning is applicable to the justification of a judge's conclusion, then an indispensable minimal condition is the idea of formal justification. And for that, the appeal to legal norms (plus the corresponding factual statements and definitions) from which the conclusion follows is sufficient. This thesis implies neither a psychological nor a moral assertion. It does not say that judges consistently follow general rules. Neither does it say that judges accept legal norms for moral reasons. The judge's psychological reasoning, and the beliefs and other internal attitudes supporting it, are relevant for the study of justification in the subjective sense and, eventually, for its substantive evaluation. But all that has nothing to do with logical justification. Confounding these concepts of justification means confounding the nature of the topics involved.

If one takes into account the different meanings of 'justification' and 'practical argument' spelled out in the first section, it becomes perfectly clear that the positivist thesis has nothing to do with those presented in reply by its critics. The positivists' thesis about judicial justification refers to justification in the formal and objective sense. From that perspective, what is at issue is whether the model of an argument in the logical sense is applicable here. It has nothing to say about justification from a judge's subjective point of view, that is, about what judges accept or believe. The positivistic approach to judicial justification also is no normative proposal concerning the reasons which *ought* to be invoked. It does not say that legal norms are substantive reasons for action. In other words, it is not a theory about substantive justification in the objective sense.

The objection presented in the above-quoted passage by Carlos Nino is based on the idea that the judges' acceptance inevitably presupposes that moral norms must intervene in their reasoning. This brings the subjective concept of justification into play. But note that, by definition, this concept is linked to the attitude of acceptance towards the norms used in the justification. In Nino's view, even when they intend to do only a formal justification, judges incur a moral commitment with the norms, i. e., they perform an action of substantive justification of their decisions. Thus, there is no formal justification without a substantive justification (in the subjective sense). In the last chapter, I have already discussed the need for such a kind of commitment with norms, which has its root in an idea of Hart. According to his proposal, the acceptance of certain standards as reasons for action is an indispensable condition for the existence of a legal system. The topic comes up again in the analysis of judicial justification because that is where, paradigmatically, that acceptance is manifested. According to most interpreters of Hart, the assertion that judges accept the norms they apply contains two decisive proofs against positivism. First, although positivists claim to defend the thesis that an objective formal justification is necessary *and* sufficient, they must assume that in performing such a justification judges also perform an act of substantive justification, accepting the norms as reasons for action. Secondly, since the accepted norms (reasons) impose duties on third parties (persons other than the one accepting them) the acceptance involved must necessarily be of a moral kind. Thus, apparently it has been shown that the formal justification positivists require presupposes a substantive justification in the subjective sense.

The argument according to which a justified sentence presupposes the performance of an act of substantive justification on the part of the judge can be rebutted in two ways. In the first place, it ignores the distinction between premise-reason and reason for action, and thus identifies the *assumption* of a premise, i. e., the formal acceptance of a statement (or a norm) with its substantive acceptance. And secondly, it ignores that even if a substantive justification were required, it could be simulated.

Those who agree that the reconstruction of a justified sentence involves an act of substantive justification refer to the psychological reasoning of a judge, i. e., the reasoning a judge accepts in order to reach a conclusion. However, the thesis they seek to defend is not of a psychological nature. They do not mean to show that a high percentage of judges does actually have certain mental attitudes. Approaches such as that of Nino, just like positivism, claim to be of a logico-conceptual nature.[24] They hold that in order to justify a sentence the applied legal norms must be accepted as moral reasons, i. e., as substantive reasons for action, and that, therefore, without such acceptance, there is no justification.

If the thesis is presented in that way, the only thing to be said is that it constitutes a change in the conceptual point of view – a shift of attention from formal to substantive justification. But the proposal is not framed in these terms. It is not seen as a new conception, independent of the positivist thesis, but as a refutation of it. And this is a claim which confounds two meanings of justification, of practical argument and of reason. In Carlos Nino's conception, an appropriate premise-reason, i. e., an adequate foundation of a practical statement, is at the same time a substantive reason for action. This also implies, as has already been observed, that the distinction between the acceptance of norms as premises (assumption) and their acceptance as substantive reasons for action is lost. By posing as a refutation, the question of the substantive justification of judicial

[24] It should be noted that, although Nino has been taken as an example, the same thesis is maintained by numerous authors, among them all those who think that the acceptance of norms on the part of judges presupposes an attitude of a moral kind. To name but a few: Philip Soper, Joseph Raz, Ernesto Garzón Valdés, Manuel Atienza, Juan Ruiz Manero, etc.

decisions, displaces the debate on the justification presented by positivism, rather than broadening it. If all formal justification is, at the same time, also a substantive justification, the distinction between the two concepts makes no sense. The unification of the notion of justification implies that the distinction between formal and substantive aspects is regarded as irrelevant. Only if the irrelevance of that distinction is presupposed can the above argument be presented as an objection against positivism. Otherwise, one would have to admit that it concerns another question than that analysed by positivism.

Finally, an important consequence of that approach deserves to be mentioned. If it is understood as the replacement of one notion of justification by another, then the result is that only judges who accept the norms as substantive reasons can justify their decisions. Those who do not accept the invoked norms in their substance have given no justification, even though their arguments (in the formal sense) may be indistinguishable from those of judges who do accept the norms in that way. This difficulty alone is already enough to reject the proposal.

Given the purposes connected with the office of a judge, the attitude of acceptance is generally attributed to those who participate in it, that is, our linguistic rules in this context permit us to impute to a judge the action of substantive justification. In that sense, those who hold that judicial justification implies an act of substantive justification seem to emphasize the existence of a linguistic convention to the effect that the acceptance of the norms they invoke as reasons for action is attributed to all judges, and no evidence to the contrary is admitted, *even when that acceptance may in fact not exist.* That is, in accordance with linguistic practice, whenever a judge invokes a legal norm in order to ground a decision, the action of a substantive justification is imputed to her, regardless of the attitude she has or ought to have. If such a linguistic convention exists, the assertion that judicial justification is a substantive justification is true – but in that case it does not refer to what judges actually do or ought to do, but to the linguistic practices of the respective community. In contrast, if the thesis is to be descriptive of what judges do, then it would need empirical corroboration in each single case of justification. As has been pointed out in Chapter II, the feature distinguishing an act of formal justification from an act of substantive justification is the agent's internal attitude. And to find out what that attitude is, i. e., whether or not there is acceptance, presents serious difficulties.

Finally, it must be said that authors like Carlos Nino hold that the reconstruction of a judicial sentence implies a substantive justification not only in the subjective, but also in the objective sense.[25] Generally, it is said that such a justification is required in order to ensure that the premises of the justificatory argument are correct. This question will be treated in the next two sections.

5. Justifying the Normative Premises of a Judicial Decision

The problems analysed under this label are different from those about the logical justification of individual norms issued in a judicial sentence. The question in this case is

---

[25] Cf. Nino, Carlos S., Respuesta a J. J. Moreso, P. E. Navarro y M. C. Redondo, op. cit.

whether the premise-reasons invoked in a sentence are adequate as substantive reasons for action.[26] From an objective point of view, the substantive justification of an individual judicial decision requires that the premises used in its foundation are materially correct. But, does the notion of 'justified judicial decision' presuppose a duty to offer a justification in that sense?

In order to avoid being imprecise, it is important to state explicitly that:

(i) the requirement of a substantive justification is generally understood as a requirement of a moral justification, where 'moral' must be read in the ideal or critical sense. It is, therefore, equivalent to the requirement of a true or correct justification;

(ii) none of the notions of 'practical argument' mentioned as strategies for ensuring or reaching that correctness is a practical argument in the logical sense. Rather, they are schemes the application of which enables one to weigh and assess the reasons involved, for instance, through the implementation of a certain procedure, or through relations of force or weight, or means-ends relations existing between them.

The foundation of the requirement of a substantive justification lies in the idea that legal arguments must be based on guaranteed premises. This idea, in turn, is a corollary of a more general principle of rationality according to which all justification must be based on reasons which are themselves justified.[27] For this kind of justification, the application of the deductive model is not considered to be useful. A practical argument in the logical sense only serves for a formal concept of justification and does not ensure that the premises are substantive reasons for action. On this, two positions deserve to be mentioned. One of them completely abandons the formal concept of justification and replaces it with a substantive concept. For this position, it makes no sense to treat the justification of the conclusion and that of the premises separately. By definition, the conclusion will only be justified if the premises are too. That means that there can be no genuine justification if the premises are incorrect.[28] The other position holds that the question of whether the premises are adequate gives rise to a kind of justification to be

---

26 In what follows, references to reasons without any further specification are always to substantive justificatory reasons.

27 Nilo Jääskinen calls this conception the 'positive notion of justification'. He sees a parallel between the concepts of justification employed in legal theory and the concepts of justification coming from the theory of knowledge, and he holds that the positive notion of justification corresponds to the concept used by those theories of knowledge which assert the existence of epistemologically basic, i. e., 'directly evident'. or 'self-justifying' propositions. Such propositions, on this view, constitute the basis for all other human knowledge. This position can be applied to the justification of normative statements. In that case, it must be recognized that there are certain basic normative principles which ground the correctness of all other statements of that kind.

These theories are opposed by coherence theories of knowledge. In their view, there are no epistemologically basic propositions and, therefore, the justification of a statement does not presuppose them. Instead, a statement is justified when it is coherent with the other statements accepted by the same person (positive coherence theories) or when it is not inconsistent with them (negative coherence theories). This idea too can be applied to the justification of normative statements. For example, Aulis Aarnio and Neil MacCormick can be qualified as advocates of a positive coherence theory. Nilo Jääskinen himself, following John Pollock, attempts to defend the application of the negative version of coherence theory. Cf. Jääskinen, Nilo, External Justification of Propositions in Legal Science, in: E. Bulygin et al. (eds.), Man, Law and Modern Forms of Life, Dordrecht: D. Reidel 1985, pp. 224-229.

28 Cf. Nino, Carlos, S., Respuesta a J. J. Moreso, P. E. Navarro y M. C. Redondo, op. cit., p. 262.

added to the formal justification of a judge's conclusion.[29] For this new type of justification, the application of the deductive argument is not entirely discarded, but the problem it is now supposed to solve is a moral problem which cannot be solved exclusively by a justification in the logical sense. In any case, whether understood as an additional justification or as the only one relevant in judicial decisions, a substantive justification requires the correctness of the factual as well as of the normative premises of the argument offered by a judge.

In this section, I will only consider the problem of the justification of the normative premises of a sentence. The question whether they are correct can be answered from different criteria. Some classical natural-law theories, for example, suggest that the premises must be in accord with a particular normative (political, moral, or religious) code, or that they must be instrumentally useful for certain ends. In contemporary moral philosophy, confidence in practical reason has located the criterion of correctness in the very idea of practical reasoning itself. According to this position, it is a necessary (and in some cases also a sufficient) condition for the choice of the correct premises that they must have been obtained as a conclusion of an appropriate practical argument.

In many legal processes, the need for a substantive justification of the chosen premises does not arise[30] – for instance, when the parties and the judge identify the applicable law through common criteria of interpretation and there is no conflict between norms thought to be applicable (or the criteria used for solving such conflicts are uncontroversial). Although it *can* always be asked whether the normative premises are correct, in fact this is done only when there is disagreement about the normative interpretation. When this is the case, two questions must be answered:

(i) Is it possible to determine *rationally* which one of two conflicting proposals is the morally correct option?

(ii) When there is a conflict in the interpretation of the law, what is the criterion judges should use in order to ensure that the right premises are chosen?

The answer to the first question depends on the meta-ethical theory one adopts, and involves a particular conception of reasons for action. The answer to the second question depends on one's theory of normative ethics.

(i) The possibility of a *rational* answer to the question about the moral correctness of a norm depends, among other things, on the position one has with respect to the existence of reasons for action in the substantive sense. Three possibilities can be mentioned. First, there is the skeptical position which rejects the existence of that kind of reasons. In the case of controversies about the correctness of a norm, the skeptic denies that the road to a solution lies in a search for reasons. Skepticism holds that the act of choice is not of a cognitive nature. Disagreements about norms or values are emotional disagreements and must be resolved as such. They cannot be overcome by searching for a correct or true answer, because there is no such thing. Discarding the existence of rea-

---

[29] Most proposed theories of legal argumentation fall into this category.

[30] Cf. Schauer, Frederick, Easy Cases, in: California Law Review 58 (1985).

sons means discarding the possibility of solving conflicts between norms in terms of their truth or correctness.

From the perspective of skepticism, the judge's question about the material justification of the premises has no rational answer. The only admissible description in terms of reasons is a description alluding to an incompatibility between premise-reasons which imposes the need for a decision. Once such a decision has been taken, it can be explained by its subjective components and formally justified relative to certain premises, like any other action. What cannot be rationally justified is that the content of the decision is *better* or *more just* than some other option. The substantive justification of a judicial decision, that is, cannot be rational.

Metaphysical realism is diametrically opposed to skepticism on the question of reasons. According to this conception, normative facts, and among them justificatory reasons for action, exist independently of all human perception and activity. Realists with respect to justificatory reasons admit their existence, just as realists with respect to empirical facts admit theirs. And if that normative world can be known, then it is also possible to find a correct solution to the problems posed on that level. Conflicts only indicate that there is a lack of knowledge about the reality and the hierarchy of objectively determined reasons.[31] The true normative theory enables one to know which decision is the correct, the best or the most just one.

Between these two extreme positions, as a third way, there is room for the proposal presented in the previous chapters. According to this point of view, moral conflict can be regarded as a theoretical problem. That is, there is a means for solving normative conflicts in an intersubjectively controllable way, without a need to believe in the truth or falsehood of statements about substantive reasons. The concept of reason for action is a theoretical concept. It is a notion stipulated in meta-ethical theory in order to refer to those data which ground normative discourse. Therefore, their conditions of existence depend on how they are conceived in each meta-ethical theory. For a realist theory, reasons exist independently of human beings. For a skeptical position, reasons don't exist at all. And for the proposal advocated in this book, they are entities which are relative to a normative theory:[32] a reason for action is a duty or a permission to act which is stipu-

---

[31] Not all realist conceptions assert the existence of objective hierarchies. Metaphysical realism with respect to moral facts is generally defined by a set of ontological, semantic and epistemic theses. The ontological thesis holds that such facts exist and that they are independent of people's attitudes or actions. The semantic thesis maintains that moral statements and terms refer to such moral facts, i. e., it is committed to a correspondence theory of truth. Finally, the epistemic thesis says that it is possible to obtain moral knowledge. Thus, realism must have a theory of the justification and discovery of moral truths. Cf. Moore, Michael, Moral Realism as the Best Explanation of Moral Experience, op. cit., pp. 4-11; also Smith, Michael, Realism, op. cit., pp. 171-173; Mackie, John L., The Subjectivity of Values, in: Geoffrey Sayre-McCord (ed.), Essays on Moral Realism, Ithaca, N. Y.: Cornell University Press 1988, pp. 95-118; Brink, David O., Externalist Moral Realism, op. cit., p. 24.

[32] Strictly speaking, this position could be called a 'constructivist' position, where this means that the existence of reasons for action depends on a human construct, namely, a theory. However, it seems preferable to avoid this label. Constructivism is a meta-ethical conception holding that moral facts depend on certain formal and substantive conditions of the practice of moral discourse. Cf. Nino, Carlos S., El constructivismo ético, op. cit., pp. 15 and 69-71. On this interpretation, moral theory attempts to reconstruct and account for the moral facts which result from human practice, and which are theory-independent. In contrast, on the

lated and justified by some normative theory.[33] A normative theory proposes a set of well-founded and hierarchically ordered duties and permissions of action. Its function is to determine, with the greatest possible precision, under what conditions a certain action must or may be performed, that is, under what conditions there is a reason for that action.[34] Hence, a normative theory is a proposal of a set of reasons for action in the substantive sense. Those reasons must serve as a parameter of criticism for the standards actually accepted. Besides, they must enable the consistent solution of conflicts between duties and permissions within its scope. From this point of view, a reason for action cannot be given outside of a normative theory. To *identify* a reason for action means to use some normative theory. Using a theory does not entail accepting it, just as accepting it does not entail believing in its truth. Throughout this book, I have not advocated a specific normative theory about duties or permissions of action, i. e., about what norms should be considered substantive reasons for action. Instead, I have proposed a meta-ethical conception about the meaning of that terms and the conditions of existence of the entities it refers to.

(ii) When there is a conflict in the interpretation of the law, what is the criterion judges ought to use in order to ensure that the chosen premises are correct? From a methodological point of view, the answer to this question can be seen either as part of a conception of normative ethics, or as part of legal theory itself.[35] Regardless of how that methodological issue is approached, the question leads to the internal point of view of some normative conception. From a positivist ideology, a correct justification is a justification according to law. Legal norms must be applied and obeyed.[36] When there is a conflict, the question of which is the best premise must be answered within the con-

---

position proposed here, justificatory reasons in the substantive sense are duties and permissions constituted by a theory which does not necessarily reconstruct a moral practice.

[33] The idea that reasons are relative to a theory must not be confused with the thesis that they are relative to some cultural or social environment. For a communitarian meta-ethics, for instance, everything must depend on a prior conception of the good which, in turn, is incomprehensible outside of the respective community. A reason for action, i. e., that which indicates what should or may be done, depends on the communitarian conception of the good. In contrast, the position I am advocating here asserts that all must depend on a theory, regardless of whether it is conceived as universally valid or restricted to some social group.

[34] The conditions a proposal must satisfy in order to constitute a normative theory depend on what an adequate epistemological theory for the respective field stipulates. What exactly the epistemological criteria of adequacy are is beyond the limits of this study. In any case, the conception of reasons for action followed here does not imply that any normative proposal is a normative theory, i. e., a set of reasons for action. However, it *excludes* the possibility that there is a true normative theory based on external reasons. To accept that possibility means to adopt metaphysical realism about reasons.

[35] According to a positivistic methodological position, it is the function of a legal theory to describe and explain the law, but not to indicate what judges ought to do with it. On this view, it is not the legal theorist's task to answer the question about what judges should do in case of conflict. The opposite position holds that every legal theory must have a descriptive and a normative part. One of the purposes of the normative part of such a theory is to help the judges in their task of applying the law, among other things, by recommending adequate ways for ensuring the correctness of their justifications. Cf. Dworkin, Ronald, Taking Rights Seriously, op. cit., pp. vii-ix.

[36] On positivism as an ideology, cf. Bobbio, Norberto, Positivismo jurídico, in: id., El problema del positivismo jurídico, op. cit., pp. 46-55.

fines of the legal system. A judge is an official of a social institution and the institution has its own rules. The moral duty to support a decision in exclusively legal reasons is the basic axiom of ideological positivism and, therefore, its main criterion for the correctness of a justificatory argument. This commitment to the established system implies that the justification of the correctness of the premises is, in the last instance, based on a principle of authority. A norm is the most adequate one when it best accords with established principles. An important consequence can be drawn from this ethical position. It admits that the legal system is a set of substantively justified standards. Legal norms, that is, are conceived as a source of authentic duties, i. e., as reasons for action.

A conception opposed to ideological positivism is that of ideological naturalism.[37] From this standpoint, only *just* norms should be applied and obeyed. That is, only morally correct norms are substantive reasons for action. The fact that a decision derives from the norms of the legal system is irrelevant for its correctness. A judicial decision is justified correctly only if it is obtained from norms the content of which is morally adequate. All legal provisions, including those of an individual nature issued through a judicial sentence, must be subordinated to the standards of critical morality. According to this ideology, no matter how hard a case may be, the judge must search for the correct norms, and in that search must not be confined to the legal system itself. The need to ensure that the argument is substantively adequate is not restricted to hard cases, but to the very concept of justification.

On this common ground, each variant of natural-law theory erects the conditions a justification must satisfy in order to be valid (i. e., substantively correct). Carlos Nino, for example, asserts on this point:

„[A] justification invoking a legal norm thought to be valid, in order to give a foundation to that validity, must, in the last instance, depend on (a) norms which are (b) categorically accepted (c) because of their content and which (d) claim impartially to take into consideration the interests of all those affected, that is, on moral norms.“[38]

The assumption of this ideology also has a noteworthy consequence. According to it, the attempt to stipulate duties and rights on the part of legal systems is subordinated to the moral adequacy of their content.[39]

From an ideological perspective (whether positivist or naturalist), the question of justification is a substantive question of a moral nature. Different moral conceptions may be maintained; but in any case legal justification is always seen as a kind of moral justification. Currently, the naturalist proposal commands a wide consensus among legal philosophers. Concerning the justification of the premises of judicial decisions, either

---

[37] Cf. Bobbio, Norberto, Iusnaturalismo y positivismo jurídico, in: id., El problema del positivismo jurídico, op. cit., pp. 67-90 (Italian original: *Giusnaturalismo e Positivismo Giuridico*, Milan: Communità 1965).

[38] Nino, Carlos S., Respuesta a J. J. Moreso, P. E. Navarro y M. C. Redondo, op. cit., p. 262.

[39] However, under certain conditions something may be a legal duty without being, at the same time, a moral duty. According to Nino, for a legal or any other practical discourse to be able to generate reasons which justify actions and decisions they must move in a space left free by moral discourse, „either because it moves in another dimension, or because it defines an area of indifference, or because some defensible principle of moral discourse is applicable which permits that some subdiscourse produce its own justification“. Cf. Nino, Carlos S., Derecho, moral y política, op. cit., p. 80 (hereafter, 'DMP').

the thesis that a moral justification is needed (i. e., that justification must always be based on morally correct contents) or the thesis that a legal justification is insufficient in hard cases is maintained.[40] Most theories of argumentation argue in the latter direction. They generally base the correctness of a decision's content on some procedure of reasoning rather than on its conformity with some code of substantive contents. These schools are confident that the design of an adequate reasoning pattern determines the substantive correctness of a justification. The ideology of so-called 'theories of argumentation' corresponds neither to that of legal positivism nor to that of legal naturalism. A consistent ideological positivism must regard all justification supported in law as correct. And a consistent legal naturalism must admit that the law is totally irrelevant.[41] Generally, theories of argumentation attempt to harmonize the principles represented by the two ideologies. On the one hand, they agree that there is a duty to justify judicial decisions on the basis of established legal norms. For this case, they accept the possibility of advancing a practical argument in the logical sense. On the other hand, when conflicts arise in the determination of the legal premises, they admit appeals to morality as the ultimate criterion for the solution of conflicts and, therefore, as a criterion for the determination of the correct premise.

Under the label of 'theories of argumentation', normative proposals with very different features are grouped together. Basically, the label applies to theories which maintain the following two principles:

(i) In easy cases, a deductive justification on the basis of legal norms is necessary and sufficient. This does not mean that they advocate a kind of legal correctness independent of moral correctness. What happens is that, *ex hypothesi*, easy cases are those in which the question about the correctness of the legal premises does not arise. Cases where there are conflicting options and where it must therefore be determined which of them is the adequate premise are, by definition, hard cases.

(ii) In hard cases, in order to determine the correctness of the chosen premises, an argument must be developed in which the reasons for and against each option are weighed. Usually, the example for such an argument is that of a balancing of reasons.

Theories of argumentation are not substantive ethical theories. They do not stipulate which reason ought to be chosen; they only say that substantive justification, i. e., the correctness of that choice, requires the elaboration of a practical argument. Such an argument is an indispensable condition if one wants to find out whether certain reasons are better or more plausible than others. Hence, they presuppose a substantive moral theory which stipulates the relative weight of the different reasons under consideration, or the different ends and objectives one ought to pursue.[42] Within theories of argumen-

---

[40] A similar characterization of two naturalist theses can be found in Moreso, J. J, P. E. Navarro and C. Redondo, Argumentación jurídica, lógica y Derecho judicial, op. cit., p. 248.

[41] This problem is related to the so-called 'paradox of the moral irrelevance of law and government'. If legal norms coincide with moral judgments, they are superfluous, because decisions can be justified directly by moral standards. And if legal norms do not coincide with those standards, then they are illegitimate and should play no role in the justification of a judicial decision. Cf. Nino, Carlos S., The Ethics of Human Rights, op. cit., Appendix iv: The Superfluousness of Law, p. 304 f.

[42] On this topic, cf. Chapter III, sect. 5. There, I mentioned two different patterns as models of practical arguments advanced with a normative purpose.

tation, strictly procedural proposals constitute a special kind. A clear example of this is Robert Alexy's conception. He presents the rules an argumentation must, in his view, obey. Compliance with these conditions as such is seen as the foundation for the correctness of a decision.[43]

It is not among the purposes of this book to analyse the particular features of each and every of those theories of argumentation. I only wish to underline the basis on which they found their thesis that a strictly legal justification is insufficient and that, therefore, it must be complemented by moral reasoning. In principle, these theories do not base their position on the arguments of classical natural-law theory, that is, that of the existence of a set of universally true standards to which the law must conform if judicial decisions are to be correctly justified. The basis of the necessary connection between legal and moral justification is, rather, to be found in a characteristic attributed to all justificatory reasoning, namely that it is of a single kind. Positivism ignores this peculiarity, it is said, when it asserts that legal justificatory arguments can correctly end in a legal premise. From this point of view, the positivist thesis implies a fragmentation of reasoning, thus violating one of the basic rules of practical reasoning. According to Carlos Nino, this fundamental rule which requires the unity of practical reasoning under a set of moral standards is the „fundamental theorem of legal philosophy".[44] The next section will be dedicated to a discussion of this idea.

6. The Principle of the Unity of Practical Reasoning

One of the thesis of legal positivism is that a legal justification is a formal justification based on legal premises. Against this position, it is objected *(i)* that a legal justification can only be a substantive justification, and *(ii)* that because of the unity of practical reasoning, it must be based on moral premises.

Concerning this controversy, first, it must be noted that it is wrong to speak of *the* 'principle of the unity of practical reasoning', because that statement has been given different interpretations.[45] It always involves at least two elements: *(a)* a general conception of rationality, according to which the different existing standards of justification are hierarchically ordered, and *(b)* acceptance of the view that there is a set of moral norms which occupies the highest rank in that hierarchy of justificatory standards.

According to the idea of unity, there is only one sense in which an argument for the foundation of a duty can be correct. This does not mean to deny that there are different kinds of practical discourse – for example, political, legal, moral or religious discourse. But all these discourses are thought to be integrated through a set of ultimate standards which are given the rank of ideal or true morality. On this hypothesis, the correctness of a judge's argument cannot be relative to the legal sphere, because that would mean to adopt a parcial or insular point of view, i. e., a fragmentation or compartmenta-

---

[43] Several objections against a procedural nature of the criterion of correctness can be found in Atienza, Manuel, Las razones del Derecho. Teoría de la argumentación jurídica, op. cit., pp. 207-209.

[44] Nino, Carlos S., Breve nota sulla struttura del ragionamiento giuridico, in: Ragion Pratica (1993) p. 32.

[45] Hereafter, in order to refer to the 'principle of the unity of practical reasoning', I will simply speak of the principle, proposal, or idea, or theorem of unity.

lization of practical reasoning. Most legal philosophers who have treated the topic of judicial justification explicitly accept this principle of unity.[46] They generally agree that compartmentalization is a mistake which is a symptom of „a profound misunderstanding of the formal rules our practical reasoning is bound to".[47]

A) DIFFERENT INTERPRETATIONS OF THE PRINCIPLE OF UNITY

The proposal of the unity of practical reasoning can be seen as a thesis of descriptive ethics, or as a meta-ethical thesis; besides, it can be understood in a subjective or an objective sense.[48] To these alternatives, one must also add the possibility of a normative interpretation, that is, the possibility that the theorem of unity is understood as the content of a standard of behaviour, supported by a certain conception of normative ethics or rationality. These different interpretations, as is important to remember, always come in some combination. The principle of unity, that is, must always be understood either in the subjective or in the objective sense, and at the same time either as a descriptive, or as a meta-ethical or as a normative thesis. Each one of these combinations can, in principle, be maintained. For our purpose, what is of interest is to see for which of them the fragmentation of practical reasoning constitutes a mistake, that is, which of them hold that the unification of different orders of justification, and especially the unification of legal and moral justification, is necessary.

First, the idea of the unity of reasoning under moral premises can be held as a descriptive or sociological thesis referring to different kinds of objectively valid justificatory discourses (practical arguments). The following passage by Carlos Nino leaves no doubt about this:

> „What I am trying to defend in this chapter is that the moral discourse of modernity has an imperialistic nature which prevents the subsistence of insular justificatory discourses. [...] Things could be different from what they are, and we could live in a culture in which there are insular discourses."[49]

This quotation points to a feature which can be confirmed empirically. In modern times, the discourse of morality has succeeded in establishing itself as an order which unifies all the other kinds of normative standards. According to this point of view, the content of morality as well as its typical ways of reasoning have imposed themselves as the predominant form for our justificatory practices. Interpreted in this way, the theorem of unity describes a contingent property and, as all descriptive statements, can be true or false with respect to a particular society in a certain time and place. But its truth cannot be invoked as proof for the mistake of a conception which admits different contexts of justification. All the assertion of the existence of that 'imperialistic' tendency of moral

---

[46] The thesis of the unity of practical reasoning is presupposed, e. g., in the works, mentioned earlier, of David Richards, Joseph Raz, Manuel Atienza, Juan Ruiz Manero, Philip Soper, Juan Carlos Bayón Mohino, and Carlos S. Nino.

[47] Nino, Carlos S., La validez del Derecho, op. cit., pp. 64 f.

[48] Cf. Atienza, Manuel, Lógica y argumentación jurídica, in: J. Echeverría, J. de Lorenzo and L. Peña (eds.), Calculamos ... Matemática y Libertad. Homenaje a Sánchez-Mazas, Madrid: Trotta 1996, 229-238, p. 235.

[49] Nino, Carlos S., DMP p. 79.

discourse can do is explain why in a specific time and place other currents are ignored or held in low regard; but it cannot prove that they are wrong.

Secondly, the principle of unity can be understood as a thesis about the subjective reasoning of agents.[50] In this case, the principle can be defended as a psychological thesis. Asserting the unity of reasoning is asserting that it is impossible for one and the same person to split up her own hierarchy of the preferences or standards in which she grounds her arguments. This idea refers to individual reasoning in some fixed point in time. In the course of time, however, a person may change the premises on which she bases her reasoning. Nothing prevents her preference order at one time to be inconsistent with her preference order at some other, earlier or later, point in time. What the principle of unity on this interpretation asserts is the unity of the reasoning of single individuals at specific points in time.

When the thesis of the unity of individual reasoning is considered to be valid without this temporal restriction, it loses its descriptive nature. The principle of unity is then defended either as a definition or as a normative standard of rationality. As a definition, it stipulates that a person cannot be qualified as rational unless she reasons consistently, according to a relatively stable preference order. A rational agent, that is, assesses and justifies his decisions on the basis of a position that is consistent with a particular scale of priorities. Whoever does not proceed in this way is not rational.

The idea of unity, understood as a normative principle, consists in the requirement that one's own internal preferences be hierarchically ranked and that one reason and act according to that hierarchy. This requirement follows the recognition that all individuals have a complex set of desires, (short-term and long-term) plans, principles, etc., which cannot all be satisfied or complied with at the same time. If an agent does not respect some order, he will probably frustrate most of his own motivations.[51] In short, a normative interpretation of the principle of unity reduces to a standard demanding consistency with the order oneself has accepted.

This subjectivist version of the principle (whether interpreted as a description, a definition, or a standard of rationality) likewise cannot prove that it is a mistake not to regard morality as the ultimate unifying parameter of all justification. Moral standards acquire that status only if they happen to be the highest-order preferences of the reasoning person. For those whose highest preferences do not consist in moral reasons, the principle of the unity of reasoning is still valid, but it is totally unrelated to critical morality. It only enables one to say that if a person undertakes a practical reasoning (and

---

[50] For example, the characteristics which, according to David Richards, define the natural attitude of rationality of all human beings presuppose the unity of practical reasoning, understood as a psychological thesis. On the one hand, this attitude of rationality includes the actual desire and the ability to formulate and carry out rational plans of action. On the other, it also includes the awareness that this ability has continually existed until the present and will continue to exist in the future. In Richards's opinion, these characteristics presuppose that the principles of rationality necessarily form part of all adequate explanations of what is to be understood as the human self. Cf. Richards, David, A Theory of Reasons for Action, op. cit., p. 68.

[51] This requirement is generally implicit in all standards of rationality. For example, one of the four principles of rational choice suggested by David Richards stipulates that of several plans of action one ought to choose that which ensures all the ends desired in the other plans. Obviously, the requirement that one should coordinate one's own purposes is part of such a proposal. Cf. Richards, David, A Theory of Reasons for Action, op. cit., p. 28.

acts accordingly) without being consistent with her own preference order, then it must either be doubted wether we are dealing with a rational human being or she deserves a reproach for being irrational.[52]

In all the interpretations mentioned so far, the only way of coming to critical morality as a unifying standard for an individual's reasoning is by emptying it of all content, i. e., attributing a moral quality to whatever principle may occupy the highest rank in that person's accepted order of preferences or standards of behaviour.[53] When morality is defined simply by occupying the highest rank, the principle of the unity of reasoning can be said, without any difference, to be either a rule of rationality demanding that individuals act in accordance with their highest preferences or a rule of rationality demanding that they act in accordance with moral principles. In both cases, we reach the desired conclusion, i. e., that morality is the ultimate unifying 'tribunal' of practical arguments. The problem is that under this interpretation the word 'morality' loses all content. Its use can be explained only by the positive emotion it evokes. To say 'the last instance of justification is morality' is equivalent to saying 'the last instance of justification is the last instance of justification'.

In any case, despite the fact that this strategy allows one to call 'morality' any ultimate content of justification, the idea of the unity of reasoning, interpreted as a standard of rationality referring to an individual's psychological reasoning, is generally accepted. But this is perfectly compatible with admitting that there are different objective contexts of justification and, therefore, with the positivist thesis which says that the schema of legal argumentation can correctly end in a legal premise, without any need to resort to moral premises.

Another way of understanding the principle of unity is as a proposal on the metaethical level, that is, as a condition all conceptions of normative ethics or of rationality should satisfy. This idea can be understood in two ways. The first refers to a requirement of systemic unity and gives rise to a weak version of the principle of the unity of practical reasoning. This requirement ensures that, within a particular normative conception, even when it includes standards of different kinds (e. g., moral, legal, political, etc.) the question about the correctness of a practical argument has one single answer. Thus, on this view, in the last instance there should be only one valid way of assessing practical arguments. All normative conceptions should be configured in a way that, all things considered, either one should or one should not do *x*. The problem is that this systemic notion of unity does not exclude that multiple normative conceptions may coexist. And some of these provide that under certain circumstances there is more than one correct way of assessing a situation. This happens, for instance, when the certain exclusionary reasons are admitted to be legitimate. In this sense, the principle of unity does not prevent that within a certain normative conception a legal justification may be con-

---

52 An example for a normative and subjectivist interpretation of the principle of the unity of practical reasoning can be found in Juan Carlos Bayón Mohino's position. He thinks that all agents rank their preferences. And such a ranking contains different kinds of reasons for action: instrumental, prudential, and moral reasons. Cf. Bayón Mohino, Juan Carlos, The Normativity of Law: Legal Duty and Reasons for Action, op. cit., chs. 3-5.

53 On this, cf. Caracciolo's critique of Garzón Valdés's view: Caracciolo, Ricardo, L'argomento della credenza morale, op. cit.

sidered correct, regardless of the corresponding evaluation 'all things considered'. In other words, a systemically unitary normative conception can still admit a kind of fragmentation of reasoning in the sense that, in one and the same situation, one is justified to do something that is different from what one is justified to do all things considered.[54]

Besides, even when the above-mentioned possibility is rejected and one insists that all normative conceptions rely on an ultimate instance of principles which unify the assessment of the objective correctness of an argument, another kind of fragmentation is not excluded. If that set of principles is different for each conception, we again have a plurality of frameworks of evaluation and, thus, compartmentalization. Only that now this fragmentation is not internal to some normative conception; rather, it derives from the existence of a plurality of normative conceptions. The critics of positivism cannot reject the thesis that a purely legal justification may be sufficient merely on the basis of the idea of the systemic unity of different normative discourses under a set of last principles. In order to show the mistake of fragmentation, they must show that it is also a mistake to agree that there exists a plurality of equally correct standpoints. The plurality of standpoints, even when each one of them constitutes a unitary systematization of different kinds of normative discourses, implies that the parameters of evaluation are fragmented in an objective sense. In order to avoid this, one must hold a strong idea of unity and require *(i)* that the set of last principles must also be a single one, and *(ii)* that within this single set there are no incompatible standards of equal rank or incommensurable standards. In other words, at the meta-ethical level one must postulate the existence of one single valid form of justification.

This meta-ethical requirement of justification is opposed, on the one hand, to skepticism about reasons for action[55] and, on the other, to the possibility that there may be a plurality of admissible proposals of reasons for action. An inevitable consequence of this is a commitment to the existence of reasons independent of any theoretical construction. This is so because if one were to admit that reasons depend on a normative theory, the plurality would reappear. If there were more than one admissible normative theory, there would be more than one set of valid reasons for action, and fragmentation would be inevitable. Therefore, in order to eliminate this possibility, the principle of the unity of practical reasoning must be interpreted in the strong sense, and as a meta-ethical postulate. Only on the assumption that there is one single correct normative conception

---

[54] According to Joseph Raz, that there is an exclusionary reason typically means that one and the same action can be assessed in two different ways which may lead to contradictory results. But according to a principle of rationality, if the exclusionary reason is valid it always prevails. What one should do on account of valid exclusionary reasons is correct even if it does not coincide with what one should do all things considered. On this, cf. Raz, Joseph, PRN pp. 35 ff. and Postscript, pp. 182 ff.

[55] The interpretation of the theorem of unity as an anti-skeptical postulate suggests the possibility of regarding it as the conclusion of a so-called 'transcendental' argument. Such arguments usually have one of two possible forms. One starts from some kind of experience a skeptic would not be willing to deny and then proceed to show that it is a necessary condition for that kind of experience to admit, for example in the present case, the unity of practical reasoning. The other one argues that the skeptic could not use the very concepts he uses to express his doubts if he would not know that at least some of the propositions within his sphere of doubt are true – in the present case, the existence of a unifying set of objectively valid principles. The general viability of that kind of arguments can, however, be criticized. Cf. Strawson, P. F., Skepticism and Naturalism, op. cit., pp. 8-25.

the justificatory fragmentation defended by legal positivism is wrong. Thus, the principle of unity must be linked to an idea usually not explicitly formulated. The two elements previously mentioned – *(i)* the existence of a rank order of the different existing justificatory standards and *(ii)* a set of moral norms as the last step in that hierarchy – are not enough for the principle of unity in the strong sense. They only guarantee the systemic unity *within* each normative conception, but *not across* normative conceptions. That is, they cannot prevent fragmentation since they do not ensure the unity of the parameter of validity of practical arguments.

Defending a postulate of unity in the strong sense does not imply that the set of correct justificatory standards must already have been identified. But since such a set is thought to exist, there is good reason to foster discussion and try to discover it. Only that this enterprise encounters an obstacle which until today has proved insurmountable. Under certain conditions, every attempt to enumerate correct moral principles constitutes a moral theory. Every moral theory is a proposal of a set of standards (criteria) for the correctness of actions. This makes it necessary to have some criterion on the meta-ethical level that would allow us to decide which moral theory really offers the correct standards. According to the postulate of unity in the strong sense, there must be one single set of standards which are true, or correct, because they correspond to a set of objective reasons. Thus, the ultimate tribunal for the justification of actions, i. e., morality, consists in a set of behavioural standards which are true because of the existence of reasons. But here, two sources of epistemic difficulties must be mentioned. The first arises from the application of the correspondence criterion of truth. The question about the truth of a set of standards (criteria) for the correctness of actions, i. e., the question about the truth of a normative theory, is equivalent to the question about what reasons for action there are. The identification of those reasons, which are the foundation of the truth of a normative theory, cannot itself, in turn, depend on a normative theory, because that would lead to a circular argument. The criteria themselves must be theory-independent, since it is through them that we can determine which is the correct theory. This point is important. Often, proposals which assume the idea of the unity of practical reasoning as a meta-ethical thesis against fragmentation then want to adopt a constructivist position concerning the ontology of objective moral reasons. But that is a mistake. If objective reasons are what enables us to verify or falsify normative theories and other current moral beliefs, then such reasons may not themselves depend on the theories or beliefs of individuals. In that sense, the idea of the objective unity of practical reasoning, together with a correspondence conception of truth, seems to require the acceptance of moral realism.

The second difficulty is related to the first. Two ways of a solution for the problems concerning our access to a knowledge of moral reasons can be suggested. Either one discards the correspondence interpretation and adopts, for example, a coherence conception of moral truth. Or one stipulates directly the reasons normative principles must conform to in order to be regarded as correct. The first option must be rejected if unity in the strong sense is to be ensured. If on the meta-ethical level all that would be required were truth in the sense of coherence, the possibility that a plurality of conceptions satisfy this condition would have to be admitted. The second option is the one adopted, for instance, when the 'correct' is defined as that which provokes an increase in overall happiness.[56] This position proposes overall happiness as the only justificatory reason, and it holds that the truth or correctness of a moral principle consists in its instrumental capacity for promoting such happiness. But, of course, one can imagine that different meta-ethical conceptions, while upholding the principle of unity, propose justificatory reasons other than overall happiness, which would give rise to different sets of morally correct principles. Hence, the same problem encountered at the level of normative ethics reappears at the meta-ethical level. Just as the existence of several normative theories creates the need for a criterion for deciding which one of them is the correct one, the existence of different meta-ethical proposals requires some parameter which enables us to determine which one is the correct meta-ethical conception. In conclusion, then, even if one would presuppose the existence of one single correct set of criteria for the validity of practical arguments, the epistemic limitations in the identification of that set would inevitably lead to the fragmentation of reasoning in the subjective sense and would make the idea of unity in the objective sense inapplicable.

The principle of unity understood as a meta-ethical thesis does not prove that fragmentation is a mistake; it only postulates it through the concepts it proposes. The idea of unity is an axiom. According to this axiom, there is one single concept of correctness and of duty. Only *after* one adopts this point of departure, fragmentation, and with it also the separation of legal and moral justifications, is wrong. The question is whether, from a philosophical point of view, it is plausible to adopt that axiom. In order to take a position on this question, we must take into account the commitments and consequences connected with it. That is what I will consider in the following section.

B) THE FOUNDATION OF THE META-ETHICAL PRINCIPLE OF UNITY

The theorem of the objective unity of reasoning, as a meta-ethical conception, is not adopted as an unfounded dogma. In one of Carlos Nino's last works, one finds an explicit reflection about this question.[57] Nino criticizes the positivist proposal and holds that the fragmentation of practical reasoning is a mistake. The idea of unity he defends is not only referred to the psychological reasoning of agents justifying a decision, but to valid patterns of argumentation, i. e., to arguments in the objective sense. The unitary nature he postulates is backed by an ultimate set of moral standards. These standards permit the solution of conflicts which may arise between the different lower-level normative discourses (aesthetic, political, legal, etc.). Among these discourses, moral discourse is the only one providing genuine justificatory reasons. Hence, a practical argument (and the justification given through such an argument) is valid or invalid (correct or incorrect) from one single point of view: that of objective morality. In other words, the principle of unity imposes a justificatory connection and a subordination of law to morality.[58]

---

[56] This meta-ethical conception corresponds to an objectivist naturalist position sometimes attributed to the normative theory of utilitarianism. Cf. Nino, Carlos S., Introducción al análisis del Derecho, op. cit., p. 357.

[57] Nino, Carlos S., DMP.

[58] This is only one of the ways of connection mentioned by Nino. He also indicates the existence of a conceptual and an interpretative connection. Cf. ibid.

A coherent defense of that principle leads to an essentialist position concerning the meaning of 'duty'. The unity of reasoning necessarily presupposes the unity of the notion of duty, and this makes it inevitable to abandon a conventionalist theory of language concerning this concept. If one would accept that the meaning of 'duty' is of a conventional nature, one would have to accept also the possibility of different senses in which something may be obligatory. There could then be as many kinds of duties as one likes, and that would contradict the principle of unity. The arguments in favour of this conception are based on two features of the notion of duty which distinguish it from most other concepts. With respect to the latter, among them the concept of law, Carlos Nino acknowledges not only the possibility, but also the convenience of having a plurality of meanings.

The foundations of that proposal are remarkable. First, Nino refers to Quine in his refutation of one of the two dogmas of empiricism.[59] In Quine's famous paper, it is suggested, metaphorically speaking, that human knowledge should be considered a „man-made fabric“, a „field of force whose boundary conditions are experience“.[60] Within that field, there are basic propositions (located at the center of the field) and other, less basic ones (located in the periphery, touching on experience). A modification in the truth-value of a statement implies a reassessment of all others logically related to it. According to Quine, all statements of the system of knowledge can be considered either as true or as false, provided the necessary adjustments in the other statements of the system are made. Of course, changing a central statement requires many more changes than modifying a peripherical statement.

Carlos Nino proposes an analogy to this and applies to concepts what has just been said about propositions. That is, in our fabric of knowledge, some concepts are more central than others. For example, concepts like duty or justice occupy a central place in the field of practical knowledge and constitute a common point of departure for several competing conceptions. However, it is hard to understand why Nino used Quine's idea as an argument in favour of an essentialist conception of the meaning of 'duty', when it seems to suggest just the contrary. According to the analogy Nino stipulates, all concepts, just as all propositions, must be open to reassessment, provided the pertinent modifications in related concepts are made. This suggests that elaborating a concept is a task of convention and that, therefore, there may be a plurality of plausible proposals. For example, in a theory of law like that of Hans Kelsen, the concept of duty used is different from the one used in Herbert Hart's theory, and both differ from Kant's concept of moral duty. Kant's concept, in turn, is not the same as that of Hume. Part of the contribution of these theories is of a semantic nature. It would be wrong to say that they only propose different conceptions or contents of one and the same concept when in fact they explicitly affirm the need to modify the concept.[61]

---

59 Ibid., pp. 30 f.

60 Quine, Willard V. O., Two Dogmas of Empiricism, op. cit., pp. 49-81, reprinted in: P. K. Moser (ed.), A Priori Knowledge, Oxford: Oxford University Press 1987, from which I quote (p. 62).

61 The controversy about whether one should adopt an essentialist conception of the concept of duty is a discussion on the semantic level, that is, about the relation between concepts and reality. In this controversy, the essentialist position holds that there is one single correct concept of duty which different proposals of definition intend to capture. There is another way of arguing in favour of the existence of concepts that are

Secondly, Carlos Nino invokes an argument very different from the one suggested by Quine in favour of unity. He points out as a characteristic feature of the concept of duty its similarity with concepts referring to natural classes, that is, concepts the properties of which are constituted by natural laws. This analogy enables him to assume that essentialist theses held about the concepts of natural classes can be extended to the concept of duty. According to the theories of Saul Kripke and Hilary Putnam, the concepts of natural classes necessarily refer to something that does not depend on a convention and, therefore, cannot be changed by conventions either. In these cases, the changes of meaning proposed by different theories are not the product of a conventional decision. Rather, they are attempts to advance in the knowledge of something which depends neither on theoretical constructions nor on tacit agreements manifested in language.

Independently of the arguments for or against conceptual essentialism, what is of interest here is to underline that this is the philosophical conception the analogy proposed by Nino is committed to. Of course, the idea to draw a parallel between the concept of duty and concepts constituted by natural properties is not new. Classical natural-law theory openly advocated the thesis that all concepts of the sphere of 'ought' allude to natural properties depending on immutable laws. The suggestion mentioned above thus brings out a connection between current and classical legal naturalism. If we were to take it literally, we would return to a controversy which Carlos Nino himself regarded as totally anachronistic with respect to other concepts. The problem is not so much that it would reopen the controversy between essentialism and conventionalism as that it would constitute a return to an identification of concepts from the sphere of 'ought' with concepts from the sphere of 'is', i. e., an identification of notions which do not designate entities subject to causal laws with notions which do designate such entities. One of the merits of positivism in this context is to have shown how unfortunate that identification is.[62] On the other hand, if the analogy is not to be taken literally, then the reason for accepting the essentialist arguments about the concept of duty, thus distinguishing it from all other ordinary concepts, disappears.

In summary, the idea of the unity of duty at the meta-ethical level implies conceptual essentialism, just as conceptual conventialism is implied in the relativistic idea of duty at the meta-ethical level. The objective interpretation of the principle of the unity of practical reasoning makes essentialism with respect to the concepts of duty, correctness and, above all, reason for action – which, on this conception, is prior to the concept of duty – necessary.

---

not based on conventions, which does not serve to support Nino's thesis. This argument distinguishes two kinds of agreements reflected in language. On the one hand, agreements adopted or abandoned merely for the fact that other individuals do the same. On the other hand, agreements backed by conviction, which are adopted or rejected for substantive reasons, regardless of whether or not others agree. The latter cannot be generated, modified, or discarded on the basis of a convention.

This thesis does not refer to a correspondence between language and reality. It is not an analysis of a semantic nature and, in that sense, does not represent a position in favour of essentialism about certain concepts. At best, it implies a generic rejection of the plausibility of semantic analysis. Cf. Dworkin, Ronald, Law's Empire, Cambridge, Mass.: Harvard University Press 1986, pp. 135-139.

62 Kelsen, Hans, Causality and imputation, in: Ethics 61 (1950) pp. 1-11; also id., Reine Rechtslehre, op. cit.

7. Conclusions

Let us return to the questions that gave rise to the preceding analysis: What kind of justification is required of a judge? What concept of justification is applied in the reconstruction of a judicial decision as a justified decision? The only kind of justification that can be required in an intersubjectively controlable way, without giving rise to controversies, is justification in the formal sense. As for substantive justification in the subjective sense, it is impossible to determine whether a judge accepts, or believes in, the norms he invokes as substantive reasons for action. Although in view of existing linguistic conventions it is common to attribute to a judge a commitment with the norms he applies, it is not at all necessary for the functions of a judge to be performed that the judge accept, or believe in, the norms he applies as substantive reasons. And as for substantive justification in the objective sense, its requirement would make sense only if there were agreement about what normative theory should be applied.

The assertion that, because of the principle of the unity of practical reason, judicial justification is a kind of substantive, moral justification is merely a rhetorical device. If the notion of unity is interpreted in the weak sense, the assertion is empty, since in that case it means only that legal justification presupposes certain ultimate premises which, for this reason alone, are called moral premises. And if unity is understood in the strong sense, it is untenable since, even if one postulates that only the criteria of critical or true morality are admissible for justification, the different attempts to identify what that morality contains inevitably lead to fragmentation. If the analysis developed here is correct, then in none of the senses proposed the principle of unity can show that in order to give a substantive justification a judge must resort to an ideal morality. Even if objective reasons (and, accordingly, a single set of standards for substantive justification) existed, such a justification could not be required. The epistemic difficulties judges would confront in trying to comply with their duty of giving *the* correct justification are the same that would arise for any attempt to assess whether they have complied with that duty.

The rejection of essentialism and, with it, of the principle of unity does not, of course, eliminate the possibility of designing normative theories, i. e., theories about substantive reasons for action, which permit the solution of practical conflicts. But only agreement with a particular theory makes it possible 'objectively' to give or criticize a substantive justification and, if found correct, to demand compliance with it.

CHAPTER VII

FINAL REMARKS

By way of conclusion, I will offer a brief summary of the main ideas and results presented in this work.

(i) Throughout the book, I have distinguished several meanings of the word 'reason': as a human faculty, as a premise of an argument, as a motive, and as a justification for an action.

I briefly analysed the notion of *reason as a faculty*, and especially the senses in which one can say that it is a theoretical or a practical faculty. Reason as a theoretical faculty is linked to an epistemic capacity based on the ability to establish relations between meaningful contents according to certain rules. Reason as a practical faculty can be understood in several ways. One of the foundations on which it rests is the ability to acquire knowledge about correct standards as guidelines for action. In that sense, its characterization as a practical capacity is merely rhetorical since this involves the same epistemic capacity as the one defining it as a theoretical faculty. The only difference is the kind of entities that can supposedly be known, namely, moral facts. A second way of interpreting the practical quality of reason is based on the ability to stipulate standards of behaviour. Here, the practical faculty of reason refers to a 'legislative' capacity, independent of any epistemic faculty. Finally, practical reason can also be regarded as a faculty which is different, though not independent from its epistemic capacity. On this view, certain mental states, of a rational origin, can intervene causally in the performance of an action.

The notion of reason as a faculty is related to the different meanings of the term *reason for action*. Concerning this topic, I have emphasized above all the need to distinguish empirical problems (linked to a *motivational* notion of reason) from normative problems (linked to a *justificatory* notion). Another point mentioned was the need to keep these matters separated from the logical aspects connected with the notion of *reason as a premise* of an (explanatory or justificatory) argument. This implies a position contrary to that which advocates one single concept of reason. This idea was rejected mainly because one single concept leads to a confusion of completely different kinds of problems – like those already mentioned – and implies the rejection of Hume's principle. If reasons are empirical entities, in accordance with Hume's principle, they cannot justify anything. And if they are abstract normative meanings, they cannot causally motivate action. Hence, if one agrees that reasons intervene in both functions (motivation and justification), then one also implicitly agrees that, according to Hume's principle, at least two meanings of 'reason' must be recognized.

(ii) The analysis of the possible motivating function of reason led to a consideration of the *intentional states* that could fulfil this function. In Chapter I, I studied different kinds of mental states. Among them, special attention was paid to desires and beliefs which enable one to analyse the internal structure of human action. Some conclusions were drawn from a review of the controversy between rationalists and Humeans about what kinds of mental states are capable of bringing about action. For action to be generated, an intentional state which merely represents states of affairs (a state with a mind-to-world direction of fit) is not sufficient. Because of the very concept of action, the purpose of effecting a change is necessary. The teleological structure of action presupposes an internal state defined by its aim of obtaining some end (a state with a world-to-mind direction of fit). Generally, those who define the concept of reason as a practical capacity hold two theses: that beliefs are intentional states produced by reason, and that they may be sufficient for producing action. Both assertions are questionable. First, it can be questioned that beliefs should be understood as rational products (cf. Chapter V). Secondly, it is also questionable that, being states defined by a claim of truth, i. e., a claim of correspondence with reality, they have the right direction of fit for leading to action (cf. Chapter I).

(iii) In Chapter II, the ambiguity of the term 'reason for action' was pointed out. We allude to reasons when we explain as well as when we justify actions. The truth of assessments which explain the performance of an action depends on explanatory reasons. The correctness of judgments justifying a duty to perform some action depends on justificatory reasons. In the theory of human action and in moral philosophy, several concepts of explanatory and justificatory reasons have been proposed. They all say that if reasons exist, then they are either empirical or abstract entities. From the point of view of the present work, an explanatory reason refers to empirical entities capable of causally bringing about action, i. e., capable of motivating it. Only in a secondary or subsidiary sense, it was admitted that external factors which are not motives of action can be called explanatory reasons. A justificatory reason, in turn, is an abstract entity both when it is understood in the formal sense (as a premise of an argument) and when it is understood in the substantive sense (as a standard in conformity with which one ought to behave). Because of Hume's principle, a justificatory reason necessarily refers to norms. Again, only in a secondary or subsidiary sense it was admitted that certain *facts* can be understood as justificatory reasons. In any case, the determination of reasons always depends on a theory. What entities can be identified as specific intentional states depends on a psychological theory. What contents may constitute premises for certain kinds of arguments depends on a logical theory. And what contents constitute reasons for action depends on a normative theory.

(iv) In the present study, I was primarily interested in the notion of *justificatory reason*. Within this category, I only considered reasons which constitute *duties* for action. No reference to reasons justifying permitted or supererogatory actions was made. I introduced two fundamental distinctions concerning justificatory reasons: first, the difference, already mentioned, between the existence of a *formal* reason (or justification) and that of a *substantive* reason (or justification); and secondly, between the *existence* of a

reason or justification and the *belief* in or *acceptance* of something as a reason. Whoever performs an act of substantive justification necessarily believes in, or accepts, some standard as a substantive justificatory reason. But that does not imply that such a reason actually exists or that, from an objective point of view, a substantive justification really has been given.

(v) The concepts of reason and justification are closely related to the notion of *argument*. In Chapter III, I have formulated several criteria for the distinction between 'theoretical' and 'practical' arguments and shown the ambiguity of the latter term. Besides the logical concept of practical argument, two other notions were mentioned: a theoretical, reconstructive notion, and a normative notion. The distinction of these three different concepts enabled me to sort out the confusions stemming from the indiscriminate usage of the term 'practical argument'. With respect to judicial justification, for instance, it was thus possible to distinguish three senses and functions of 'practical arguments': *(a)* an argument which reconstructs the deductive steps of a justification, *(b)* an argument which represents the judge's psychological process, and *(c)* an argument which claims to ensure a correct substantive justification. These three schemata of 'practical reasoning' are directly related to the distinctions pointed out with respect to the meanings of 'reason'. All practical arguments in the logical sense mention premise-reasons. All practical arguments in the theoretical, reconstructive sense, when applying to an action, mention explanatory reasons. And all practical arguments in the normative sense stipulate how substantive reasons should be assessed.

(vi) In the second part of the investigation, I have analysed the notions of *norm, acceptance* and *judicial justification*. In the currently predominant legal theory, the analysis of these concepts presents two common elements. First, their reconstruction provides the basis for arguments which claim to prove that there is a necessary connection between law and morality; and secondly, they are all analysed in terms of reasons for action.

Regarding the characterization of *legal norms*, there have always been two rival methodological proposals in legal theory: that which defines them independently of any duty of acting accordingly, and that which regards this valuational element as a defining characteristic of the concept. Something similar applies to the question of *normativity*, understood as the practical nature of ought-provisions. An *externalist position* conceives the concept of duty independently of its practical nature, i. e., its nature of a reason for action. An *internalist position* regards being a reason as a defining characteristic of duty. For the externalist conception, an ought-provision is 'normative$_a$' because it qualifies conduct deontically; but it is a contingent matter whether it constitutes, or is accepted as, a reason for action, i. e., whether it is 'normative$_b$'. For the internalist conception, ought-provisions are normative only in one sense: if and only if they constitute, or are accepted as, reasons for action. Hence, from an internalist point of view the existence of norms of obligation implies the existence, or a belief in the existence, of a moral duty. From this standpoint, if we want to understand in what sense the law establishes duties, we must understand its relationship with reasons for action, that is, its relationship with moral duty. Generally, there are two common lines of argument on this topic. In some cases, normativity is defined in terms of the *existence* of justificatory reasons. On this interpretation, if one does not want to adopt an extreme ideological positivism, one must deny that normativity is a characteristic of legal provisions. In other cases, it is defined in terms of *beliefs* in justificatory reasons. On this view, normativity is usually considered a necessary condition for the existence of legal systems. On the one hand, it is held that this feature permits one to present legal systems as regimes which possess legitimation, in contrast to others based exclusively on the exercise of force. On the other hand, it is said, it permits one to show the necessary connection between law and morality.

(vii) The latter line of reasoning claims to show that the law is grounded in the moral approval of the citizens or at least of the officials of a system. According to this view, when judges apply norms they accept them as substantive reasons for action. This means that they believe that they are correct standards of behaviour, or that there are correct reasons for which these norms ought to be applied. The idea can be criticized from two perspectives. First, even when there is a linguistic practice which imputing acceptance without demanding any evidence for it, it is still contingent whether or not judges actually do accept legal provisions as substantive reasons. Secondly, even if judges accept them, the analysis of the notions of belief and acceptance has shown that the two concepts must not be identified. Acceptance of a norm does not imply belief in its moral correctness and must not necessarily be based on moral beliefs. If acceptance were necessarily conditioned by beliefs, it would depend on involuntary mental states and could not be qualified as a rational attitude that can be deliberately chosen. Besides, even if acceptance implied moral beliefs, it would still be questionable whether on this basis one could establish a connection between law and critical morality.

(viii) Finally, I have discussed the different meanings of justification which are applicable to the reconstruction of legal decisions. This involved basically the question of what kind of justification should be required of a judge in his sentences. Despite the difficulties it presents, justification in the formal and objective sense is generally required. The justification of a sentence in this sense can be controlled by the parameters of logic. Things become really problematic, however, when judicial justifications are to involve the two senses of substantive justification. According to the conclusions of Chapter V, substantive justification in the subjective sense cannot be regarded as a necessary condition for the justification of a judge. First, if the *act* of a substantive justification is defined by a commitment to some moral belief it makes no sense to require it since beliefs cannot be adopted voluntarily. Secondly, such a commitment, if it could be adopted voluntarily, could be simulated.

Much of Chapter VI was dedicated to the discussion of the thesis which requires a substantive justification in the objective sense. On this view, what ought to be required is the moral correctness of the premises of judicial arguments. Some conceptions hold that this requirement exists in all cases. Others admit that in easy cases a formal justification on the basis of the norms of the legal system is necessary and sufficient, and only in hard cases substantive justification from a moral point of view must be ensured. All these standpoints share the idea that morality is a normative order which unifies practical justifications. In other words, for these theories the need to resort to morality is based on the *principle of the unity of practical reasoning*. This principle can be interpreted in different ways. However, the only way of interpreting it as a critique of the idea of the fragmentation of reasoning is on an essentialist meta-ethical conception of the concepts of duty, justification and reason. The meta-ethical idea of unity makes it necessary to assume the existence of (external, theory-independent) reasons as elements which enable one to assess the truth or falsehood of proposed normative theories. In contrast, the thesis I have defended in this book asserts that the existence of reasons itself depends on a normative theory. According to the conclusions of Chapter VI, even if a postulate of the objective unity of reasoning were true, it would be irrelevant for the judge (and, indeed, for any agent) because of the epistemic difficulties connected with it. I argued that only agreement about a normative theory would make it possible to require a substantive justification of judicial decisions. Such a justification would then be 'objective' only relative to that theory. If those who carry out the task of justification and those who control their attempts do not consent to one and the same normative theory, their discussions about the correctness of a justification cannot be rational.

Concerning the two features of the predominant legal theory mentioned before, the analysis I have offered leads to the following conclusion: The concept of reason can be useful as a starting point for the discussion of a number of legal topics of theoretical and practical relevance. The different meanings of 'reason' are helpful tools for the analysis of notions such as those I have proposed, and the problems connected with them. When these meanings are confounded, however, the approach loses its analytical force and can only be regarded as a strategy for 'showing' an already presupposed necessary connection between law and morality.

BIBLIOGRAPHY

AARNIO, Aulis (1977): *On Legal Reasoning*, Turku: University of Turku.

AARNIO, Aulis (1987): *The Rational as Reasonable. A Treatise on Legal Justification*, Dordrecht: Kluwer.

ALCHOURRÓN, Carlos E. (1994): Para una lógica de las razones prima facie, mimeo.

ALCHOURRÓN, Carlos E. and BULYGIN, Eugenio (1971): *Normative Systems*, New York and Vienna: Springer.

ALCHOURRÓN, Carlos E. and BULYGIN, Eugenio (1975): *Introducción a la metodología de las ciencias jurídicas y sociales*, Buenos Aires: Astrea.

ALCHOURRÓN, Carlos E. and BULYGIN, Eugenio (1976): Sobre el concepto de orden jurídico, in: *Crítica. Revista Hispanoamericana de Filosofía* (Mexico-City) VIII:23.

ALCHOURRÓN, Carlos E. and BULYGIN, Eugenio (1979): *Sobre la existencia de las normas jurídicas*, Valencia, Venezuela: Universidad de Carabobo, OLIJS.

ALCHOURRÓN, Carlos E. and BULYGIN, Eugenio (1981): The expressive conception of norms, in: R. Hilpinen (ed.), *New Studies in Deontic Logic*, Dordrecht: Reidel.

ALCHOURRÓN, Carlos E. and BULYGIN, Eugenio (1984): Pragmatic Foundations for a Logic of Norms, in: *Rechtstheorie* 15.

ALCHOURRÓN, Carlos E. and BULYGIN, Eugenio (1989): Limits of logic and legal reasoning, in: A. A. Martino (ed.), *Pre-proceedings of the III International Conference Logica – Informatica – Diritto*, Vol. II, Florence [Spanish original: Los límites de la lógica y el razonamiento jurídico, reprinted in: Alchourrón/Bulygin 1991].

ALCHOURRÓN, Carlos E. and BULYGIN, Eugenio (1991): *Análisis lógico y Derecho*, Madrid: Centro de Estudios Constitucionales.

ALCHOURRÓN, Carlos E. and MARTINO, Antonio (1990): Logic Without Truth, in *Ratio Juris* 3:1.

ALEXY, Robert (1978): *Theorie der juristischen Argumentation. Die Theorie des rationalen Diskurses als Theorie der juristischen Begründung*, Frankfurt/M.: Suhrkamp.

ALEXY, Robert (1989): On Necessary Relations Between Law and Morality, in: *Ratio Juris* 2:2.

ANSCOMBE, G. E. M. (1957): *Intention*, Ithaca, N. Y.: Cornell University Press.

ANSCOMBE, G. E. M. (1968): Intention, in White, A. R. (ed.), *The Philosophy of Action*, Oxford: Oxford University Press [first published in: *Proceedings of the Aristotelian Society* 57 (1956-57)].

ARISTOTLE: *Nicomachean Ethics*.

ATIENZA, Manuel (1990): Para una teoría de la argumentación jurídica, in: *Doxa* (Alicante) 8.

ATIENZA, Manuel (1991): *Las razones del Derecho. Teorías de la argumentación jurídica*, Madrid: Centro de Estudios Constitucionales.

ATIENZA, Manuel (1993a): *Trás la justicia. Una introducción al Derecho y al razonamiento jurídico*, Barcelona: Ariel.

ATIENZA, Manuel (1996): Lógica y argumentación jurídica, in: J. Echeverría, J. de Lorenzo and L. Peña (eds.), Calculamos ... Matemática y Libertad. Homenaje a Sánchez-Mazas, Madrid: Trotta.

AUDI, Robert (1991): *Practical Reasoning*, London: Routledge.

AUNE, Bruce (1977): *Reason and Action*, Dordrecht: Reidel.

AUSTIN, John L (1953): How to talk – Some simple ways, in: *Proceedings of the Aristotelian Society* 53.

AUSTIN, John L (1955): *How to Do Things With Words*, The William James Lectures, 2nd ed., eds. J. O. Urmson and Marina Sbisà, Oxford: Oxford University Press 1990.

BAYÓN MOHINO, Juan Carlos (1991): *La normatividad del Derecho: deber jurídico y razones para la acción*, Centro de Estudios Constitucionales, Madrid, (English transl.: *The Normativity of Law: Legal Duty and Reasons for Action*, Dordrecht: Kluwer, forthcoming).

BLANKE, Richard (1986): Objective Reasons and Practical Reasons, in: *Metaphilosophy* 17:1.

BOBBIO, Norberto (1991): *El problema del positivismo jurídico*, transl. E. Garzón Valdés, Mexico-City: Fontamara.

BRATMAN, Michael (1992): Practical Reasoning and Acceptance in a Context, in: *Mind* 101.

BRINK, David (1986): Externalist Moral Realism, in: *Southern Journal of Philosophy* 24, Supplement.

BROWN, Harold (1977): *Perception Theory and Commitment. The New Philosophy of Science*, Chicago, Ill.: Precedent.

BULYGIN, Eugenio (1963): El concepto de vigencia en Alf Ross, in: *Revista del Colegio de Abogados de La Plata* (reprinted in: Alchourrón/Bulygin 1991, 339-353).

BULYGIN, Eugenio (1966): Sentencia judicial y creación de Derecho, in: *La Ley* 124 (reprinted in: Alchourrón/Bulygin 1991, 344-369).

BULYGIN, Eugenio (1981): Enunciados jurídicos y positivismo jurídico: respuesta a Raz, in: *Análisis Filosófico* 1:2 (reprinted in: Alchourrón/Bulygin 1991, 427-438).

BULYGIN, Eugenio (1982): Norms, normative propositions and legal statements, in: G. Fløistad (ed.), *Contemporary Philosophy. A New Survey. Vol 3: Philosophy of Action*, The Hague: Martinus Nijhoff.

BULYGIN, Eugenio (1990): An Antinomy in Kelsen's Pure Theory of Law, in: *Ratio Juris* 3:1.

BUNGE, Mario (1985): *La ciencia, su método y su filosofía*, Buenos Aires: Siglo XXI.

CARACCIOLO, Ricardo (1988a): Justificación y pertenencia, in: *Análisis Filosófico* 2.

CARACCIOLO, Ricardo (1988b): *El sistema jurídico. Problemas actuales*, Madrid: Centro de Estudios Constitucionales.

CARACCIOLO, Ricardo (1991): El concepto de autoridad normativa. El modelo de las razones para la acción, in: *Doxa* (Alicante) 10.

CARACCIOLO, Ricardo (1993): Entrevista a Eugenio Bulygin, in: *Doxa* (Alicante) 14.

CARACCIOLO, Ricardo (1994a): *Autoridad sin normas y normas sin autoridad*, manuscript.

CARACCIOLO, Ricardo (1994b): L'argomento della credenza morale, in: P. Comanducci and R. Guastini (eds.), *Analisi e Diritto 1994. Ricerche di Giurisprudenza Analitica*, Torino: Giappichelli.

CARACCIOLO, Ricardo (1996): Sistema jurídico, in: E. Garzón Valdés and F. Laporta (eds.), *Enciclopedia Iberoamericana de Filosofía, Vol. 11: El derecho y la justicia*, Madrid: Editorial Trotta, Consejo Superior de Investigaciones Científicas and Boletín Oficial del Estado.

CARNAP, Rudolf (1958): *Introduction to Symbolic Logic and Its Applications*, New York: Dober.

CARNAP, Rudolf (1963): Intellectual Autobiography, in: P. Schilpp (ed.), *The Philosophy of Rudolf Carnap*, The Library of Living Philosophers, La Salle, Ill.: Open Court.

CARNAP, Rudolf (1952): Empiricism, Semantics, and Ontology, in: L. Linsky (ed.), Semantics and the Philosophy of Language, Urbana, Ill.: University of Illinois Press.

CARRIÓ, Genaro (1987): *Cómo estudiar y cómo argumentar un caso*, Buenos Aires: Abeledo-Perrot.

COHEN, L. Jonathan (1988): Acceptance and Belief, in: *Mind* 98.

COHEN, L. Jonathan (1992): *An Essay on Belief and Acceptance*, Oxford: Clarendon.

COHEN, Morris (1945): *A Preface to Logic*, New York: Henry Holt.

COHEN, Morris and NAGEL, Ernest (1934): *An Introduction to Logic and Scientific Method*, New York: Harcourt, Brace and Company.

COHON, Rachel (1986): Are External Reasons Impossible?, in: *Ethics* 96.

DANCY, Jonathan (1993): *Moral Reasons*, Oxford: Blackwell.

DANTO, Arthur (1968): Basic Actions, in: A. R. White (ed.), *The Philosophy of Action*, Oxford: Oxford University Press 1968.

DAVIDSON, Donald (1982): Actions, Reasons and Causes, in: id., *Essays on Actions and Events*, Oxford: Clarendon Press.

DWORKIN, Ronald (1975): Hard Cases, in: *Harvard Law Review* (reprinted in: id. 1977, 81-130).

DWORKIN, Ronald (1977): *Taking Rights Seriously*, London: Duckworth.

DWORKIN, Ronald (1986) *Law's Empire*, Cambridge, Mass.: Harvard University Press.

EDGLEY, Roy (1969): *Reason in Theory and Practice*, London: Hutchinson.

EDGLEY, Roy (1975): Practical Reason, in: J. Raz (ed.), *Practical Reasoning*, Oxford: Oxford University Press.

FALK, W. D (1947-48): 'Ought' and Motivation, in: *Proceedings of the Aristotelian Society* 98.

FRANKENA, William (1958): Obligation and Motivation in Recent Moral Philosophy, in: A. I. Melden (ed.), *Essays in Moral Philosophy*, Seattle, Wash.: University of Washington Press.

GANS, Chaim (1986): Mandatory Rules and Exclusionary Reasons, in: *Philosophia* 15.

GARRIDO, Manuel (1983): *Lógica simbólica*, 2nd ed. Madrid: Tecnos.

GARZÓN VALDÉS, Ernesto (1987): *El concepto de estabilidad de los sistemas políticos*, Madrid: Centro de Estudios Constitucionales (German transl: *Die Stabilität politischer Systeme*, Munich: Karl Alber 1988).

GARZÓN VALDÉS, Ernesto (1990): Algo más acerca de la relación entre Derecho y moral, in: *Doxa* (Alicante) 8 (English version: More on the relation between law and morality, in: A. Aarnio, K. Pietilä, J. Uusitalo (eds.), *Interests, Morality and the Law*, Tampere: University of Tampere, Research Institute for Social Sciences 1996, 123-143).

GAUTHIER, David (1963): *Practical Reasoning*, Oxford: Clarendon.

GIBBARD, Allan (1985): Moral Judgement and the Acceptance of Norms, in: *Ethics* 96.

GOLDMAN, Alvin (1970): *A Theory of Human Action*, Princeton, N. J.: Princeton University Press.

GONZÁLEZ LAGIER, Daniel (1993): Clasificar acciones. Sobre la crítica de Raz a las reglas constitutivas de Searle, in: *Doxa* (Alicante) 13.

GREEN, Leslie (1985): Authority and Convention, in: *Philosophical Quarterly* 35:141.

GRICE, G. R. (1975): Motive and Reason, in: J. Raz (ed.), *Practical Reasoning*, Oxford: Oxford University Press.

GUIBOURG, Ricardo (1986): *Derecho, sistema y realidad*, Buenos Aires: Astrea.

HARE, Richard (1989): Ontology in Ethics, in: id., *Essays in Ethical Theory*, Oxford: Clarendon.

HARMAN, Gilbert (1977): *The Nature of Morality. An Introduction to Ethics*, New York: Oxford University Press.

HART, Herbert L. A. (1994): *The Concept of Law* (1961), 2nd ed. Oxford: Clarendon.

HART, Herbert L. A. (1982): *Essays on Bentham*, Oxford: Clarendon.

HART, Herbert L. A. (1982a): Legal Duty and Obligation, in: id. (1982).

HART, Herbert L. A. (1982b): Commands and Authoritative Legal Reasons, in: id. (1982).

HART, Herbert L. A. (1983): American Jurisprudence Through English Eyes: The Nightmare and The Noble Dream, in: id., *Essays on Jurisprudence and Philosophy*, Oxford: Oxford University Press.

HOFSTADTER, Albert and MCKINSEY, J. C. (1939): On the Logic of Imperatives, in: *Philosophy of Science* 6.

HUMBERSTON, Lloyd (1992): Direction of Fit, in: *Mind* 101.

HUME, David (1739-40): *A Treatise of Human Nature*, London: John Noon.

HUND, John (1991): Wittgenstein versus Hart. Two Models of Rules for Social and Legal Theory, in: *Philosophy of the Social Sciences* 21:1.

JÄÄSKINEN, Nilo (1985): External Justification of Propositions in Legal Science, in: E. Bulygin *et al.* (eds), *Man, Law and Modern Forms of Life*, Dordrecht: D. Reidel.

KELSEN, Hans (1945): *General Theory of Law and State*, Cambridge, Mass.: Harvard University Press.

KELSEN, Hans (1960): *Reine Rechtslehre*, 2nd ed., Vienna: Franz Deuticke.

KELSEN, Hans (1971): *What is Justice? Justice, Law and Politics in the Mirror of Science*, Berkeley, Calif.: University of California Press.

KELSEN, Hans (1950): Causality and imputation, in: Ethics 61.

KENNY, Anthony (1965-66): Practical Inference, in: *Analysis* 26.

KLARKE, D. S. (1994): Does Acceptance Entail Belief?, in: *American Philosophical Quarterly* 31:2.

KLIMOVSKY, Gregorio (1985): El método hipotético-deductivo y la lógica, in: J. Gracia *et al.* (eds.), *Análisis filosófico en America Latina*, Mexico-City: Fondo de Cultura Económica.

LEMMON, John (1965): *Beginning Logic*, London: Thomas Nelson.

LEWIS, C. Irving (1971): *An Analysis of Knowledge and Valuation*, La Salle, Ill.: Open Court.

LEWIS, David (1988): Desire as Belief, in: *Mind* 97.

MCBRIDE, William (1965): The Acceptance of a Legal System, in: *The Monist* 49.

MACCORMICK, Neil (1978): *Legal Reasoning and Legal Theory*, Oxford: Clarendon.

MACCORMICK, Neil (1981): *H. L. A. Hart*, London: Eduard Arnold.

MACCORMICK, Neil (1986): The Limits of Rationality in Legal Reasoning, in: MacCormick/Weinberger (1986).

MACCORMICK, Neil and WEINBERGER, Ota (1986): *An Institutional Theory of Law*, Dordrecht: Reidel.

MACINTYRE, Alasdair (1984): The Claims of After Virtue, in: *Analyse & Kritik* (Wiesbaden) 6:1.

MACKIE, John (1977): *Ethics. Inventing Right and Wrong*, London: Penguin.

MACKIE, John (1981): Obligations to Obey the Law, in: *Virginia Law* Review 67.

MACKIE, John (1988): The Subjectivity of Values, in: G. Sayre-McCord (ed), *Essays on Moral Realism*, Ithaca, N. Y.: Cornell University Press.

MOORE, Michael S. (1989a): Authority and Razian Reasons, in: *Southern California Law Review* 62.

MOORE, Michael S. (1989b): *Moral Realism as the Best Explanation of Moral Experience*, paper presented at the Saturday Discussion Group of Southern California Legal and Political Philosophers, January 1989, manuscript.

MORESO, José Juan (1996): On Relevance and Justification of Legal Decisions, in: *Erkenntnis* 44.

MORESO, José Juan (1998): *Legal Indeterminacy and Constitutional Interpretation*, Dordrecht: Kluwer.

MORESO, José Juan and NAVARRO, Pablo E. (1993): *Orden jurídico y sistema jurídico*, Madrid: Centro de Estudios Constitucionales.

MORESO, José Juan, NAVARRO, Pablo E. and REDONDO, Cristina (1992): Argumentación jurídica, lógica y decisión judicial, in: *Doxa* (Alicante) 11.

MOSER, Paul (1987): Introduction, in: id. (ed.), *A Priori Knowledge*, Oxford: Oxford University Press.

MOSTERÍN, Jesús (1978): *Racionalidad y acción humana*, Madrid: Alianza.

MOSTERÍN, Jesús (1984): Sobre el concepto de modelo, in: id., *Conceptos y teorías de la ciencia*, Madrid: Alianza.

MOYA, Carlos (1990): *The Philosophy of Action. An Introduction*, Cambridge: Polity Press.

MOYA, Carlos (1992): Introducción a la filosofía de Davidson: mente, mundo y acción, in: D. Davidson, *Mente, mundo y acción*, transl. by Carlos Moya, Barcelona: Paidós/I. C. E. – Universidad Autónoma de Barcelona.

NAGEL, Thomas (1970): *The Possibility of Altruism*, Princeton, N. J.: Princeton University Press.

NAVARRO, Pablo E. (1993): Sistema jurídico, casos difíciles y conocimiento del Derecho, in: *Doxa* (Alicante) 14.

NAVARRO, Pablo E. and REDONDO, Cristina (1991): Aceptación y funcionamiento del Derecho, in: *Doxa* (Alicante) 9.

NINO, Carlos (1984): *Introducción al análisis del Derecho*, Buenos Aires: Astrea.

NINO, Carlos (1985): *La validez del Derecho*, Buenos Aires: Astrea.

NINO, Carlos (1985a): Normas jurídicas y razones para la acción, in: id. (1985).

NINO, Carlos (1986): El concepto de Derecho de Hart, in: A. Squella (ed.), *H. L. A. Hart y el concepto de Derecho*, Revista de Ciencias sociales (Universidad de Valparaíso) 29.

NINO, Carlos (1987): *Introducción a la filosofía de la acción humana*, Buenos Aires: Eudeba.

NINO, Carlos (1989): *El constructivismo ético*, Madrid: Centro de Estudios Constitucionales.

NINO, Carlos (1991): *The Ethics of Human Rights*, Oxford: Clarendon (Spanish original: *Ética y derechos humanos. Un ensayo de fundamentación*, Buenos Aires: Astrea 1989).

NINO, Carlos (1993a): Respuesta a J. J. Moreso, P. E. Navarro y M. C. Redondo, in: *Doxa* (Alicante) 13.

NINO, Carlos (1993b): Breve nota sulla struttura del ragionamento giuridico, in: *Ragion Pratica* (Genova) 1.

NINO, Carlos (1994): *Derecho, moral y política. Una revisión de la teoría general del Derecho*, Barcelona: Ariel.

PAP, Arthur (1949): The Verifiability of Value Judgments, in: *Ethics* 60.

PAP, Arthur (1958): *Semantics and Necessary Truth*, New Haven, Conn.: Yale University Press.

PERRY, Stephen (1987): Judicial Obligation, Precedent and The Common Law, in: *Oxford Journal of Legal Studies* 7.

PETTIT, Philip (1987): Humeans, Anti-Humeans, and Motivations, in: *Mind* 96.

PLATTS, Mark (1979): *The Ways of Meaning*, London: Routledge & Kegan Paul.

PRICE, Huw (1989): Defending Desire-as-Belief, in: *Mind* 98.

QUINE, Willard V. O. (1953): Two Dogmas of Empiricism, in: id., *From a Logical Point of View*, Cambridge, Mass.: Harvard University Press (reprinted in: P. K. Moser (ed.), *A Priori Knowledge*, Oxford: Oxford University Press 1987).

RADFORD, Colin (1990): Belief, Acceptance and Knowledge, in: *Mind* 99.

RAMSEY, Frank P. (1929): Philosophy, in: id., *Philosophical Papers*, ed. by D. H. Mellor, Cambridge: Cambridge University Press 1990.

RAWLS, John (1971): *A Theory of Justice*, Cambridge, Mass.: Harvard University Press.

RAZ, Joseph (1979): *The Authority of Law. Essays on Law and Morality*, Oxford: Clarendon.

RAZ, Joseph (1975): Introduction, in: J. Raz (ed.), *Practical Reasoning*, Oxford: Oxford University Press.

RAZ, Joseph (1984): Hart on Moral Rights and Legal Duties, in: *Oxford Journal of Legal Studies* 4:1.

RAZ, Joseph (1986): *The Morality of Freedom*, Oxford: Oxford University Press.

RAZ, Joseph (1989): Facing Up: a Reply, in: *Southern California Law Review* 62.

RAZ, Joseph (1990a): *Practical Reason and Norms* (1975), 2nd ed., Princeton: Princeton University Press.

RAZ, Joseph (1990b): Introduction, in: id. (ed.), *Authority*, Oxford: Basil Blackwell.

RAZ, Joseph (1990c): Authority and Justification, in: id. (ed.) *Authority*, Oxford: Basil Blackwell.

RAZ, Joseph (1994), Authority, Law, and Morality, in: id., *Ethics in the Public Domain. Essays in the Morality of Law and Politics*, Oxford: Clarendon.

REDONDO, Cristina (1993): Las normas jurídicas como razones protegidas, in: *ARSP* 79.

RESCHER, Nicholas (1969): *An Introduction to the Theory of Value*, Englewood Cliffs, N. J.: Prentice Hall.

RICHARDS, David (1971): *A Theory of Reasons for Action*, Oxford: Clarendon.

ROSS, Alf (1941): Imperatives and Logic, in: *Theoria* 7.

ROSS, Alf (1968): *Directives and Norms*, New York: Humanities Press.

RUIZ MANERO, Juan (1990): *Jurisdicción y normas*, Madrid: Centro de Estudios Constitucionales.

SCHAUER, Frederick (1985): Easy Cases, in: *California Law Review* 58.

SCHAUER, Frederick (1991): *Playing by the Rules. A Philosophical Examination of Rule-Based Decision Making in Law and Life*, Oxford: Clarendon.

SCHUELER, G. (1989): *The Idea of a Reason for Acting. A Philosophical Argument*, Lewiston: Edwin Mellen.

SEARLE, John (1969): *Speech Acts: An Essay in the Philosophy of Language*, Cambridge: Cambridge University Press.

SEARLE, John (1983): *Intentionality: An Essay in the Philosophy of Mind*, Cambridge: Cambridge University Press.

SEN, Amartya (1985): Rights as Goals, in: S. Guest *et al.* (eds.), *Equality and Discrimination: Essays in Freedom and Justice*, ARSP, Beiheft 21.

SHINER, Roger (1992): *Norm and Nature. The Movements of Legal Thought*, Oxford: Clarendon.

SMITH, Michael (1987): The Humean Theory of Motivation, in: *Mind* 96.

SMITH, Michael (1988): On Humeans, Anti Humeans, and Motivation: A Reply to Pettit, in: *Mind* 97.

SMITH, Michael (1994): Realism, in: P. Singer (ed.), *Ethics*, Oxford and New York: Oxford University Press.

SOPER, Philip (1984): *A Theory of Law*, Cambridge, Mass. and London: Harvard University Press.

SOSA, Ernesto (1966): The Logic of Imperatives, in: *Theoria*.

STRAWSON, Peter (1985): *Skepticism and Naturalism. Some Varieties*, London: Methuen.

VERNENGO, Roberto (1987): Relativismo ético y justificaciones morales, in: *Doxa* (Alicante) 4.

WALLACE, Jay (1990): How to Argue About Practical Reason, in: *Mind* 99.

WELLMAN, Vincent (1985): Practical Reasoning and Judicial Justification: Toward an Adequate Theory, in: *University of Colorado Law Review* 57:1.

WHITEHEAD, Alfred (1966): *The Function of Reason*, Princeton, N. J.: Princeton University Press.

WILLIAMS, Bernard (1973): Deciding to Believe, in: *Problems of the Self. Philosophical Papers 1956-1972*, Cambridge: Cambridge University Press.

WILLIAMS, Bernard (1991): Internal and External Reason, in: id., *Moral Luck. Philosophical Papers 1973-1980*, Cambridge: Cambridge University Press.

VON WRIGHT, Georg Henrik (1963): *Norm and Action. A Logical Enquiry*, London: Routledge & Kegan Paul.

VON WRIGHT, Georg Henrik (1971): *Explanation and Understanding*, Ithaca, N. Y.: Cornell University Press.

VON WRIGHT, Georg Henrik (1980): *Freedom and Determination*, Acta Philosophica Fennica xxxi, Amsterdam: North Holland.

VON WRIGHT, Georg Henrik (1983): *Practical Reason, Philosophical Papers*, Vol. I, Ithaca, N. Y.: Cornell University Press.

VON WRIGHT, Georg Henrik (1983a): Practical Inference, in: id. (1983).

VON WRIGHT, Georg Henrik (1983b): On So-Called Practical Inference, in: id. (1983).

VON WRIGHT, Georg Henrik (1983c): Determinism and the Study of Man, in: id. (1983).

VON WRIGHT, Georg Henrik (1983d): On The Logic of Norms and Actions, in: id. (1983).

WRÓBLEWSKI, Jerzy (1971): Legal Decision and Its Justification, in: H. Hubien (ed), *Le raisonnement juridique*, Proceedings of the World Congress on Legal and Social Philosophy, Brussels.

WRÓBLEWSKI, Jerzy (1974): Legal Syllogism and Rationality of Judicial Decision, in: *Rechtstheorie* 5.

INDEX OF NAMES

MIX
Papier aus verantwortungsvollen Quellen
Paper from responsible sources
FSC® C105338

If you have any concerns about our products,
you can contact us on
ProductSafety@springernature.com

In case Publisher is established outside the EU,
the EU authorized representative is:
Springer Nature Customer Service Center GmbH
Europaplatz 3, 69115 Heidelberg, Germany

Printed by Libri Plureos GmbH
in Hamburg, Germany